AN INEBRIATED HISTORY OF BRITAIN

PETER HAYDON

SUTTON PUBLISHING

First published in the United Kingdom under the title
Beer and Britannia in 2001 by
Sutton Publishing Limited · Phoenix Mill
Thrupp · Stroud · Gloucestershire · GL5 2BU

Originally published in 1994 by Robert Hale Ltd as *The English Pub: A History*.

This new edition first published in 2005

British Library Cataloguing in Publication Data
A catalogue record for this book is available from the British Library.

ISBN 0 7509 4256 8

Chapter emblem: detail from *Sir John Barleycorn – Miss Hop – (and their only child) – Master Porter*. Anonymous etching, *c*. 1800. Guildhall Library, Corporation of London.
P. 287: 'The Man That Waters The Workers' Beer', by Paddy Ryan, courtesy of the Workers' Music Association.

Typeset in 9.5/12 pt Photina.
Typesetting and origination by
Sutton Publishing Limited.
Printed and bound in England by
J.H. Haynes & Co. Ltd, Sparkford.

CONTENTS

FOREWORD TO THE 2005 EDITION

Sadly it would appear that few members of the Association of Chief Police Officers, Conservative parliamentary party, or editorial staff of the *Daily Mail* have read the previous edition of this book. If they had their reaction to the Labour government's plans to liberalise the country's licensing laws at the start of 2005 might have been less strident, hysterical and generally wide of the mark.

Readers will quickly pick out two recurrent themes in this brief history of Britain as shaped by drink: firstly, as is said below, he who tries to legislate against a Briton and his right to drink is either a fool or a fanatic. Second, whilst, laws and wars, kings and codpieces come and go, the people remain stubbornly constant.

This book is an attempt to assess the contribution that beer, alehouses and pubs have made to the nation's history. It was written because virtually all other history books are silent on the matter, yet the impact of ale and beer on this country has been immense. Take them away and every other history book would have to be entirely re-written, or most likely would never have been written at all, for without ale and beer there would have been no British history as we recognise it.

As a nation we have forgotten our traditional and ancient drinking culture. Our ancestors would be amazed at this, prior to the nineteenth century it would have been as unthinkable for anyone in Britain not to have understood the significance of beer to their lives as it would have been for them to consider breathing unnecessary.

Today we drink without thinking. Beer is a commodity product, the production of which is ever more divorced from people's everyday experience. Increasing numbers of people cannot say what it is made of and do not care. They may not even drink beer, as it is quite likely that their first drinking experiences will be 'alcopops' or premixed spirits; sweet, unchallenging flavours that are easily approached by the young.

As they demand little so they offer little. As lager continues to eat up more and more 'share of throat' as the marketeers put it, it becomes ever blander. Drinks that offer little by way of challenge in the way of bitterness or flavour and which are served ever colder (the colder something is the less flavour it has), have only one appeal – they get you drunk.

'Binge drinking,' in these increasingly puritan times, are *les mots de nos jours*. Well, in that case this book is the story of a 1000 year drinking binge, for the British truly are world class binge drinkers, which rather suggests that if the issue is to be seriously addressed it needs rather more profound insight and revelation than are to be found amongst the indignant posturings of the *Daily Mail* and the front bench of the Tory Party. When the shadow Home Secretary says that the relaxation of licensing laws should be suspended until binge drinking is put under control he is really saying that they should be suspended for another 1000 years, because he offers no analysis of how people's habits should be moderated and, in truth, he has none.

So why, at the start of the 21st century is government planning to change a licensing regime that has lasted for the entire lifetime of virtually everyone? Put simply, it is because our habit of shutting pubs and 11.00 pm on the dot look increasingly silly when we are a part of a Europe in which people can drink whenever they like. Our licensing laws were introduced in 1915 as part of the drive for efficiency during the First World War, in order to keep munitions workers in remote parts of the country at their lathes and out of the pubs that offered their only recreation (as Chapter 21 describes). Now it may come as a surprise to the journalists and readers of the *Daily Mail*, but the First World War is over. The question that a right of centre newspaper should be asking is what is the reason why, in a free country, mature responsible adults should not be free to go to the pub when they wish. The answer is that there is none.

Critics of licensing law relaxation, who like to refer to it as 24 hour drinking, though no pubs wish to open for 24 hours to sell liquor (some supermarkets do, however, but these do not attract the same opprobrium), cite binge drinking as justification for retaining the status quo. It needs very little intellectual effort to see that binge drinking is neither a necessary nor sufficient reason for opposing licensing reform. In the first place, binge drinking is already a problem. This is why the police were initially behind the reforms, as it meant that people would not all be coming out onto the streets at the same time and competing for the same buses and taxis. It would appear that we have learnt little in 200 years from the days when the only effect of closing pubs during Divine Service was to turn reluctant drunks out onto the street into the paths of those going to church.

In the second place binge drinking will never be tackled whilst the debate centres solely on where and when people drink. The solution to addressing the unenviable problem of police chiefs who regularly and predictably see our weekend town centres turned into violent latrines is to understand the factors that have shaped the drinking environment over the last 90 years. These include looking at what we drink; changes in diet and nutrition; changes in the national palate; changes in lifestyle; changes in culture and changes in drinking patterns. It seems harsh to hold publicans entirely responsible for drunkenness when much of the alcohol their customers consume was bought from the supermarket and drunk before going out.

Above all changes in the ownership of the pubs needs to be looked at. The break up of the vertically integrated industry where pubs were owned by breweries has had significant effects on what and how we drink. Only a few years after Britain's largest pub owner was the late and once mighty Bass it was the Japanese bank Nomura. Its shareholders are not interested in manufacture, heritage or company values built up over centuries. They are interested in maximising returns from a raft of investments. They care little if in order get them pubs are induced to sell alcoholic fruit juice to teenagers. Nomura are no longer major pub owners and their time as Britain's biggest publicans was short lived. They had an exit strategy, as most financiers do, but they did leave the pub landscape much altered when they left. Now I would not suggest that Nomura are responsible for Britain's youth getting drunk every Saturday night, but I would say that that the consequence of the changes in the pub landscape of a quick succession of owners who regard pubs merely as sweatable assets to be bought, exploited and sold has been to make it easier for Britain's youth to get drunk. Relations between publicans and their landlords are at their lowest for 100 years, whilst some of the panicked responses thrown out by the Department of Culture Media and Sport suggesting the necessity of levies on the trade call forth other comparisons with the turn of the last century.

If the Jeremiahs of the *Daily Mail* are determined to question the desirability of the licensing reforms they are, as usual, looking in the wrong place. Much of the course of drinking in Britain has been shaped by the activities of the licensing magistrates. Their role is to end. After 750 years local authorities are to take on the magistrates' licensing functions. No one knows why. Local authorities have not sought their new powers and in the latter half of the twentieth century the licensing bench was at last doing the job it was designed to do in the thirteenth century. It was doing it well – for the first time – and was lean, cost effective and expert. These are not adjectives usually applied to local authorities.

One reason for the changes has been suggested. Magistrates have already lost their regulatory authority over gambling. Take away licensing and all that is left is pre-custodial hearings and administration of justice in the lower courts. Magistrates are famously independent and obdurate. Their lay status makes them impervious to patronage – unlike, for example, their professional colleagues, the stipendiary magistrates. It has been suggested that the shift in licensing from the bench to the council chamber is part of a wider attack on an independent magistracy. Something, one would imagine, that would exercise the *Daily Mail*, had it the wit to notice.

What goes around comes around, however. Amongst the other contemporary trends that have been played out before in the following pages are the wholesale destruction of the inn sign – never has the branding of pubs been done so cheaply as at the present day. Sadly there is no Hogarth to come to their rescue and *The Times* (see Chapter 22) is not the force it used to be. We see shadows of the pre and post first world war era in trends in pub food and pub refurbishment. Though this time round the reconnection of drink and food is wholly to be applauded and the present determination that a pub can look like anything so long as it doesn't look like a pub, is, for the most part, confined to the buildings' interiors.

Good old pubs are being ruined at a faster rate than good new pubs are being created. Around 20 pubs a week are closing in Britain at the present time. Of these six a week are country pubs, which continue to have a tough time as the countryside continues to have a tough time. One third of English parishes now have no pub. These trends have been going on for several decades now and show no sign of abating.

We must not be downcast however. The pub is a remarkably resilient old dog. The real threat to the pub is not the new puritanism, the government, the crisis in the country or the greed of pub companies. When the ice caps melt and the nation disappears under the waves, we should take comfort in the fact that the last Briton clinging to the last rooftop will probably be determined to be sitting atop a pub. Poetically he will be following Hillaire Belloc's profound instruction.

Chapter 1

THE ORIGINS OF ALE TO THE ORIGINS OF THE ALEHOUSE

There were deep bowls
Carried along the benches often,
So likewise cups and pitchers
Full to the people who were sitting on couches;
The renowned shielded warriors
Were feted, while they took thereof.

Anglo-Saxon poem 'Judith'

In AD 361 the Emperor Julian described the Teutonic northern European races as 'sons of malt'. Big drinkers they were, but none so much as the British. This book traces drinking in England from its earliest days through the entirety of its history. It is, if you will, a history of England seen through the bottom of a pint glass.

In pre-Roman times wild honey was plentiful to a degree never since known. The making of 'mead', a word derived from the Sanskrit *madhu*, was an easy matter. With the growth of settlement, deforestation and cultivation, honey became ever scarcer. We know how important honey was because we know that fines were often levied in the form of honey. A cheaper substitute had to be found, to which honey could be added as flavouring and to provide a finish. Malted grain was the obvious choice. The honey content gradually declined and the grain content rose, so much so that a new word was needed to distinguish between the pure honey mead, that was now solely for the rich, and the common drink. In Prussian this word was *alu* in Saxon *ealu* and in English ale. The origin of the word 'ale' is very different from 'beer', which comes from the Sumerian/Hamitic languages and was used to describe the infusions of malted bread drunk in Egypt over 3,000 years ago.

When the Romans colonised Britain in AD 43, they brought with them the embryonic pub. Until that time we had shared a common Aryan culture, and like the Norsemen of legend the cup was the centrepiece of cultural activity.

In Valhalla the fallen Vikings were served ale by the Valkyries in the skulls of their enemies as it flowed from the bounteous udders of the she-goat Heidron. Although the Britons had no Valhalla, for them, too, drinking was an expression of identity, but it was an expression of local cohesion rather than of untamed prowess. Our Aryan cousins never went on to develop pubs as we did, with the result that the *bier kellers* remain essentially little Valhallas.

The Romans brought two innovations that affect our story. The first was roads, the second wine. Roads mean travel, travel means distance, distance means time and time brings the necessity for refreshment and sustenance. With the roads the Romans built *mansiones* and *diversoria*. These buildings were probably of a two-storey design with a galleried upper floor where the Romans would have sat rather than reclined to eat and where the drinking vessels may well have been of a standard capacity and the flagons chained to posts. Chess was probably played and the Chequers is the country's oldest inn sign. The *mansiones* were spaced along the roads, while in the towns the Romans had their *tabernae*, identifiable by a bush of vine leaves displayed above the door, which gives us the saying 'a good wine needs no bush.'

Between the departure of the Romans and the arrival of Christianity there occurs another short event that deserves mention. Sometime during AD 450, at the Kentish hamlet of Ebbsfleet, two Jutish chieftains, Hengist and Horsa first set foot in Britain. They arrived as allies of the Kentish King Vortigern to assist in his battles against the picts and celts, and initially, at least, all was cordial.

And after that he – King Vortigern – had been entertained at a banquet royal, the damsel stepped forth from her chamber bearing a golden cup filled with wine and coming next the king bended her knee and spake saying 'Laverd King, wacht heil.' But he, when he beheld the damsel's face was all amazed at her and his heart was enkindled of delight. Then he asked of his interpreter what it was that the damsel had said. Whereupon the interpreter made answer, 'She hath called thee "Lord King" and hath greeted thee by wishing thee health. But the answer thou shouldst make unto her is "Drinc Heil".' Whereupon Vortigern made answer 'Drinc Heil!' and bade the damsel drink. Then he took the cup from her hand and kissed her and drank; and from that day unto this hath the custom held in Britain that he who drinketh at a feast saith unto another 'Wacht Heil' and they that receiveth the drink answer 'Drinc Heil'.[1]

King Vortigern went on to marry the beautiful Rowena, presumably dispensing with the interpreter, and ensuring that the custom of wassailing survived, and while our modern cry of 'cheers' may lack the romantic vigour of our ancestors' 'wassail', the tradition of pledging and toasting has been with us, unbroken, for 1,500 years. With the arrival of Christianity, the tradition became formalised. The wassail bowl became an essential component of Christmas and, accompanied by singing, was taken from house to house on New Year's Eve, filled with warm ale, spiced with nutmeg and apple and with crusts of toast floating therein.

> Wassail, Wassail, Over the town,
> Our Toast it is white, our ale it is brown,
> Our bowl it is made of the maplin tree,
> We be good fellows all, I drink to thee.

As early as AD 616, Ethelbert, King of Kent, was forced to regulate the number of ale sellers and Edgar, father of Edward the Martyr (himself assassinated while in mid-draught) in AD 975 restricted the number of alehouses per village to one. He also learned a lesson that has had to be relearned countless times during the subsequent thousand years. To legislate between an Englishman and his ale is to court disaster and certain to produce a result opposite to the one intended. Where King Edgar went wrong was to decree that drinking vessels in alehouses be of a standard size – to whit, the pottle (four pints) – and that each pottle should be subdivided into eight parts by means of pegs set inside the tankard and that no one was to drink down further than one peg at a sitting.

Far from viewing this as a restriction favouring sobriety, Englishmen everywhere took it as a challenge and commenced – as we still do today – to take each other down a peg or two, so that by the start of the twelfth century drinking to pegs was a serious problem. Gauging the peg was not simple and manners decreed that if you overshot the peg you had to drink down to the next, lest you short measure the person after you. A man might easily intend to drink down a half pint and end up drinking four. Thus did Edgar's decree backfire, and as we shall see, the man who tries to regulate drink is either a fool or a fanatic.

On the whole it is through canon law that we get our best picture of life in the alehouse in the years before Hastings. St David in the sixth century decreed that: 'Those who get drunk through ignorance must do penance fifteen days, if through negligence 40 days, if through contempt three quarntains.'[2] The Breton monk Gildas lamented 'Not only laity, but the Lord's own flock and its shepherds, who ought to have been an example to the people, slumbered away their time in drunkenness as if they had been dipped in wine.'[3]

The introduction of Christianity in AD 597 did little to moderate the habits of the population. Much of its proselytising success was due to its ability to absorb pagan ritual. Since so much pagan ritual was drink related, much of English Christianity became drink related too. Christmas, of course, still is. Wakes are the best example of pagan festivities taken over by Christianity, with the birthdays of the holy martyrs usurping the pagan deities. Intended as vigils, people quickly discovered that the long, cold hours passed more agreeably with the assistance of 'cakes and ale', to such a degree that

The people fell to lechery and songs and dances with harping and piping and also to gluttony and sin and so turned the holyness to cursedness.[4]

In AD 745 Ecbright, Archbishop of York, had to prohibit priests from entering taverns for food or drink. St Dunstan – who appears today on several inn signs, tweaking the Devil's nose – was fighting a losing battle. Canon 26 states, 'let no drinking be done in Church.' Canon 28 says, 'let men be very temperate at Church wakes and pray earnestly and suffer there no drinking or unseemliness.' Dunstan's prohibitions were largely ignored. Canon 56 warns priests to 'beware of drunkenness and be diligent in warning and correcting others in this matter.' However, he had only got as far as Canon 58 before he felt obliged to insist that 'no priest be an ale-sop nor in any wise act the gleeman.'

Still it was to no avail. The tenth century archbishop, Aelfric, was forced to complain 'Yet men often act so absurdly as to sit up all night and drink to madness within God's house and to defile it with scandalous and lewd discourse.'[5] Of course they did. The church was also the centre of secular as well as spiritual life, largely because it would have been the only substantial building in a community. The ale houses were indistinguishable from any other domestic dwelling, and while they had custom – some clerical – that imbibed inside, much of its business was off sales, and much of this would well have found its way across the village green, or up the hill to the churchyard and nave.

The church's view of immoderation would have differed from the layman's, and we must not assume that intemperance was at the levels it was to be in later centuries. For many, prior to the Black Death, ale was beyond their means. The poet William Langland wrote of the poor, 'it would be a charity to help them; bread and penny ale are a luxury.'

Nor was ale ubiquitous. Permanent alehouses only start to appear in significant numbers in the thirteenth century, matching the increase in population and the number of new settlements. Before this time much brewing would have been done on a communal level, as with the church ales or the numerous other ales where communities would pool resources for a feast and the proceeds would go to some worthy cause or other; in the case of *bede* ales, *help* ales, or *give* ales, to some unfortunate bankrupt; with *bride* ales the beer was given in return for small gifts, which we now call wedding presents; *clerk* ales were for the benefit of the parish clerk and *cuckoo* ales were general festivities for an event now only celebrated in the Letters Page of *The Times*; while the revenue from church ales went to the church. For all these feasts the merrymaking would probably have taken place in the church, and they were well-organised affairs.

For the Church-ale, two young men of the parish are yerely chosen by their last forgoers to be wardens, who, dividing the task make collection among the parishioners, of whatsoever provision it pleaseth them voluntarily to bestow. This they employ in brewing, baking and other actes, against Whitsuntide, upon which holding the neighbours met at the Church home, and there merrily fed on their owne victuals, each contributing some petty portion to the stock, which by many smalls groweth to a meetly greatness, for there is entertayned a kind of emulation between these wardens, who, by his graciousness in gathering, and good husbandry in expending, can best advance the Churche's profit. Besides, the neighbour parishes at these times lovingly visit one another and frankly spend their money together.[6]

What exactly would our Saxon ancestors have drunk and how did they drink it? Most of the drinking vessels would have been made of wood, either the tankard-style pot ordered by Edgar to be standard, which would have been made like a small barrel, of slats of wood bound with wooden hoops. Slightly larger jugs were of a square construction with a handle at each corner to facilitate their being passed round. The most common, however, would have been the mazer or bowl, the most prized of which were made from the part of the branch that joins the trunk, or 'bole', producing the most decorative grain. Elm, box and holly were all popular alternatives. Frequently larger mazers would have had a lid and usually a metal medallion would be set in the centre to identify ownership or express some religious sentiment. Even after they passed out of common usage it was still traditional to serve mead in mazers until the 1660s. Earthenware was uncommon. It was too bulky to transport far from its few centres of production and for many centuries leather bottles, blackjacks and bombards, even metal, were more popular choices for drinking vessels, though there was a surprisingly large amount of ornate glass available.

Monks and the rich would have had access to wine. The *Domesday Book* tells us that there were thirty-eight vineyards in England in 1086, though the amount of wine they yielded was insignificant compared to the amount imported. There was a variety of acid wine mixed with honey and spices – called *piment* – which was allegedly popular with King Arthur. Aside from mead and a close relation, *mürt* – made with added mulberry juice – there were various ales identified by the flavourings added, such as ground ivy (ale hoof), or costmary (ale-cost). Contrary to popular belief the hop – called hymele – was occasionally used as a flavouring even before 1066; the village of Himbleton, in Worcestershire, is really Hop Town. The monks were great flavourers of ale. Spiced ales they often called *cicer*, or infused with potions of herbs they were termed *gruits*. The ale was simple to make: malt barley, boiled with liquor (water) and yeast. The concoction was strained and left to stand, with the residue being fed to pigs. After two days it was thick, strong, sweet and ready to drink and was called new ale. The problem was keeping it from going sour, and the only solution was to drink it quickly, which, if you think about it, is a very practical solution.

The skilled brewers in monasteries and grand houses would have produced a fine brew, but the product of the poor village brewster would have been an inferior one. Wheat, oats and corn were used as well as barley, and fermentation was often an unreliable process. Not for nothing was ale described in the fourteenth century as, 'For muddy, foggy, fulsome, puddle stinking / For all of these ale is the only drinking.' Apart from those occasions when a community pooled its resources, many folk could only brew when chance provided the ingredients and they could borrow the utensils. Between the months of May and October brewing became very difficult. It was frequently impossible to keep the brew cool enough for fermentation to be ensured and impossible to safeguard against pollens, spores and wild yeasts infecting the results.

This summer difficulty, which many a modern home brewer will have experienced, poses a major unanswered question for the pub historian. For Britons in the Dark Ages ale was a luxury, albeit frequently enjoyed, rather than a necessity. Water and milk were available alternatives. By the late Middle Ages, however, with an increasingly large and dense population, plague, and early polluting industries, such as butchers and tanners, ale was the only safe liquid to drink. People drank it morning, noon and night. For breakfast they would have drunk 'small beer', a weaker, non-dehydrating brew made from a second boiling of the barley mash; at other times, strong ale. For women and children, young and old alike, there was no alternative until the popularisation of tea at the end of the eighteenth century. Wine was too expensive. Ale was central to life, on an equal footing to bread, if not higher. The king who could not guarantee its safe supply at a price the people would tolerate was taking big risks. Consequently, monarchs were careful to ensure that people got their beer.

Ancient Welsh chronicles record the tendency of British chieftains to go into battle drunk. This *may* explain why, between the Roman departure in AD 409 and 1066, just about anyone who fancied himself as anyone in northern Europe came over and thumped the British at one time or another. The Normans were no exception. At Hastings, on the eve of the most famous battle in British history, the Normans, under William the Bastard, settled down to a night of sober prayer and contemplation. The English, however, having defeated the Viking Harold Haadrada at Stamford Bridge, 'being revelling before, had in the morning their brains arrested for the arrearages of the ingested fumes of the former night, and were no better than drunk when they came to fight.'[7]

It is sad to admit, but the English lost the battle of Hastings because they were in no fit state to fight. Having lost the battle, they won the war. Like all invaders before them, the Normans succumbed to the English way of life. John of Salisbury felt obliged to remind William the Bastard that, 'he would have deserved more renown had he rather promulgated laws of temperance to a nation which he would not have subdued by arms had it not already been conquered by excess of luxury.'[8] The knight, Peter of Blois, lamented: 'When you behold our barons and knights going on a military expedition, you see their baggage horses loaded not with iron but wine, not with lances but cheeses, not with swords but bottles, not with spears but spits. You would imagine they were going to prepare a great feast rather than to make war.'[9]

Henry I was reputedly mortified by the death of his son William. History cannot enlighten us as to whether his son's White Ship would not have run aground and sunk had not the prince given three casks of wine to the crew. This event may or may not have prompted Henry's contemporary, William of Malmesbury, to comment,

Drinking in particular was a universal practice in which occupation they passed entire nights as well as days. They consumed their whole sustenance in mean and despicable houses, unlike the Normans and French, who in noble and splendid mansions lived in frugality. . . . They were accustomed to eat till they became surfeited and to drink till they were sick. The latter qualities they imparted to their conquerors.[10]

Despite huge imports of wine into Britain, a sizeable amount of English ale went abroad. In 1158 Thomas à Becket led a mission to the French king, the baggage train of which consisted of seventy-five horse wagons, two of which were piled high with tuns of ale bound in iron hoops as gifts for his majesty. Becket's impact upon the drink trade was not, however, the result of his diplomacy.

The assassination of Becket in Canterbury Cathedral started a mass movement of people that lasted 400 years. Pilgrimage became an important activity, both socially and economically. Becket's shrine and the eleventh-century shrine of Our Lady at Walsingham were of sufficient importance to attract pilgrims from overseas; so much so that many ports had *maison dieu* to cater for pilgrims entering and leaving the country. Domestically, the other important pilgrimages were to the tomb of Edward the Confessor at Winchester; the Thorn Tree of Joseph of Arimathea at Glastonbury; and, subsequently, the tomb of Edward II at Gloucester, though Norwich, York, Lincoln, Hereford and Oxford were all destinations for pilgrims. At Winchester pilgrims would have been able to rest at the Hospital of St Cross, founded in 1136 by Bishop Henry de Blois, and today it is still possible to receive alms, known as the 'wayfarers dole', every day except Sunday, merely by knocking at the door of the porter's lodge.

There were two important results of this increase in pilgrimage. First, it helped make the monasteries very rich, and second, it started to strain the resources of traditional hospitality provided at monasteries and in the homes of the gentry until the Reformation. A new institution was needed to cater for the needs of pilgrims and other travellers emboldened to chance the risky paths of medieval England: the inn.

The usual route to Canterbury was from Winchester, via Farnham, Guildford, West Malling, Aylesford, Maidstone and Charing. Many ancient pilgrims' hostels were to be found: St Mary's Abbey in West Malling; Bishop Boniface's Hospital, Maidstone; Boxley Abbey; Hollinghourne Priory; the Archbishop's Palace, Charing; and in Canterbury no less than two abbeys, two friaries and two hospitals. More comfortable accommodation was to be had at the pilgrims' inns interspersed along the road; the Cat and Fiddle, Hinton Admiral, Hampshire, was an eleventh-century hospice for the monks of Christchurch Priory; the Church House, Rattery, Devon, is not coy about its origins; the Weary Friar at

Pillaton, Cornwall, probably started life as lodgings for the twelfth-century masons building the neighbouring St Odulph's church; while at Goudhurst, Kent, the Star and Eagle was actually a monastery during the fourteenth century, becoming a notorious smugglers' den four hundred years later. The Bush at Farnham and the Angel in Guildford, both have monastic origins; Ye Olde Bell, Hurley, dates back to 1135, as a guest house of Hurley Priory, and several original features remain. The Old Mint, Southam, Warwickshire, was also a monks' hospice, though it acquired more fame by being used as a mint by Charles I to produce coin with which to pay his army at Edge Hill. The Star, Alfriston, East Sussex, with its famous carved lion corner post, was part of the demesne of Battle Abbey, whose monks ran it as a hospice for those travelling to the shrine of St Richard at Chichester. There was the White Hart, Bletchingly; the Crown, Oxted; and in Canterbury the Chequers, the White Hart, the Sun and the Fountain, which, until Geoffery Chaucer immortalised the Tabard in Southwark, was arguably the most famous inn in England.

Pilgrimages apart, the growth of towns and the number of alehouses required some form of practical regulation. In 1189, as a fire precaution, the London city council forbade all unlicensed alehouses not made of stone, with the provision that 'no baker bake, or ale wife brew by night, either with reeds or straw or stubble, but with wood only.'

Note that it was expected that persons engaged in brewing would be female. Ale wives or 'brewsters' were held in fairly low esteem, and the brewster who brewed bad ale was the lowest of the low, likely to be ducked, or like the brewster depicted on the misericords in the parish church at Ludlow, who was found guilty of lining her pots with pitch to give short measure, destined to be punished by eternal damnation with plenty of fire and brimstone.

> Of cans I kept not true measure,
> My Cups I sold at my pleasure
> Deceiving many a creature
> Though my ale was nought.

In fact an alewife was ducked at Kingston in 1745, and another at Chelmsford as late as 1801. Not surprisingly the displacement of women by men as brewers was not the result of any major social change, but rather due to the gradual increase in the potential profits to be made by brewing. It was women's work to provide the village with liquid sustenance; it was men's work to extract a profit from the same task and produce the modern industry.

At this time it was not unrespectable for women to be seen in alehouses, though comparatively early on it would have been unusual for married women to patronise alehouses without their husbands, and single women in towns could well be mistaken for prostitutes. This was partly due to the unfeminine nature of drinking at the time. By the end of the twelfth century the fashion for drinking was very much for drinking in bouts. This was not assisted by the fact that many drinking vessels, horns, bowls and tumblers could not be set down once filled without spilling. The only remedy was to see off the entire contents. Canon 6 of Archbishop Edmund, in 1236, deplores 'the ill practice by which all that drink together are obliged to equal draughts, and he carries away the credit who hath made most drunk and taken off the largest cups, therefore we forbid all forcing to drink.'[11]

It is not known whether the famous thirteenth-century Abbot of Burton, whose excellent ale he would never touch, 'whilst he could get at his neighbours,' was ever given to drinking bouts. The opportunity was there, not least because of the abundant supply available to him. Fountain's Abbey in Yorkshire had a malt house with a capacity to brew 900 barrels of strong ale per annum (230,400 pints). At a meal in a monk's refectory in Canterbury in the late twelfth century we are told that 'there was such an abundance of wine and strong drink, of pigment and claret, of new wine and mead, and mulberry wine and all intoxicating liquors in so much abundance, that even ale which the English brew excellently – especially in Kent – found no place; but rather ale stood as low in this matter as the pot-herbs among other dishes.'[12]

The monks were to enjoy their luxury for another 350 years or so, but already there were signs that the ancient tradition of 'hospitality' could not survive under an ever increasing population. The seeds of a nascent growth were producing two quite different strains, the humble alehouse and the lofty inn, which would take over the role of provider for the needs of the nation.

Chapter 2

THE GROWTH OF THE INN: 1215–1400

This is what I now Propose:
In a Tavern I shall die
With a glass up to my nose
And God's angels standing by
That they may indeed declare
As I take my final tot
May God receive with loving care
Such a decent drunken sot.

Fourteenth-century toast

Article 35 of the Magna Carta decreed that there shall be a standard measure for 'wine, ale and corn'. King John may have found standardisation a means of spreading the rule of law, for in the village there was no standardisation. The alewife who was thought to give short measure would soon be the alewife floating in the village pond, and very few villagers travelled far enough to worry about regional practices and variations. The article in Magna Carta must have been to facilitate an expanding trade, especially in malt.

King John assisted trade interests as a means of curbing the power of the very barons who forced him to Runnymede. A particular ploy was to make grants of land in France on condition they were cleared and planted with vines. He also encouraged wine consumption by price fixing, favouring wines from English-ruled France: Anjou and Poitou. Often, however, the market would not tolerate the ceiling of 20s per cask for Poitou or 24s per cask for Anjou, and frequently even the king found himself paying over the odds to secure his supplies.

The fourteenth century saw a rapid rise in the number of alehouses and the formalising of the traditions of alehouse, tavern and inn. Early on in his reign Edward III was getting alarmed at the fact that the growing numbers of alehouses were distracting the good yeomen of England from spending their Sundays practicing at the butts, as they were duty bound to do. As it was commonly reckoned to take a good six years of consistent practice with the longbow to achieve the kind of standard which so decimated the French cavalry at Crecy, neglect of the butts was seen as a real threat to national security. The king was forced to outlaw cards, dice, games of chance, throwing of stones, football, handball and club-ball, while bull baiting and cock fighting were condemned as worthless.

The most important event of the thirteenth century was the Assize of Bread and Ale of Henry III in 1266.

When a gallon of wheat is sold for 3s or 3s 4d and a ¼ of oats for 15d, then brewers in Cities ought and may well afford to sell two gallons for a penny and out of cities sell 3 gallons for a penny. And when in a town 3 gallons is sold for a penny, out of town they ought and may sell 4. And this assize ought to be holden throughout the land.[1]

Holden throughout the land it certainly was. The 1266 assize was important for several reasons. It was the first attempt to relate the price of ale and bread to the cost of wheat and barley, to produce a system that would guarantee supply of bread and ale but also have an element of consumer protection built in. The Leet Courts were full of people being charged with selling ale against the assize – though rarely with selling bread. The fines extracted were used as an early form of licensing and were a means by which the feudal authorities could extract some benefit in the same way as the church extracted a profit from church ales. Alewives and brewers would expect to be arraigned quite frequently, and it soon became an occupational hazard with no stigma attached.

Sir Steward, the bailiff Robert complaineth of William Tailor, that against the ordinance of the Lord and his free assize, he hath broken the assize of beer in every brewing since Michelmas till now, for the ordinance is that no brewer or

breweress upon pain of forfeiture of half a mark should brew
beer whereof the gallon shall be sold at more than ½d the gallon
between Michelmas and All Saints, unless it be so good and
approved according to the ale testers that it may be
conveniently sold at ¾d without complaint, and the said William
wrongfully and in spite of the Lord and without the assay of
the ale testers hath sold beer that was flat ever since Michelmas
at ¾d a gallon to the great prejudice of the Lord, so that he hath
incurred the forfeiture of half a mark and damage to the
amount of 6s. And William defendeth the suit and avers that
he hath not broken the assize as the bailiff saith. Fair friend
William the court awardeth thee that thou be at law six handed
to aquit thee of the charge.[2]

The position of ale-conner was a very important one for several
hundred years. Shakespeare's father was appointed ale-conner for
Stratford in 1557. It was the custom for brewsters and brewers to
display an ale stake in front of their premises when there was ale
for sale. This was a descendant of the bush hanging outside
Roman Tabernae, but had extra significance. It was an offence to
offer for sale a brew without displaying an ale stake, as the stake
was the signal to the ale-conner to perform his duty. It was also an
offence to offer more than one brew under the same stake, since
this would also deny the conner the opportunity to decide which
quality of ale the second brew fell into. We hear, for example, of
one Kentroppe being fitted 6d in 1461 for brewing three times
under the same ale stake. At Ashburton officials appointed by the
local Leet Courts still tour the town during the annual Ale Tasting
in July. The Portreeve and Ale Tasters taste the beer and,
if satisfactory, they present the landlord with a branch of
evergreen to display over his door.

To modern eyes this redisplaying of the ale stake would seem
bizarre, since one would assume that the stake would be removed
and replaced almost immediately. This is far from the truth.
Brewing would have been fairly intermittent for a host of reasons.
In the first place, ale was still fairly expensive. At least until the
late thirteenth century there were also many periods when
alewives were forbidden to brew, notably when the church was
holding a church ale. These feasts were not as popular as others
since they were compulsory, and because the aim was to maximise

revenue for the church all other brewing was banned. The parishioners of Okebrook, Derbyshire must have concluded that they had been given the short end of the stick.

> The parishioners of Elveston and Okebrook agreed to brew four ales, and every ale of a ¼ of malt, betwixt this and the feast of St John Baptist next coming. And that every inhabitant of the said town of Okebrook shall be at the several ales. And every husband and his wife shall pay two pence, every cottager one penny and all the inhabitants of Elveston shall have and receive all the profits and advantages coming from the said ales to the use and behoof of the said Church of Elveston, and the inhabitants of Elveston shall brew eight between this and the feast of St John Baptist at which ales the inhabitants of Okebrook shall come and pay as before rehearsed, and if he be away at one ale to pay at the other one forthwith.[3]

In those parts of the country covered by forest a different type of ale grew up. Villagers would gather together, donate their scots (shares) to the common pot and revel for days in the forest outside the jurisdiction of the church and without the church enjoying any of the profit. Not surprisingly the church hated the fact that people were getting off 'scot free'. They managed to persuade King John to prohibit these revels in 1213, but to no effect, as Robin Hood demonstrated, crown law held no sway in the forests. The church prohibited scot-ales in 1220, 1223, 1230, 1237, 1240, 1255 and 1256, and continued to do so until 1364.

Naturally, all types of ale could be boisterous affairs and gradually the church began to look on them less favourably. In 1468 bride-ales (wedding receptions) were forbidden to be held in church on pain of excommunication. Even in Henry VIII's reign wedding services were little more than debauches, a commentator noting that 'Early in the morning the wedding people begin to exceed in superfluous eating and drinking and when they come to the preaching they are half-drunk, some altogether.'[4]

The non-compulsory ales were undoubtedly very popular events attracting neighbours from villages far and wide.

> No man telle yn tale
> The people that was at thates Brede Ale.

In 1500 the priest of Lymington, near Yeovil – one Thomas Wolsey – got so plastered at a village ale that the magistrates had him placed in the stocks. This event seems not to have impeded his rise to both cardinal and chancellor to Henry VIII.

The alewife was by no means the only source of drink. Most feudal employment would have been either for manorial or monastic landlords. In the thirteenth century ale would have formed a large part of a labourer's wages, possibly as much as two-thirds, and the decline of this practice in the thirteenth and fourteenth centuries contributed greatly to the rise of the alehouse.

Finally, for everyone except the poor of a village a certain amount of hospitality was still available, and hospitality was still seen as a primary Christian virtue.

> In a village there may be
> Men of some nobility
> Five or six or even more
> Who keep a hospitable door
> For a guest it is but meet
> To offer bread that is made of wheat.

A further advantage of the ale stake was the transient nature of the brewsters. In any community the established brewsters would have been the wives of wealthier men who brewed for domestic needs and sold off the surplus. Poorer folk would brew to keep the wolf from the door. As time progressed there was an increasingly mobile class of itinerant poor, many of whom may have set up an alehouse in a village before moving on.

The various records and laws that come down to us regarding ale stakes are fairly confusing. As early as 1292 signs were replacing ale stakes in London, and the reason is not too hard to discover. Stakes extended too far into the streets, impeding riders and waggoners. In 1375 they were restricted to no more than seven feet in length. It was not, however, until 1393 that Richard II decreed that every alehouse should display an ale stake, a statute that seems to have caught poor Florence North, alewife of Chelsea, unawares and landed her in court. Perhaps this was a case of the law catching up with popular practice, or perhaps people were becoming lax in displaying ale stakes and authority needed to be re-stamped; certainly it seems a little late to legislate in the matter.

Various myths attach to the ale-conner. He may well, like Chaucer's, have been identified by his big red nose, but more frequently he was supposed to wear his badge of office – his leather breeches. He would visit a house where a new ale stake was displayed and pour a sample on a stool. He would then sit on the stool, endeavouring not to move for half an hour, after which he would attempt to rise. If his breeches stuck to the stool there was too much residual sugar, and the ale was deemed not fully brewed and not fit to drink. If the ale passed the breeches test the conner would then taste the ale to see if it was the first or second quality, thereby determining at what price it would be sold. If the ale-conner deemed the ale unfit to drink it was poured away and the ale stake forcibly removed.

The duties of the ale-conner are, perhaps, best described in the terms of his oath. This example comes from Canterbury in 1377, where there were very many inns, alehouses, hostels, herbergeours and religious houses, all busy brewing.

You shall swear, that you shall know of no brewer or brewster, cook, or pie baker in your ward, who sells the gallon of best ale for more than one penny halfpenny, or the gallon of second for more than one penny, or otherwise than by measure sealed and full of clear ale; or who brews less than he used to before this cry, or withdraws himself from following his trade the rather by reason of this cry . . . and that you, so soon as you shall be required to taste any ale of a brewer or brewster shall be ready to do the same, and in case that it be less good than it used to be before this cry, you by assent of your Aldermen, shall set a reasonable price thereon, according to your discretion, and if any one shall afterwards sell the same above the said price, unto your said Alderman you shall certify the same. And that for no gift, promise, knowledge, hate or other cause whatsoever, no brewer, brewster, huckster, cook, or pie baker, who acts against anyone of the points aforesaid, you shall conceal, spare, or tortuously aggrieve, nor when you are required to taste ale, shall absent yourself without reasonable cause and true, but all things which until your office pertain to you, you shall well and lawfully do. So God you help and All the Saints.[5]

Notice that in 1377, once you had decided to brew you were obliged to brew. Ale had become a necessity and a supply had to be guaranteed. Anyone who brewed less than they used to, or who decided to cease brewing at that price, was liable for punishment.

A herbergeour was analogous to the publican of today. They were differentiated from the hostlers by the fact that they offered no lodging or stabling. The *Liber Albus*, which chronicles much of London life until the middle of the reign of Richard II, tells us that hostlers and herbergeours were mostly freemen of the city, but that it was not unusual for 'foreigners' – non-freemen – to be admitted to the freedom for the purpose of becoming herbergeours. These newcomers were then obliged to keep house within the city, but were scrupulously excluded from the banks of the Thames which were the most fashionable and lucrative sites of the hostelries and cookshops of London. Clearly the herbergeour was superior to the alehouse keeper in that he provided food and, like the hostler, was a 'licensed victualler' in the true sense. As a freeman of the city he was a citizen of a fair degree of standing, not at the top of the social scale, but not at the bottom.

A huckster was a woman, usually an agent of the alewife, who sold ale in the street. Since ale did not keep it was necessary to dispose of it before it went sour, and if the alehouse custom was insufficient the huckster would have peddled it in the street. In the early Middle Ages this activity was perfectly legitimate, but later as the numbers of alehouses became a problem the huckster too became a nuisance. Moreover, it became increasingly likely that the huckster was not an agent of the alewife but a 'regratress', a woman who bought the ale and then resold it on her own account, and the middleman or woman was as detested in those times as much as they are loved today.

In 1368 the Mayor of London ordered that, 'No regratress shall buy ale of anyone to sell again by retail on pain of forfeiture and that the vendor forfeit the value of the ale and suffer imprisonment; and anyone coming and encouraging any regrator or regratress to act contrary to the ordinance shall for the first offence forfeit half a mark, for the second a mark and for the third 20*s*.'[6]

It is clear that the mayor was determined to stamp heavily on the regratress. This was, however, a time of an increasing number of alehouses, and the rate of growth was causing concern. It is likely that hucksters would have attracted increasing opprobrium and the propensity of the authorities to be willing to differentiate between hucksters and regratresses would seem to have declined. That being said, in 1375, we hear of one William Felle convicted of posing as an officer of the Serjeants in order to extract money from hucksters, so presumably they had some form of protection under the law.

Prior to the 1266 assize, there had been many statutes concerning ale, but they were nearly all avoided or ignored. The 1266 assize, however, was clearly a success, in part because it was a sensible measure, linking price to supply. However, the main reason for its success was that everyone knew where they stood, and it was sufficiently flexible. In 1283 there was an ordinance to raise the prices of ale to 1½d per gallon for double (best) ale and 1d per gallon for single ale. This may have been a response to the harvest for that year, but the same prices applied in Canterbury over a hundred years later.

People brewed, broke the assize, were amerced and the manor gained a revenue, which encouraged it to protect the ale-sellers, lest it could not amerce them again come the next petty sessions. In practice the sessions would seem, in this respect at least, to have been quite friendly affairs. In 1288–9 the Norwich Manorial Rolls show that of £6 6s in fines levied only £2 19s were paid.

> Of John the Bailiff and his wife, for not observing the assize of ale and of J de Morley and his wife for the same; of L the Clerk and his wife for the same 2d each – each paid one shilling the rest is excused.
>
> Of R de Dalby for the same, 2s excused. Of Beatrice de Irestead for the same and for a muck heap 2s, paid 6d, rest excused at request of Master John Mann out of carnal friendship. Of John de Sibton and his wife for the same 3s excused because he is gate keeper.[7]

To maintain local harmony, therefore, the practice seems to have been to pay as much as you could afford. It would have been silly for John de Sibton to pay, since as a manorial employee it would have amounted to him paying his own wages and may have reduced his loyalty to the manor. Beatrice de Irestead's charms were obviously not reduced by her muck heap; however, what point of jurisprudence is being invoked by pleading carnal friendship is unclear.

The 1266 assize also distinguished between the price in the town and elsewhere. There is little doubt that from early on the ale of the town was superior to that of the country. In the towns there was more likely to be greater competition and greater economies of scale to be derived. Better quality malt was probably available and brewing expertise disseminated more quickly. In 1247 we are faced with the slightly pathetic sight of 'customary' residents of Houghton and Wyton being charged at court with 'having gone to Huntingdon for penny ale at other times than a fair'. Clearly the residents preferred the town ale to their own, though it would have been a fine sight to have seen the entire population of two villages standing sheepishly in the dock at the sessions. Who would have been left to sit on the jury?

Another factor affecting the quality of ale in towns was the rise of the common brewer. Already there was a tendency for the alehouse keeper to buy in his supplies. In Oxford in 1319 we find that the 'ale-drapers' were allocated a space in the market between St Edward's Lane (Alfred St) and the Chequers Inn. Here then are a body of wholesale brewers selling their wares to retailers.

In the same year there was a very early tied house – the Bear at Bridge Foot, Southwark, which reigned as one of the country's most famous inns until 1761 when it was demolished, as were so many of our great inns, to widen the road. From its earliest days down to the seventeenth century it offered archery as a pub sport. Sir John Howard, who died with Richard III at Bosworth, is reported to have lost 20*d* over an archery wager at the Bear, skill at arms seemingly not one of his strong points. When, in 1633, many of the riverside inns were suppressed and forced to close their waterside doors, because they were seen as convenient escape routes for the many criminals who swarmed the riverside, the Bear was notably excluded, being an important embarkation point for the tilt boats – canopied passenger boats – to Greenwich and Gravesend. Ned Ward gave this description of a Billingsgate inn in his *London Spy* of 1704, though life at the Bear would have been similar.

Next came in a spruce blade with a pretended wife, ask'd what time the boats went to Gravesend, they told him about four in the morning. 'Alas', says he, 'it will be too long to sit up; can't my wife and I have a bed here?' 'Yes, yes, if you please,' replied the pious Beldam. 'God forbid else, we have couples above in bed that wait for the tide as well as you Sir.' So up they were lighted post haste to the old trade of Basket Making.[8]

In 1319 Thomas Drinkwater granted a lease to James Beaufleur for the Bear, in return for which Beaufleur undertook to buy all his wines from Drinkwater – an early form of the tie.

Buying in ale, as well as wine for the larger taverners and innkeepers, was an attractive proposition, since for many alehouse keepers ale selling was not the principal occupation. In 1325 Gilbert de Mardone of Oxford kept an alehouse in Crooked Lane but he was also a fishmonger. He had a ward named Emma, and one Walter de Bengyton attempted one time to assail the alehouse with a band of followers, to make off with Emma. Gilbert managed to stave off the attackers until the sound of fighting aroused neighhours who rallied to his side. De Bengyton was felled by a blow from a quarterstaff and left insensible in the street. He died two days later. There are two possible accounts of this tale, depending upon your disposition. Firstly, Walter was madly in love with the beautiful Emma and, his advances having been rejected by the protective Gilbert, he sought to win the girl in the only way he knew. Secondly, Emma was not particularly beautiful and almost certainly smelt of fish, but her attraction for both Walter and Gilbert was that she was an heiress, hence her wardship, and was soon to come into a small fortune. You may choose your fancy.

A further consideration for the alehouse keeper in deciding whether to buy in his ale was his busy schedule. A typical day for a London alehouse keeper would start at 6 a.m., shopping for victuals. At 9 a.m. the malt market would open, and at 11 a.m. non-freemen were permitted to buy. Noon saw the customary lunchtime rush – *Noonschenche* – and the ale house would have remained open until 9 p.m. when the church bells rang *Initegium*, the call for all fires to be doused. As early as 1189 only brewhouses made of stone could brew at night, so without a large family or domestic service night was, for many, the only time available to brew.

Alehouse keeping at this time was a very low occupation, barely one step away from absolute poverty. This situation changed little in 300 years. In the early seventeenth century the *Ballad of the Industrious Smith* contains the perennial lament:

> I see by my labour but little I thrive,
> And that against the stream I do strive.
> By selling off ale some money is got,
> If every man honestly pay for his pot.
> By this we may keep the wolf from the door.

In towns, the poor smith or labourer, or leather worker would buy a decent quantity of ale from the common brewer and retail it to supplement his income. He may possibly have brewed it himself, or have got his wife to do so, but some considerable capital outlay was necessary for any serious brewing with the aim of producing ale of a quality acceptable to fastidious town palates. In the country equipment was much ruder.

A further factor behind the rise of the common brewer was that throughout the fourteenth century ale became more of a staple. It was already forbidden to malt wheat for ale production when crops were bad, so the harvest of 1375 must have been exceptionally so since the rising price of grain put ale and bread out of the means of the poor, as Langland testifies. Edward III instructed the brewers and bakers to make farthing measures of bread and ale, forbidding them to refuse to serve these small amounts. He then backed up his measure by introducing £80 worth of farthings into circulation – some 76,800 coins!

In addition to the alehouse in the town, the tavern was also enjoying a period of rapid growth. In 1272 London was reputed to have had three taverns, at Chepe, Walbrooke and Lombard Street, but by 1309 it reputedly had 354 taverns among its 1,334 alehouses. Most taverns were meant to sell wine only, but with time they came to sell ale as well, to such an extent that by the seventeenth century many taverns had an alehouse downstairs in the basement. Outside London taverns were few, even though in 1194 vintners were fined in Wiltshire, London, Southampton and Aylesbury for selling above the assize. Most taverns not in London were in ports.

In London the wine trade quickly became very influential. In 1356 London's Lord Mayor – Sir Richard Pachard – was a vintner, and no doubt his influence was instrumental in getting a hall built for the vintners in 1357. In addition, an entire area of the city – Vintry – was reserved for the conduct of the trade. Regulation of this trade, too, proved necessary at an early date. A charter of

1311 prohibits wholesale wine merchants from being tavern keepers, as a means of preventing lees from finding their way back into casks. Taverns were also obliged to operate with their cellar doors open – cellars were on the ground floor so that the customer could see the wine being drawn and know that it was free from adulteration. It has already been mentioned that attempts were made to regulate wine prices as well as ale, though largely unsuccessfully. In 1316 Henry de St Antonine was arraigned for having sold wine at 6*d* per gallon, one penny over the assize. The fact that he was very leniently treated by the court bears testimony to the general feeling that the assize was unrealistic, as well as demonstrating the general hostility felt towards foreign wine traders, de St Antoine being a freeman. The liberties extended to the wine traders of Aquitaine and Bordeaux were much resented by city freemen, and the traders were occasionally forced to violence to defend their rights. In the long term, in the face of protracted antagonism, they simply withdrew and refused to supply wine, as they frequently did during the reign of Edward III. This sanction invariably had the desired result.

The assizes often presented the taverns with a choice: either sell the wine at a loss or adulterate it, a dilemma that caused much popular concern in the 1890s when publicans found themselves in a similar position over their beer. In the fourteenth century the authorities were less prepared to accept adulteration than they were in the nineteenth.

By reason of the multitude of wines now [1330] brought to the said City it was ordered that the gallon of best Gascon wine shall be sold from hence at 4*d*, and the gallon of Rhenish wine at 8*d*: and that all taverners of the City shall keep the doors of their taverns and of their cellars open so that the buyers of their wine may be able to see where their wines are drawn . . . and thereupon the said Mayor, Aldermen and Sheriffs were given to understand that all the taverns of the City, making a confederacy and alliance among themselves and would not allow their wines to be sold . . . upon which hearing the Mayor and Sheriffs went through the middle of Vintry and Chepe and through other streets and lanes of the City that they might know the truth to the same: and they had the names of the taverners so closing their taverns written down.[9]

Outside London similar measures were being taken.

> Because there be more taverns in the realm than there wont to
> be, selling as well corrupt wines as wholesome, and have sold
> the gallon at such price as they themselves would, because there
> was no punishment ordained for them, as hath been for them
> that sold bread or ale, to the great hurt of the people, it is
> accorded that a cry shall be made that none be so hardy as to
> sell wines but at a reasonable price, regarding the price that is at
> the ports where the wine came in; and the expenses as in
> carriage of the same from the said ports to the places where
> they be sold. The town authorities were to make an assay twice
> a year and all wines found corrupt were to be shed and cast out
> and the vessels broken.[10]

It would seem that 130 years after King John had come up against
the problems of accurately assaying wines, his later Plantagenet
descendents were no closer to a solution. The assay took place
twice a year. The wine fleet left France once in the autumn, to
return before Christmas with the new wine, and once in January
returning before Easter and bringing the 'racked', the better quality
wines. These fleets must have been quite substantial, for in 1272–3
no fewer than 8,846 tuns of wine were legitimately taxed and
imported.

There was occasional wine trade with other countries too. A
Portuguese ship that was intending to land wine in England in
1318, was wrecked on the Cornish coastline. The fact that the
local Cornishmen sailed out under cover of darkness and cut its
anchor ropes may have been a significant factor in the ship's
misfortune. Further along the coast the Cinque Ports were mere
pirates' dens and no ships were safe. Considering that the French
wine fleets travelled *en masse* to afford protection against acts of
piracy perpetrated by their clients, it was a miracle that any wine
was delivered at all. It did get through, however, and in
considerable amounts – enough in 1392 for the public conduits of
London to flow with wine when Richard II returned from abroad.

Anyone could buy wine from the foreign importers in the Vintry,
who were forbidden to retail, though only vintners could supply
sufficient capital to buy up enough stock to supply towns all year
round. The capital available to the taverns meant that they

confined themselves to buying a few casks in the spring and autumn from the importers and at other times relied upon the vintners. Occasionally this manifested itself in early tie arrangements such as at the Bear. In an earlier example Christian the taverner pledged himself and his chattels to William Varache, on 16 August 1281, in lieu of six casks of wine at £13 and four silver cups, on credit. Relations were improved by the mutual benefits derived from the adulteration of wines, prohibited by Edward III on the 8 November 1327. The most common form was the mixing of new and rack wines. It became an offence to mix them together, to sell rack wines before new wines were exhausted, and to sell them together with the view of the cellar obstructed.

The golden age of the tavern was in the sixteenth and seventeenth centuries. However, as early as 1329 their numbers were starting to cause alarm, 'Whereas misdoers, going about by night, have their resort more in taverns than elsewhere, and there seek refuge and watch their hour for misdoing we forbid that any taverner or brewer keep the door of his tavern open after the hour of curfew.'[11]

It wasn't just footpads and cut-throats that made taverns unwholesome places. In Oxford, on 10 February 1354, a party of university clerks went to Swyndlestock Tavern – later to become the Mermaid Tavern. The taverner, John de Croydon, served wine to the students, who quarrelled with it and threw the jug at his head. At this point the locals and the freeholder, the former Mayor, John de Beresford, sided with him against the clerks. Several days rioting ensued, at the end of which, several university clerks lay dead.

Many medieval inns were built as investment opportunities. Westminster College built the Angel at Arlesford in 1418 and another at Andover in 1445. New College, Oxford, built the Golden Cross, in about 1490. Osney Abbey improved the Star Inn, Oxford in 1550. The brewhouse of the abbey at Dorchester-on-Thames eventually became the George Inn, the buildings surrounding three sides of its inner courtyard date from around 1500.

The abbey at Glastonbury built the famous George at the instigation of Abbot John Selwood (1457–93), and at Gloucester Abbey John Twynyng built the galleried New Inn in 1457 as a pilgrims' hostel for those travelling to the tomb of Edward II. Despite the high initial outlay, inns were ideal uses for property when returns on much urban property were low. Other notable inns of the period were built, not as investments *per se*, but as improvements – for example, the famous George at Norton St Philip.

The Carthusian and Cistercian monks were traditionally involved with the wool trade. The Carthusian monks of Hinton Charterhouse owned the Manor of Norton St Philip, which, under their patronage, hosted an important cloth and cattle fair every April from 1293. The George was built and added to between 1350 and 1400, functioning both as an inn and a warehouse. Its long, open single room on the first floor was an ideal wool exchange. A fire around 1500 resulted in part of the frontage being replaced in the half-timbered style, and the galleried courtyard at the rear was a late sixteenth century addition with which Oliver Cromwell would have been familiar. The George was the setting for an attempt on the life of the Duke of Monmouth during the abortive rebellion of 1685. When in the nineteenth century the railway largely did for the inn, history came full circle and the George's long room enabled it to survive as a carters' warehouse, a common fate among the great galleried inns.

Such a fate befell the most famous inn of all – the Tabard at Southwark – immortalised by Chaucer and Shakespeare. Its earliest history is uncertain. Evidence suggests that in 1304 it came under the demesne of the Abbot of Hyde. In 1388 Chaucer introduces us to the landlord, Henry Bailey.

> A semely man our hoste was with alle
> For to han been a marshal in a halle.
> A large man was he with even stepe,
> A fairer burgeys is ther noon in Chepe
> Bold of his speehe; and wys, and wel y-taught
> And of manhood him lakkede right naught,
> Eek thereto he was right a merry man.

Bailey was a man of some repute who twice represented Southwark at Westminster, whose inn was already widely famous as a starting point for pilgrimages – a reputation it maintained until the Dissolution. Thereafter it was leased to the Master brothers for £9 per annum.

Borough High Street, serving as the approach to London Bridge, then and for centuries the only bridge across the Thames, was an exceptionally busy thoroughfare, lined on either side with many inns such as the Bear at Bridge Foot. The layout of the Tabard when Chaucer's pilgrims met one April morning in 1388 is not known, but several likely features can be deduced. The inn was galleried, as was the fashion of the day. (Galleries are thought to have been brought back from Palestine by the Crusaders. This is a nice idea, since it is likely that the Saracens adopted the idea from the Byzantines, who took it from the Romans who had already used it in Britain.)

As the Tabard's neighbours grew more dense, frequently back to back, the gallery became more practical. In a row of chambers only one wall would have been able to have a window to admit light, as well as house the door. Chambers tended to be on the first and second floors, the ground floor being taken up with kitchens, parlours, stabling, the hall and communal rooms. Therefore a gallery was essential for the provision of both access and light. The only alternative was an arrangement of rooms sharing common staircases, as was adopted by the university colleges, where it better suited a suite rather than a single chamber.

The original shape of the inn is uncertain. Chaucer's pilgrims all rode, so stabling was necessary. Internal trade was starting to expand, but there is little evidence that the carting and waggoning trades that so helped the development of the inn in the fifteenth century had evolved to any degree. It was the association of coaches and wagons with inns that gave them their characteristic layout, with very long courtyards and entrances to front and rear, shaped by the fact that coaches and wagons cannot reverse. In essence the medieval inn fell into two categories. First the 'courtyard' style, typified by the New Inn, Gloucester, where the inn surrounds the courtyard, galleried upper floors being accessed by stairs on opposing sides of the yard. The second type is the 'gatehouse', such as the George, Norton St Philip, or the Angel, Grantham. The Angel is an ancient and historic inn. Built on the site of a manor house belonging to the Saxon Queen Elith, it became a hostel of the Knights Templar and King John held court there in 1213. It was rebuilt as an inn in the mid-fourteenth century and again in the fifteenth. It was there that Richard III signed the death warrant of the Duke of Buckingham on 19 October 1483.

The gatehouse inn is confined within one building, with a courtyard at the rear. It is likely that the early Tabard was a courtyard inn, as that is what all the Southwark inns became. So it is likely that it was not much different from a sixteenth-century description of its layout. The ground floor contained a dark parlour, or cellar, a hall and a dining room – possibly with wooden partitions of snugs. On the first floor there was a middle chamber, a corner chamber, the landord's chamber under garrets and cocklofts, as well as four other chambers. These chambers would have been quite spacious and would have been identified by names such as the Sun, Moon, Rose, or Dolphin. Another feature would have been a garden, even in town inns, fulfilling the dual role of herb garden and as Chaucer tells us, a quiet place of retreat.

> The wyff of Bath was so wery, she had no will to walk
> She take the Prior's by the hand; madam will ye stalk
> Pryvely into the garden to see the herbis grow?
> And aftyr, with our hosts wyff, in her parlour rowe.

In many respects the gatehouse inn would have resembled the manor house, as regards size and layout, and indeed many inns were manor houses doubling up while the occupant was absent. Goldsmith's comedy *She Stoops to Conquer* relies on the ability to confuse the two.

In the inns of the fifteenth century, however, there was one important design difference which indicated a major change in popular habit. The halls in these inns were considerably smaller than their manorial counterparts. This was a clear departure from the communal life of the manor hall. The guests may well have eaten in their rooms or in separate dining parlours. The hall was more for the feeding of retainers and the inn staff, and even then not necessarily all at one sitting. Class distinction emerges very early on at the inn, and for the next 400 years class dictated both the standing of any particular inn in a community and how you would expect to be treated there.

The Tabard was rebuilt in 1628 and it is likely another floor was added. The inn was destroyed in the Southwark fire of 1676, but rebuilt on almost identical lines, though renamed the Talbot. Like so many inns its heyday ended suddenly when the railways came along, and it finished its days as a warehouse for carters, for whom the galleries were fine loading bays. Before its demise Chaucer's inn was properly renamed the Tabard, but that was not enough to save it. In 1875 – despite a huge public outcry – the property developers, as ever, got their chance to destroy something of great value and replace it with something of none.

The Tabard suffered a sad fate, for our oldest inns were of a religious nature, and those like the George and Dragon, Codicote, Hertfordshire, founded by St Albans Abbey in 1297; the Green Dragon, Limnchurch, formerly the hospice of St Catherine's Priory until the early fourteenth century; the Crown, Chiddingfold, Surrey, a monks' rest home until 1383; or the Pilgrims' Rest, Battle, Sussex, a fourteenth-century hospice for the abbey, have frequently survived where their younger coaching cousins have not. The Tabard was a religious inn that just happened to become indistinguishable from the coaching inns that grew up around it, and as a result suffered their fate. All that remains of the once great Southwark inns is a tiny galleried fragment of the George, preserved only a stone's throw from the site where Chaucer

> Bifel that, in a season on a day,
> in Southwark at the Tabard as I lay.

Chapter 3

HOPS AND BEER: THE FIFTEENTH CENTURY

And in very deed, the hops but a weed
Brought over against the law, and set here to sale,
Would the law were removed, and no more beer brewed
But all men betake them to a pot of good ale.

The Hop for his profit,
It strengtheneth drink and it flavoureth malt;
And being well brewed, long kept it will last,
And drawing abide – if ye draw not too fast.

Thomas Tusser (c. 1520–80)

The story of the hop is a mysterious and intriguing one. No one is actually sure when it made its first commercial appearance in England. There are various rhymes which are supposed to educate us on this point.

> Hops, Reformation, Bays and Beer
> Came into England all in one year.

This couplet would indicate a date around 1520, which is clearly nonsense.

The hop – *Humulus Lupulus*, from *lupus*, the Latin for wolf, the hop being as destructive among willows as a wolf among sheep, and *Humularia*, the name given to the hop gardens of France and Germany in the eighth and ninth centuries – may have been introduced into England by the Romans. They certainly cultivated it as a vegetable and greatly enjoyed eating the shoots, preparing them very much as we would prepare asparagus.

A member of the hemp family, there can be few plants that have been as useful as the hop. It has been employed in medicine as a herbal remedy and a sedative. Its sap has been used as a dye and as a preservative for photographic plates; the bines, when not added to beer, make good silage; its roots can be used to make sugar or alcohol; its fibrous stems can be turned into hemp or pulped into paper, and its ash can be used in the making of glass. Strangely enough, however, in this country the hop was despised and prohibited right down through the fifteenth century until, gradually, beer began to usurp traditional ale.

As an adjunct to brewing its history goes back a long way too. The ancient Jews believed that hopped ale was a defence against leprosy. In England its use in brewing was certainly known prior to the Norman invasion and it was one of many herbs used as a flavouring in brewing, since brewing was a risky process and, if less than perfectly concluded, the result could have been pretty unpalatable. As techniques for brewing improved the use of flavourings generally declined and eventually the use of anything other than water, malt and yeast to make ale was regarded as adulteration – a serious offence.

Many authorities favour 1400 as the most likely year for the (re)introduction of hops to England. This would, however, appear to be the year that hopped beer was first imported into Britain, via Winchelsea, rather than when hops were first cultivated. Just as the marriage of Henry II to Eleanor of Provence opened up the Bordeaux wine trade in the twelfth century, so the marriage of Edward III to Phillipa, daughter of William, Count of Holland and Hainault, was responsible for the introduction of hops to England on a large scale. England's wealth was founded on the wool trade and much of our wool left via Norwich and Ipswich to be finished in Flanders. It was Phillipa who perceived the extra value to be gained by finishing the cloth here and then exporting it, and so she encouraged an influx of Flemish weavers. It was to satisfy Flemish palates that the cargo of beer arrived at Winchelsea.

The ascendancy of hopped beer over unhopped ale was by no means an inevitable or rapid matter. Beer was bitterly resented from the outset. Some regarded it as poisonous, others as adulterated. Henry VIII ordered the Royal Brewer of Eltham to put neither hops nor brimstone in his ale.

The process of the diffusion of beer was very easy to trace, and even 230 years after its first importation the picture was clear.

> I generous wine am for the court,
> The citee calls for beer,
> But Ale, bonnie Ale, like a Lord of the Soile,
> In the country shall domineer.

Rural areas clung to their ale until well into the eighteenth century, especially in the more remote corners of England, for while there was much popular prejudice against beer it had certain geographical and economic advantages on its side. It is not certain whether beer brewing was actually illegal, as this seems to have been very much a case of local enforcement. In 1487 beer brewing was well established in Canterbury while places like Norwich and Shrewsbury still prohibited adulteration by hops. The addition of hops had several commercial advantages. As it acted as a preservative it meant that beer would keep longer, and this meant economies of scale derived from brewing in larger amounts, which in turn was attractive to the growing number of common brewers in the towns.

Much rural brewing was intermittent, carried out by the semi-itinerant poor or by poorer labourers as a means of providing or supplementing a meagre income, and this practice continued until the eighteenth century in some areas. Sporadic outbreaks of plague in the fourteenth century had hugely reduced the population. Agricultural wages rose and a labour shortage followed. Ale became affordable and the numbers needing to brew to survive fell. All this played into the hands of the common brewer. Indeed, it helped to create the phenomenon of the common, or wholesale, brewer, and so helped maintain the propagation of beer.

As a rule of thumb it is probably safe to conclude that where beer brewing was illegal there were sufficient numbers of people prepared to chance their arm, aware of the gains to be made, to gradually make the law a dead letter. Elsewhere beer brewing was legitimate, provided that brewers were careful to differentiate between ale and beer. It must be stressed that from the outset of the introduction of the hop, ale and beer brewing were different processes. Beer was not merely ale with added hops, and those who thought otherwise were quickly accused of adulteration.

The amount of equipment needed was much greater for beer brewing. A copper was needed as well as the traditional mash tuns. Boiling took much longer and was therefore more fuel intensive. In addition hops had to be obtained, which was outside the scope of many ale brewers in the fifteenth century. However, an important advantage of hopped beer was that it was easier to brew and keep throughout the summer, a fact that caused great resentment among the City of London ale brewers whose attacks on Flemish brewers in 1436 prompted Henry VI to proclaim

> A Writ to Sheriffs to make proclamation for all brewers of biere within their bailiwick to continue to exercise their art as hitherto, not withstanding the malevolent attempts being made to prevent natives of Holland and Seeland and others who occupy themselves in brewing the drinke called biere from continuing their trade, on the ground that such a drink is poisonous and not fit to drink, and caused drunkenness, whereas it was a wholesome drink, especially in summertime, such attacks had already caused many brewers to cease brewing and would cause greater mischief unless stopped.[1]

The proclamation suggests the existence of a propensity to vary drinking habits. Just as many drinkers today drink bitter during the winter and convert to colder lager during the summer, so there may have been similar fluctuations between ale and beer drinking.

The brewers probably had cause to be upset, though the attacks did cease, for the following year Henry rewarded the Brewers' Company with their charter. The penalties for adulteration were severe and the ale brewers were strictly regulated. Yet here was a body of 'foreigners' – non-freemen of the city – who escaped penalty and regulation by, in their eyes, adulterating their ale but calling it something else, and, what was even worse, selling it more cheaply too.

In August 1418, when Henry VI asked London for supplies to assist him in the siege of Rouen, among the provisions shipped to Harfleur and then down the Seine to Henry's army were thirty butts of sweet wine and 1,000 pipes of ale and beer as well as 2,500 cups. As well as being an impressive volume of liquid what is notable is that while the ale was priced at 20s a tun, the beer was only charged at 13s 4d per tun: a considerable difference.

The basis of the ale brewers' grievance would appear to have been acknowledged, for in 1441 similar regulations to those governing ale brewing were applied to beer, with the exception that beer should not leave the brewery for eight days after racking. In addition, an assize of beer was introduced: 'When malt was 3s 4d a quarter a barrel of "double coyt" [double cooled] beer containing 36 gallons should be sold for 2s 8d and the price should vary – as in the case of ale – by a farthing a gallon to each shilling on the quarter of malt. Barrels of 'single coyt' beer, however should always be sold for 2s.'[2]

While ale and beer co-existed throughout the fifteenth and sixteenth centuries in the larger towns, there is no doubt that the headway being made was all in favour of beer. In 1464 the beer brewers petitioned for ordinances to standardise their barrels, an important act of recognition. It is important to note that it was deliberate policy to keep ale and beer barrels of different capacities. This may have been to enable easy differentiation of ale and beer barrels in warehouses and cellars, or to emphasise that ale and beer were different drinks. At any rate, the beer barrel was thirty-six gallons and the *kilderkin* – a Dutch term – eighteen gallons, while the ale barrel was thirty-two gallons and an anachronistic ale *kilderkin* was sixteen gallons.

By 1478 the beer brewers of London were finding that demand for their product was such that they could inflate the price of the assize, which prompted the city authorities to permit outside brewers to enjoy the right to sell in the city, until the price fell again, a course of action they were forced to repeat in 1492.

There is no doubt, given examples of this form of growth in demand, that traditional ale brewers were feeling the pinch. The beer brewers' product was equally as strong as their own, of a more consistent quality, kept longer, was cheaper and was gradually finding favour with the popular palate. By the 1480s hops were starting to find their way into ale. A petition by the ale brewers in 1485 complains:

Whereas by the sotill and crafty means of foreigners dwelling withoute the franchises . . . a deceivable and unwholesome fête is bruyng of ale within the said citee nowe of late is founde and practised, that is to say in occupying and putting of hoppes and other things in the said ale, contrary to the good and wholesome manner of bruyng of olde tyme used. Please it therefore your goode lordshippe to forbid the putting into ale of any hops, herbs or any such like thing, but only licor, malte and yeste.

The petition was granted, which was by no means a certainty, since even by this late date brewing was still seen as a very lowly occupation, unlikely to attract much sympathy. A fine of 6s 8d was levied per adulterated barrel, though this was shortly halved for adding hops to ale but retained for other adulteration.

There were frequent prosecutions for adulteration of ale with hops up until 1522, where we hear the injunction against ale brewing with hops repeated in Coventry. There is some confusion as to what is intended, or for what people were being amerced. It is quite possible that, as in the fourteenth century, breaking the assize was an institutionalised but improvised form of control and local taxation so that similar attempts to benefit from the law were being tried. It is unclear whether people were charged with adulteration who were intentionally trying to brew beer and not ale, but at 20s a time the local authorities could not resist the opportunity to levy fines.

If there is one sure indicator of the growth in beer production it must be the boom in beer exports which occurred during the early part of the sixteenth century. By 1543 the volume of exports was such that there was concern about the quantities of wood leaving the country as casks and never returning. It was decided that nothing bigger than a barrel should be used for export and that exporters should be under an obligation to import sufficient supplies of timber to balance the amount lost as exported casks. This does not seem to have been a successful measure, since Mary I felt obliged to ban beer exports altogether in 1555.

It is unclear how well this prohibition was observed. However, given the skill the English traditionally displayed at smuggling illicit liquor into Britain, it would have posed no great problem to them to smuggle it out. At any rate, we learn that in 1591 the export volume of just twenty breweries stationed along the Thames between Milford Stairs and St Catherine's was some 26,400 barrels (7.3 million pints). Beer was becoming big business.

Beer was not without its detractors, however. Andrew Boorde, writing in 1542, came up with a typically British argument. Beer, he said, was fine in its place. It was just that its place was not in Britain.

Ale is made of malte and water; and they which do put any other thynge to ale than is rehearsed, except yest, balme godisgood doth sofysticat theyr ale. Ale for an Englysshe man is a natural drinke. Ale must have these properties: it must be freshe and cleare, it must not be ropey or smoky, nor must it have no weft or taile. Ale should not be drunke under five dayes olde. Newe ale is unwholsome for all men. Barley malte maketh better ale than other malte or any other corn doth; it doth ingendre grosse humorie, but yet it maketh a man strong.

However,

Beer is made of malte and hoppes and water; it is the natural drinke for a Dutche man, and nowe of late dayes it is much used in Englande to the detriment of many Englisshe people; specially it killeth them the which be troubled with the colic and the stone and the strangulation, for the drink is a cold drinke, yet it doth make a man fat, and doth inflate the belly, as it doth appeare by the Dutch-men's faces and belyes. If the bere be well served and be fyned and not new, it doth qualify heat of the liver.[3]

Sixty years later there were still those prepared to champion ale over beer and mourn its decline: 'Ale made of barley malt and good water doth make a man strong, but nowadies few brewers doth brew it as they ought, for they add slimy and heavy baggage unto it thinking thereby to please tosse pots and to increase the vigour of it.'

By the end of the sixteenth century ale brewing was apparently sufficiently uneconomic to render adulteration necessary. By the first decade of the eighteenth century a hop shortage made beer adulteration a problem too. An act of parliament of 1710 forbade the use of any bittering agent other than hops 'in brewing any *beer* or *ale* which is intended for sale'.

It would appear that it was not just a few of the crustier types of Englishmen who felt that the change to the stronger beer and increased consumption that accompanied it was deleterious of the national character, as the French observation of 1620 suggests.

The English have a drink they call Ale and which is thought the wholesomest liquor that could be drunk; for whereas the body of man is supported by natural heat and radical moisture, there is no drink conduceth more to the preservation of the one and

> increase of the other than ale; for while Englishmen drank Ale
> they were strong, brawny and able men and could draw an
> arrow an ell [45 in] long; but when they fell to wine and beer
> they were found to be impaired in their strength and age.[4]

These sentiments were unlikely to have been mere reactionary
prejudice either. It was universally felt that ale was a warm,
sustaining, bodily drink, compared with the thinner, often stronger,
colder beer. An Englishman would no more have put spiced beer
into his gracecup or wassail bowl than a modern day publican
would serve lager through a handpump.

In Farquhar's play of 1707, *The Beaux' Stratagem*, the landlord
of an inn in Lichfield claims never to have eaten more than eight
and fifty ounces of meat. 'At one sitting judging by your bulk,' says
his startled guest. To which Boniface replies, 'Not in my life, Sir; I
have fed purely upon ale, I have ate my ale, drank my ale, and
I always sleep upon my ale.' Likewise there is no shortage of
popular testimony to the superiority of ale over beer.

> He who drinks small beer goes to bed sober,
> Falls as the leaves do fall that fall in October,
> He who drinks strong ale goes to bed mellow,
> Lives as he ought to live and dies a jolly good fellow.

While our French commentator may have lamented the inability
of the inebriated English to 'draw an arrow an ell long' – no mean
feat – Henry VII, like Edward III 170 years previously, was alarmed
not so much by the inability of the English to draw a bow but at
their disinclination to have a go in the first place.

After 400 years of obligatory archery practice at the butts the
novelty was wearing off, and new and different forms of recreation
were being sought. Naturally, one had to look no further than the
alehouse door to find a skittles game in progress, or a few idle
soaks preparing to kick a pig's bladder around for a bit.

In acts of 1495 and 1504 Henry VII gave to two justices the
power of suppression of any alehouse. In addition, licences had to
be renewed and alehouses could be suppressed for bad behaviour.
Of course no one took the slightest notice, but the acts were
important in that they made licensing a responsibility of justices,
which is, of course, where such power resides today.

Chapter 4

SECULARISATION AND SPECIALISATION

Wherever God erects a House of Prayer,
The Devil's sure to build a chapel there,
And 'Twill he found upon examination
The latter has the larger congregation.
'The True-Born Englishman', Daniel Defoe (1660–1731)

Along with the diffusion of the hop there were two other major trends occurring in the fifteenth and sixteenth centuries: secularisation and specialisation. In the first case brewing utensils and techniques were becoming more developed. The inventory of a brewer of 1335 would resemble the kit of an enthusiastic home brewer, but this inventory of a 1486 brewhouse would be more familiar to a professional brewer.

A bruying ketyll copper with a courke of waynscot, a mash fatte with a lowse bottom and a tappe trowe of ledde; a wort fatte, two kelers for wort, three gutters of tree, three hand ketils of brass; two sesterns of ledde for liquore, a fyrehole, a rake and a pyke of iron; 20 little tubbes for yeast, a little masshe tubbe; a water tubbe, and a flete [float], a clevying axe, a fanne, a stepyng sestern of lead, 24 kilderkyns and a malt mill, with all apparel, a beere dray, with two pair wheles and a blacke haire for a kiln.[1]

We do not need to get as far down the list as the beer dray to realise that this is a commercial operation.

The increase in commercial brewing meant that an increase in standards was expected. Measures were taken to ensure the quality

of the ingredients and product. In 1432 regulations governing the
quality of malt were produced, while in 1441 beer tasters were
appointed, much as ale-conners were. Officials were appointed to
hunt out and destroy diseased or defective hops. Good malt was to
be 'clere, swete and dry and wele made, not cupped in the sakkes,
nor raw dried malte, dank or wete malte or made of mowe brent
barley [overheated in the mow], belyed malte, edgrove malte
[germinating], accrespied malte [sprouting at both ends] wyvell
eten malte or medled.'

An Act for the True Making of Malt of 1548 stipulated that
malt must dry at least three weeks – seventeen days in the
summer. Indeed, in 1455 Kent was such a predominant centre for
the production of both hops and malt that a five year prohibition
on individuals producing more than 100 quarters of malt per
annum was passed to protect the malt trade in other parts of the
country.

It is not known how many people such a prohibition would have
covered, but an idea can be got from the amount of beer involved.
In the 1500s the Percy family were brewing 576 gallons of beer
from six quarters of malt. Their brew was very strong and it is
likely that most commercial brewers would have stretched their
ingredients slightly further. If this ratio is accepted then at a
conservative estimate each Kentish maltster was still allowed to
produce enough malt to brew 768,000 pints of a brew strong
enough, by today's standards, to take your head off.

That seems a staggering quantity of ale, but then the English did
drink a staggering amount. In 1464 the guests at a banquet to
celebrate the inauguration of the new Archbishop of York
managed to consume 300 tuns of ale and 100 tuns of wine, that
is, 360,000 pints of ale and 18,700 bottles of wine. When those
attending the Installation Banquet of the Archbishop of
Canterbury in 1504 managed to consume six tuns of red wine,
four tuns of claret, one tun of white wine, one tun of white wine
for the kitchen (187 bottles), one butt Malmsey, one pipe of Ossay,
two tierces of Rhenish wine, four tuns London ale, six tuns Kentish
ale and twenty tuns of English beer, it must merely be concluded
that the archbishop asked fewer guests.

The volumes mentioned give some indication as to the scale the
drink trade was beginning to assume. In the fifteenth century the
infrastructure needed to support a mature trade came into being.

The coopers and bottle makers had been around since the fourteenth century. The pewterers were incorporated in 1468 and the innkeepers in 1515. In cities like London and Coventry there was the additional trade of water bearers who supplied the brewers with their water. As early as 1312 London cooks, brewers and fishmongers were taxed on their water consumption, while in Coventry the brewers could take water from the public conduit for their victualling functions only.

Nor was the monarchy slow to take advantage of the growing drink trade. Henry VII noticed the deficiency of British shipping and the number of foreign vessels that brought trade to our ports. He decreed that Gascony and Guienne wines could only be imported in English ships with English crews. For the English the choice was simple: give up drinking or learn to sail. They have been a powerful maritime nation ever since.

Various monarchs from Henry VII to Elizabeth I assisted the trade in other ways too, by banning the export of tanned leather and the import of drinking vessels, so that the bottle makers would have no excuse for not providing ample supplies of bottles, blackjacks and bombards; or by protecting the supplies of wood used for casks.

A glance at the municipal records of any large town will show that the attitude of the authorities also was becoming more sophisticated. There are constant revisions of the assize to match supply to demand, prohibitions against selling from anything but approved measures, and ways to prevent merchants from forestalling the market and creating monopolies. Ordinances ensured that when malt prices rose brewers should not cease to supply ale. In Coventry from 1448, innkeepers were obliged to keep a lantern outside their premises till 9 p.m. for the benefit of passers, upon pain of 6s 8d. Coventry later decided to keep a register of alehouses so that they would be able to suppress the worst behaved and inferior houses first if they became a nuisance.

The second theme of the era – secularisation – occurs hand in hand with the first. As alehouses multiplied and as inns took over monastic responsibilities, there was a reduction in the central role that the Church played in society. A certain primacy was maintained in rural areas, but even then there were conscious efforts to separate the ales and wakes from the actual church building. Under Henry VI various unsuccessful attempts, were made to enforce Sunday observance – in 1428 Hull corporation ordered Sunday closing, and in 1444 an order of Common Council outlawed all Sunday trading. Both were ignored.

Obviously, part of the reason for secularisation was that alehouses were capable of providing many of the services formerly offered by the Church: a common meeting place, a focus for the dissemination of news, and a warm room with a fire. An unusual inn for its time, the Chequers in Calcot's Abbey, Lambeth, actually had an oratory in the house and a chaplain celebrated Divine Service. Today there are still pubs where church services are performed. For most people, one attraction of the alehouse was the absence of religion. You might not escape the priest in the alehouse, as priests were all too frequent customers, but you did know that at least he was unlikely, unless drunk, to start mumbling interminably in Latin.

Worse in popular reputation than priests were the 'clerics' – lay scribes employed in copying or writing manuscripts, since they had not taken holy orders.

> But if thou begin to drink to call or crave,
> Thou for thy calling such good rewards shalt have,
> That none shall call thee malopert or drunke
> Or an abbey lowne or limber of a monke.

Intemperance by monks, nuns, priests and clerics was to end with the Dissolution. Not all houses were dissolute, but clearly the excesses of some assisted Henry VIII in his ends.

Chapter 5

SPIRITS: THE ELIZABETHAN INNOVATION

Waters of capons, as men call them, are given to drinke to restore the strength to women in childbed or cold sickmen in diseases of great weaknesse, or through too much evacuation. They are want to seeth the capon very long in water, that all the flesh may fall from the bones and be distilled together with the liquor, either by itself or other precious waters put unto it, and spices, gold, silver and precious stones. Some allow the capon the more the elder he is, neither do they cut his throat, but strangle and choke him; and [when] he is cut up in small pieces they distill him.[1]

In Renaissance Europe men were making new discoveries, and reaching new heights in art, music, medicine, architecture, physics and mathematics. Renaissance man in England was wrestling with the intricacies of distilling chickens. No doubt there was much academic infighting involved with two highly acrimonious schools developing – the one pro-throat slitting, the other neck wringing.

Distilling a chicken is, however, not as daft as it seems. It was already quite common to take an old rooster, pulverise him till every bone was broken, stick him in a cloth bag with a pound of raisins and boil him up in a batch of cock ale. Chicken distilling, incredibly, was not nearly as stupid as some of the others things they distilled – for example, egg yolk, worms and scorpions; while the more zealous exponents of the new art would distil just about anything they could lay their hands on in their experiments to connect this new science with the mysteries of the Arcana and the Cabbala.

These concoctions were for the most part quack medicines, but probably tasted foul enough to convince the patient that they were efficacious. They were, however, widespread, and perhaps it was the bad taste and the smack of alchemy that stopped people catching on even faster to something potentially very good.

Irish immigrants had brought with them their own 'Usquebauch' or 'water of life' in the early part of the sixteenth century, but it does not seem to have found much favour outside their own enclaves. The fashionable water of life was 'Aqua Vitae', which was usually made from distilling the dregs from the brewer's mash tun. In 1559 it was acclaimed to be jolly useful stuff.

It helpeth red and duskish eyes. It is good for them that have the falling sicknesse [epilepsy] if thee drink it. It cureth the palsy if they be annointed therewith. It sharpeneth the wit, it restoreth memory. It maketh men merry and preserve youth. It putteth away fracins, ring worms and all spots of the face. It is merveylous profitable for frantic men and such as be melancholy. It expelleth poison. The smell thereof burnt killeth flies and cold creeping beasts. It restoreth wine that is turned or putrified. It is most wholesome for the stomach, the hart and the liver, it nouresheth blood, it agreeth merveylously and most with men's nature.[2]

Sadly the recipe for this wonder tonic is lost. The recipes for Aqua Vitae that were passed down show that it was an early form of brandy, from the Dutch for 'burnt wine'.

For ye distilation of Aqua Vitae, or burning water, a man must chuse the best wyne, blacke, red or white. Black and old yields more plenty and also better water than any other. The fire at ye first must be light and soft and after more vehement. The water that is gotten thereout is surnamed burning or the soul of life of the wine and when it is distilled twice or thrice, then they call it flaming water.[3]

The early distillers were extremely resourceful and experimental. They used to smear the heads of their stills with honey and laudanum, or insert bundles of herbs, such as musk, cloves, or camphura in the mouth of the still, so the vapours would filter through them. At this time it is unlikely that spirits would have been drunk neat. Most likely a few drops would have been added to wine or water, or mixed with juices, or spices to produce cordials, which were fashionable female drinks.

Already in 1565 the distillers were reporting very satisfactory results with juniper berries, but it was not until 1586 that gin was properly introduced into England. It was brought back by troops returning from an expedition to the Netherlands under the Earl of Leicester. It didn't catch on immediately, and for most of the seventeenth century French brandy was the country's most popular spirit, much to the satisfaction of the smugglers of the south coast who clandestinely imported huge quantities to supply the gentry and taverns. In the sixteenth century spirits were still a novelty and the majority of distillers were producing for medicinal purposes or to provide a base for perfumes, although we hear of a recipe from the 1560s for a 'water for the dying of the hairs of the head and others'.

This being England, it was not long before people discovered that drinking these waters was much better than rubbing them on your head, or even elsewhere, and in 1572 an Aqua Vitae house opened in Barking. The idea caught on and in 1584 three Aqua Vitae houses were licensed in Salisbury. Numbers throughout the country remain uncertain, but in London by 1600 there were 200 houses just distilling. The industry really took off when the Admiralty decided that spirits' lack of bulk and long life were what the navy required.

Throughout the seventeenth century the story of spirits was one of quiet growth. The Civil War and the Puritanism of the Commonwealth were hardly likely to favour the greater diffusion of such a novelty as spirits in a nation where, in some places, hops were still unknown in the 1640s.

At any rate, the distillers managed to incorporate themselves into a livery company in 1637. They received their royal charter the following year, along with prohibitions against the use of inferior goods such as returned ale, lees, or sour wine. In competition with the newly fashionable but expensive beverages of coffee (1650), chocolate (1657) and tea (1660), the distillers were managing to sell some 527,492 gallons of gin by 1684.

From slightly bizarre beginnings the distilling industry developed cautiously throughout the seventeenth century. Even so, it could

not have foreseen what was to happen after the Glorious
Revolution. The year 1688 brought William of Orange to the
throne of England. William was a Dutchman and gin was a Dutch
drink. William was also a Protestant, ruling a Dutch province with
a bitter legacy from the Thirty Years War. In 1690 and 1701
William passed laws encouraging distillation of gin in England,
partly to provide a market for inferior barley and partly to increase
trade with Holland, but mainly to end the brandy trade with
Catholic France. The measures were very successful. By 1751 gin
consumption had reached 7,049,822 gallons. and that was just
the legitimately produced product. One in four houses in London
was a dram shop and virtually the entire population was semi-
permanently drunk.

Chapter 6

THE STUART CENTURY

Nothing in nature's sober found,
But an eternal health goes round.
Fill up the bowl then, fill it high,
Fill all the glasses there for why
Should every creature drink but I?
Why, men of morals, tell me why?

'Drinking', Abraham Cowley (*c*.1650)

The Stuart century was full of contradictions and opposing forces. The Civil War, the Commonwealth, the Restoration and the Glorious Revolution were all monumentally important events in Britain's development, but their immediate effects upon the development of the inns, taverns and alehouses were either temporary and localised, transient or non-existent. In the lives and habits of the English drinking public there were other forces at work, deeper forces which were irresistible and inevitable and indifferent to the execution of a king. Yet these forces derived their volition from the same causes and changes in England that provided the momentum to swing the executioner's axe outside the Banqueting Hall on 30 January 1649.

It may be one of the great ironies of the seventeenth century that the inns and alehouses which closely copied the Stuart fashions and shaped the popular mood – and from which came the armies that rallied around the Royalist standards – may well have played a large part in the downfall of this unhappy family. The latter part of the sixteenth century saw an increase in the number of strident and persistent Puritan voices. Many attacked avarice, sloth, gluttony and other deadly sins, but drunkenness was their favourite target, and no one was safe from their fury.

> Of all the trades in the world a brewer is the lodestone which draws the customs of all the functions to it. It is the mark or upshot of every man's ayme, and the bottomlesse whirlpoole that swallowes up the profits of rich and poore. The brewer's art (like a wild kestrel) flies at all games, or like a butler's boxe at Christmas, it is sure to win, whosoever loses. Your innes and alehouses are brooks and rivers and their clients are small rills and springs, who all (very dutifully) do pay their tribute to the boundless ocean of the brewhouse. For all the world knows, that if men and women did drinke no more than sufficed nature, if drinking were used in any reason, or any reason used in drinking, I pray you what became of the brewer then? Surely we do live in an age wherein the seven deadly sins are every man's trade and calling. Every stiffe pint valiant drunkard is a post beam which holds up the brewhouse, for as the barke is to the tree so is a good drinker to the brewer.[1]

The rapid rise in supply which occurred in the latter part of the sixteenth century and early part of the seventeenth, accompanying the steady rise of the common brewers and the concentration of the industry, would have been part of the reason for the brewers attracting the increasing opprobrium of the Puritans. However, in the absence of a formal tie vitriol was directed more specifically at alehouses and their clients.

> There are in London drinking schools; so that drunkenesse is professed with us as a liberal arte and science. . . . I have seen a company among the very woods and forests drinking for a muggle. Six determined to trie their strengths who could drink most glasses for the muggle. The first drinks a glass of a pint, the second two, the next three, and so every one multiplieth till the last taketh six. The first beginneth again and taketh seven and in this manner they drink thrice a piece round, every man taking a glass more than.[2]

It is easy to visualise this story being related on the floor of a Puritan meeting, to the accompaniment of much raising of eyes,

gnashing of teeth, tearing of beards and all round wailing. If any
of the congregation had stopped their breast beating for long
enough to ponder the scene they would have found it instantly
bizarre. This cannot be a drinking competition for the first man is
automatically the loser. Attempting to drink thirty-six pints (the
last man's consumption) with a beer of 1617 strength would
constitute a suicide attempt. What is interesting is that they drank
pints for the exercise at a time when the quart was still the
standard measure. At any rate, the muggle must have been quite
desirable for them to have undergone such self-inflicted discomfort,
but alas all that is known is that a muggle was a prize for drinking
and our correspondent feels no need to enlighten us further.

While some testimonies are unreliable, the sheer volume of
indictments bears out the case that there was a considerable
amount of over-indulgence prevalent.

What immoderate drinking in every place! How they flock to the
tavern! As if they were born to no other end but to eat and
drink, as so many casks to hold wine; yea worse than a cask,
that mars wine and is itself not marred by it. . . . 'Tis now come
to pass that he is no gentleman, a very milksop, that will not
drink fit for no company. . . . How they love a man that will be
drunk, crown him and honour him for it, hate him that will not
pledge him, stab him, kill him; a most intolerable offence and
not to be forgiven.[3]

In plain truth there was no social stigma attached to getting
drunk. Everyone did it. When the royal court decamped to Oxford
in 1605 to escape the plague, they took the new fashion with them
and it caught on.

The behaviour of the court as setter of fashion was positively
deleterious, as the accounts of the state visit of King Christian of
Denmark to James I, in 1606, illustrates.

Those whom I never could get to taste good liquor now follow
the fashion and wallow in beastly delights. The ladies abandon
sobriety, and are seen to roll around in intoxication. After
dinner, the representation of Solomon, his temple and the
coming of the Queen of Sheba was made, or, as I may better say,
was meant to have been made. . . . The lady who did play the

Queen's part did carry most precious gifts to both their majesties, but forgetting the steppes arising to the canopy overset her caskets in his Danish Majesty's lap, and fell at his feet, though I rather think it was on his face. Much was the hurry of confusion, cloths and napkins were at hand to make all clean. His Majesty then got up and would dance with the Queen of Sheba, but he fell down and humbled himself before her, and was carried to his inner chamber, laid on a bed of state which was not a little defiled with presents of the Queen. The entertainments and show went forwards and most of the presenters went backwards or fell down, wine did so occupy their upper chambers. Now did appear in rich dress Hope, Faith and Charity. Hope did assay to speak, but wine did render her efforts so feeble she withdrew. Faith was then left alone. For I am certain she was joined with good works – left the court in a staggering condition. Charity came to the King's feet and seemed to cover the multitude of sins her sisters had committed; in some sort made obeyance and brought gifts.[4]

This behaviour would not have been tolerated under the previous monarch. Herself a drinker of great repute, of ales of a strength that few men could handle, Elizabeth did not approve of drunkenness. Asking a lord why he was late and getting the reply that, 'I, faith, madam, drinking your majesty's health,' she replied, 'So I thought, and I am sorry for it, for I never fare worse than when my health is drunk.'

There were many causes of complaint for the Puritans. An Elizabethan survey of 1577 into the number of retailing premises had provided the anti-drink lobby with evidence that they were multiplying out of control. Extrapolated estimates of the survey suggest that there were around 24,000 alehouse keepers in England. In 1585 it was stipulated in the city of Westminster that there was to be a maximum of 100 alehouses. By 1631 there were 551.

The population was increasing rapidly. In 1577 the population of England was approximately 3.4 million. By 1636 it was around 4.9 million and by 1688 it stood at 5.5 million, over half of whom were on poor relief, a further reason why their presence in alehouses was a grievance for the Puritans. In 1577 the ratio of retail outlets to population was approximately 1:126

(alehouses alone – 1:142); by 1636 it was in the region of 1:95. In urban areas this ratio was even lower. While the population of Cambridge rose by 50 per cent between 1587 and 1620, the number of outlets (licensed and illicit) doubled in the years between 1610 and 1625, giving a ratio of 1:52. In London 61 taverns were constructed between 1612 and 1633, making a total of 211. Indeed, during the reign of James I a walk from Charing Cross to the Tower would go past a tavern every 80 yards.

> On the way from Whitehall to Charing Cross we pass: the White Hart, the Red Lion, the Mermaid, Three Tuns, Salutation, the Greyhound, the Bell, the Golden Lyon. In sight of Charing Cross: the Garter, the Crown, the Bear and Ragged Staff, the Angel, the King Harry Head, the Fleur-de-Luce, Angel, the Holy Lambe, the Bear and Harrow, the Plough, the Shippe, the Black Bell, another Harry Head, the Bull Head, the Golden Bull, a 'sixpenny ordinarye', another Fleur-de-Luce, the Red Lion, the Horse, the White Horse, the Prince's Arms, Bell Savage's Inn, the St John the Baptist, the Talbot, the Shippe of War, the St Dunstan, the Hercules or the Owld Man Tavern, the Mitre, another Three Tuns Inn and a Three Tuns Tavern and a Grayhound, another Mitre, another King Harry Head, Three Tunnes and the Three Cranes.

In rural areas increases seem to have been more in line with demographic trends, but then this would hardly be surprising given the migration to the towns. One would not have had to live very long in a particular area in the early seventeenth century, therefore, to be convinced that there was a growth in real terms in the numbers of alehouses and inns, even if the increased drinking among one's neighbours had not already attracted one's attention. Little wonder, then, that in 1629 Durham magistrates lamented that it was impossible to count the number of alehouses because they were so numerous.

Neither should we be surprised to hear the Nottingham sessions jury intone, in 1619, the old truism, that 'when all trades fail people turn tipplers'. Nor was it a case of new houses springing up as towns grew. Existing houses of some substance were converted. Alehouses were becoming larger, taverns were offering food.

In 1612 the Lords of the Council complained to the Lord Mayor that 'there is almost no house of receipt, or that hath a back door, but, when it cometh to let it is taken for a tavern.'

The authorities found they were helpless when up against the traditional liberties of a freeman of London. In 1623, having denied Robert Burchmore a licence and warned him not to convert his house into a tavern, they were adjudged to have illegally confined him after he had ignored their injunction. Outside London it was not necessary to claim ancient guild privileges to circumvent the law. In the first decade of the seventeenth century James Hayhall owned a Mendip alehouse named Green Oare. It was suppressed in April 1607, but complaints were received again in January 1608. It was complained of in 1613 and again in 1619, by which time it had passed into the hands of John Helpass. In that year it was suppressed, though the landlord, Peter Bush, was following the traditions of his predecessors and was giving grounds for complaint again in 1620.

If all this was not enough to make the most placid of Puritans apoplectic, they then had to cope with the drinking habits that came into vogue at the time. Chief among these were the practices of Healths and Toasts.

Of all the wiles, the projects, plots and policies which that subtle serpent Satan has brought forth and practised in these last and sinful producing times, of purpose to entrap the soules of men in the labyrinths and snares of sinne; there are few more dangerous, hurtful and generally pernicious than this one of drinking and pledging healths, which now of later times hath purchased such a general and common approbation in City, Court and Country that it is become a usual ordinary and daily gueste at most men's tables; and a familiar, customary and assiduous complement at every banquet, feast, nay common meeting though it be held in a taphouse or tavern.[5]

A French commentator observed that 'anyone in England who drank at table without doing so to the health of some person present would be considered as drinking on the sly, and that it would be regarded as an act of incivility'. This attack on toasting above, entitled *Healthes' Sicknesse*, was dedicated to Charles I. By the time he had acceded to the throne his father had already passed four separate statutes concerning drunkenness. The first, in 1604, declared:

> Whereas the loathsome and odious sin of drunkenesse is of late grown into common use, being the roof and foundation of many other enormous sins, as bloodshed, murder, stabbing, swearing, fornication, adultery and such like, to the great dishonor of God, and of our own nation, the overthrow of many good arts and manual trades, the disabling of divers workmen, and the general impoverishment of many good subjects abusively wasting the good creatures of God.[6]

The act of 1606 imposed a 5s fine for drunkenness, or six hours in the stocks and a further 3s 4d, or four hours in the stocks for drinking within one's own neighbourhood, for as the act pointed out, 'the ancient, true and proper use of inns and ale houses is for the receipt, relief and lodging of wayfaring people . . . and not meant for the entertainment and harbouring of lewd and idle people to spend their time and money in lewd and drunken manner.'

The 1604 act was an important piece of legislation since it ended the medieval principle that the innkeeper was responsible for the behaviour of each of his guests, and while he could still be presented for keeping a disorderly house it was the drunkard who now paid for being drunk. James went on to remind his Privy Council that, 'the keeping of an alehouse . . . is none of those trades which it is free and lawful for any subject to set up and exercise.'[7] The act also granted labourers and craftsmen an hour per day to take their lunch in an alehouse as a recognition of the decline of the old medieval tradition of payment in kind. Further measures strengthened the hand of the common brewers, but prohibited them from selling to unlicensed alehouses. A law of 1609 enabled an alehouse licence to be revoked for three years for the offence of keeping a drunken house, and a further act of 1625 charged all town and village officials to act as informers, even against travellers.

None of these statues was very successful, either in curbing drunkenness or in reducing the number of unlicensed houses, though an act of Charles I in 1627 was more effective. It permitted local authorities to administer a public flogging to tipplers who did not pay their fines, and stipulated that fines could be used to supplement the poor rate – a big incentive for a parish to enforce the law. It was a measure which may have taken its inspiration from the results of an experiment of 1622 in Dorchester where a municipal brewhouse was established, the profits going to offset the poor rate. On the whole, however, the population were not really interested in listening to their monarch lecturing them in a 'do as I say, not as I do' fashion, and were far keener on aping James's debauched exploits. Indeed, in 1617, when the Board of Green Cloth took the common brewers to task for brewing beer of excessive strength – as Elizabeth had done – the brewers bluntly told the court that its advice would carry more weight if it were a little more reliable in settling its bills.

Despite the Civil War and the zealotry of the Major-Generals it would appear that toasting remained an entrenched and popular custom in 1657.

We drink as if we were nothing but sponges to draw up moisture. There are many, like Claudius, which seldom go sober over their own thresholds. . . . And would to God this were only a masculine sin, but it hath spread itself to both sexes; neither the bashfulness nor modesty of women can restrain them from participating in their guilt . . . for we among ourselves may find a multitude of those intemperate sottish women, which will quaff with the most riotous, and give pledge for pledge, and take of cup for cup. Oh, blemish of the nation, and affrightment to the very heavens.[8]

Naturally, after the Restoration there was a tremendous anti-Puritan backlash, and toasting the king's health took on more significance than before. Refusing to take part in a toast was considered a sign of being a Commonwealth sympathiser, and was, in the wrong company, an extremely foolhardy action.

In the first year of his reign Charles II felt obliged to publish a Proclamation Against Drunkenness: 'There are likewise a set of men of whom we have heard much, who spend their time in taverns and tippling houses and debauches, giving no other evidence of affection for us but in drinking our health, and in inveigling against all others who are not of their own dissolute temper.'[9]

In the general euphoria that followed the Restoration, Cavalier behaviour became an exaggerated parody of itself, as a means of emphasising the demise of the Commonwealth and the hated Cromwells. Slightly more foppish toasting habits developed, such as reviving an old Roman custom of drinking as many cups as there were letters in the name of the woman being toasted. When toasting women it was often the done thing to cut yourself and mix blood with the wine. At least the English never adopted the habit, popular among certain Prussian Army officers of the time, of draining off a toast from the muzzle of a loaded pistol, before discharging the pistols in a volley, reloading and repriming the next toast. Presumably the Prussian army was either full of officers with a steady hand, or short of officers.

In Charles II the English had a king who was very much a man for the time. Ward tells us of a report he read about the number of drink-related deaths. The report is not so much of interest as the footnote, which explains that the statistics exclude those deaths resulting from carts and wagons passing over the bodies of inebriates lying in the streets, as these are too numerous to record.

James I was notorious for the selling of titles, favours and patents. He may have stripped Sir Walter Raleigh of his monopoly for wine licensing, but he was not slow to grant similar favours to others. Always strapped for cash, and somewhat humiliated by Parliament in 1610 when they declared his 1608 plan to tax victualling licenses at 8*s* 'uncustomary', James instituted a scheme of revenue gathering via means of patents. In 1618 Sir James Spence was patented to collect fines from tipplers in breach of licenses, and Sir Giles Mompesson, a notorious patent holder, bought, for £1,350, a patent to license inns, which were exempt from the licensing legislation of 1552 which required alehouse keepers to be licensed on bond. Between 1618 and 1621 Mompesson licensed 1,200 inns. The majority were, of course, alehouses that had been suppressed by local magistrates, who then petitioned Mompesson to grant inn status. The high price – £5 – of an inn licence was probably the reason why there were not even more, though Mompesson was nothing if not resourceful and had plenty of means of drumming up trade. An alehouse keeper by the name of Cooke was approached by a man aptly named Ferrett, who asked him for lodging. Cooke replied that he was not an inn, and though he had kept the house for fifty years he had lodged no one. Evidently Ferrett was a persistent man, and at length Cooke relented. The next morning Ferrett declared himself to be an agent of Mompesson, denounced Cooke for keeping an inn, and presented him with a ticket to appear before His Majesty's Commissioner for Inns and Hostelries.

In 1621 Parliament impeached Mompesson. His and Spence's patents were abolished and Parliament, unimpressed with the smallness of the revenues that came the Crown's way, declined to accept Mompesson's plea that 'it was not the profit that tied me to it, but the hope of reformation'. Mompesson was forced into exile and a major obstacle to the suppression of alehouses removed.

In fact many obstacles were disappearing and other factors were swinging the balance of advantage towards the Puritans. Whereas people had been able to license alehouses and petition in their favour as a means of keeping others off the poor rate, such that, 'if one or two justices be ready to put the [alehouses] down, that be too bad, by and by other justices be ready to put them up again', polite society was beginning to adopt the modern view that alehouses probably kept other people on the parish, even if it kept the alehouse keeper off it.

There was at the same time a concerted rise in Sabbatarianism, as the behaviour of the educated classes reacted faster to the new scientific and mercantile vigours of the Stuart Age than the illiterate masses. With the Puritan ascendancy the influence of class started to make itself felt. Then, as today, the self-appointed guardians of morality came from small and vociferous, though untypical, sections of society: the non-established clergy, the minor gentry and those parts of the nascent bourgeoisie who would, in time, come to form the 'professional' classes.

From the seventeenth century down to the early twentieth, therefore, we enter a phase when literate, minority elites sought to prescribe the activities of the masses, in the way that previous feudal, aristocratic and monarchical elites had. Needless to say, they too failed, for they never actually gave much consideration to the wants and needs of the English rural and urban masses, except to express disapproval.

Of the 270 signatories to the twenty-four petitions surviving among the sessions papers for Essex between 1600 and 1650, only 26 per cent were illiterate, at a time when male illiteracy was at over 60 per cent. These petitioners tended to sign themselves as the 'chief' inhabitants, or the 'better sort', or the 'principal' and 'honest' among the community. Frequently their complaint was not that disorder was occurring, but rather that the Sabbath was being profaned and that Divine Service was being ignored. There is no doubt that the Puritans had decided that the 'nests of Satan' must be eradicated.

What was new, however, was the intensity of their actions. Ancient kings and feudal lords may have disapproved of immodest intemperance as ungodly, or as a distraction from the butts, but they understood the social and cohesive nature of popular culture and drinking culture – as if the two were really divisible – and were aware of their responsibilities as well as their position in that culture.

Puritanism in the seventeenth century – like later teetotalism – was not concerned with social cohesion or the maintenance of culture. For the Puritans 'custom' was an insufficient *raison d'être* if its manifestations were in conflict with the values of thrift, diligence, respect for authority, sobriety and piety that were preconditions for the new economic order that was to emerge.

The alehouse stood as anathema to all that Puritanism sought to achieve. It was the product of a social order based on self-sufficiency, subsistence husbandry and communal living. This product transposed very well to the medieval towns. Rural links were strong, and while one might argue that communal loyalties faced more conflicting rivalries between neighbours and guild brethren, many trades stuck to their own quarters of the towns and town life retained its own homogeneous culture. The Puritans stood for change, while the alehouse stood for continuity. Indeed, as the post-Reformation church withdrew from many of its traditional functions, the alehouse was strengthened as an institution which bound people to each other and to their past.

As an institution the alehouse, therefore, was unsuited to act as a social tool for the new productive order, and was dismissive, if not downright contemptuous, of the religious fervour underlying the new order. As a levelling influence it was an obstacle to the creation of alienated and divided labour. Thus it may well have been for economic as well as for religious reasons that Lord Coventry, Charles I's Lord Keeper, declared, 'I account alehouses and tippling houses the greatest pests in the Kingdom.'

Where the seventeenth century differed from previous centuries was in the emergence of an organised class bent on alehouse suppression. However, the suppressors did not have it all their own way. The apparatus for the enforcement of suppression was far from complete, though as time passed it fell into place. Ironically, the mechanism was not constructed by Puritan justices, or by social changes, but instead evolved out of much more traditional concerns – the shortage of royal revenues.

In 1620 a Royal Commission recommended that the complexity of the trade was a hindrance to revenue maximisation and so proposed concentration of the drink industry. In the face of this threat rural brewers also promised to accept the 1614 levy. In 1623 a 1 per cent valorum hop duty was imposed, rising twice in 1635 to 2s 6d per cwt and to 5s. By 1657 it stood at 10s per cwt and double this by 1690. Apart from these direct fiscal measures the main emphasis was on maximising licence revenues by reducing avoidance by suppressing unlicensed houses. In the 1620s this policy was given a fillip by a succession of bad harvests. Since it was already known that the number of alehouses rose in times of depression and fell in times of plenty, an order in council was passed in 1622 requiring magistrates to suppress all unnecessary houses and required those that remained to moderate the strength of their ale. Many localities needed few such spurs. Ripon, in 1623, reported to the Privy Council that having counted its alehouses and 'finding the number to be great we have reduced them to half the number.'

An example of the way things were to go comes from 1629 when Staffordshire justices 'ordered constables to produce at petty sessions certificates of acceptable tipplers signed by the ministers and up to six of the most discretist and substantial inhabitants.'[10] This was a substantial change of policy. An alehouse's acceptability was now to be determined by individuals unconnected with either the trade or the local authorities and whose credentials for judging 'acceptability' were wealth and propriety, i.e. those people who would never have patronised the premises that they were being called upon to assess.

There is no doubt that the persistence of the magistrates was also effective in bringing public opinion round to their point of view. Between 1590 and 1603 the yeomen of the village of Terling, in Essex, who sat on the jury for their Hundred, brought only two presentments in connection with alehouse behaviour – one in 1590 for running a disorderly house, and one in 1603 for non-attendance at church. Their successors between 1609 and 1623 made presentments regularly and as part of a policy. In the same village between 1590 and 1649 there were, at one time or another, twenty-six individuals selling ale without a licence. Only one of them seems not to have attracted any official attention. The remainder 'allowed disorderly gatherings in their houses on Sundays or holy days, tolerated gaming, tippling, drunkenness, fighting and swearing. Three sold their ale too dear, three harboured sexual miscreants, two harboured thieves and one abused the constables.'

In 1633, when it was being complained of that 'a whole street is in some places but a continuous alehouse, not a shop to be seen between red lattice and red lattice' – the traditional sign of alehouses after ale stakes but before painted signs – the London authorities suppressed all taverns and alehouses with doors or stairs on the river, as these were felt to provide an easy getaway for criminals. At the same time they also attempted to suppress many of the taverns near Covent Garden, and impose a levy on those that remained as a means of providing compensation for those tavern keepers who were suppressed. The plan was never enforced, but the idea of a levy to provide compensation was a novel one, although it was not taken up until the Licensing Act of 1902.

If the frenzy of suppression were not enough, the justices were determined to interfere in the affairs of those premises they permitted – most notably in the strength of ale.

Certain Justices of the Peace, being informed of the odious abuses committed by drunkennesse in their jurisdictions did, according to their places and duties, meet at a market town and sate two days hearing information, and working reformation. At last, they concluded that the ale and beer were too strong, and therefore, commanded that from thence forth smaller drinke should be brewed, whereby unruly people might sometimes go to bed sober. But one mad tossepot fellow being much aggrieved at this order . . . asked them if they had sat two days about the brewing of small drinke; to who one of the Justices replied, yes. Why then, quoth the drunkard. I pray you sit three days more to know who shall drink it, for I will none of it.[11]

In certain areas of the country the zeal employed in suppression must have had the atmosphere of a witch-hunt. In 1631 Somerset magistrates instituted a programme of wholesale suppression. Yet 1631 was also a famine year. In times of bad harvest the alehouse became essential as a means of survival for many rural and labouring poor. Ale was, as the brewers argued in 1647, 'most cherishing to poore labouring people, without which they do not well subsist, their food being for the most part of such things as afford little or bad nourishment.'

Suppression in times of bad harvest was particularly vindictive and certain to result in increased poverty, misery and starvation for both the ale sellers and their customers. It is likely that certain sections of society viewed the suppression policy of the Puritans as dangerous and excessive. In July 1631 Judge Richardson ordered the suppression of all ales and wakes, time honoured customs which were centuries old. The Church was immediately upset at this loss of revenue and ordered a reversal of this ruling, which was denied. A highly acrimonious argument was only defused by the intervention of the king.

> In some counties of our Kingdom we find that under pretence of taking away abuses there hath been a general forbidding, not only of ordinary meetings, but of the feast and dedications of the Churches, commonly called wakes. Now his Majesty's express will and pleasure is that these fetes with others shall be observed, and that his Justices of the Peace shall look to it both that all disorders may be presented or punished.[12]

The alehouse was, therefore, in the vanguard of the conflicts and tensions exercising themselves in England at this time, and was a visible and tangible manifestation of old England standing in the way of the new. All these tensions came to a head with the Civil War, and the alehouse had a crucial role to play during the course of that war.

Most immediately the war caused a halt to policies of suppression. Demand for ale and beer rose to satisfy the thirst of armies on the move. The Petition of Right of 1628 exempted private householders from the onerous burden of billeting troops. This role, therefore, fell heavily on the alehouse and inn. It was not good logistical sense to suppress the houses that were victualling the troops, though the unlikelihood of the publican being recompensed for these costs drove so many of them to the wall that a form of surrogate suppression may be said to have been operating.

Alehouses were also an important source of revenue for fighting the war. In 1643 the Parliamentarians imposed an excise duty on ale and beer, replaced the following year by an easier to collect malt duty of 2s per quarter. This was not repealed until 1880. In 1645 the Royalists imposed identical duties to the Roundheads.

Many of our old pubs date from the Civil War, indeed many of them owe their preservation to events that happened under their roofs during that time. At Thame there is the Nag's Head (known as the King's Head during the war) where a Parliamentary soldier who had deserted to the Royalists was recaptured by Roundheads who hanged him from the inn sign, saving as they did so, 'You must have one word to the King before you go!' Also at Thame, though no longer an inn, is the Greyhound, where John Hampden died after his pistol exploded in his face. At Uxbridge there is an inn, built in 1575, where, in 1645, commissioners from each side met, unsuccessfully, to sue for peace. Hence, it is now known as the Crown and Treaty. Charles I stayed at the Red Lion at Hillingdon after his escape from Oxford, and many pubs can claim similar patronage. Some, like the Saracen's Head, Southwell, Nottinghamshire, can in fact claim his patronage on more than one occasion. Charles stayed there on 17 August 1642 en route to raise his standard against parliament, and again on 5 May 1646 on the eve of his surrender to the Scots. This is by no means an exhaustive list – there are, after all, all the inns that reputedly hid Charles II on his flight to France – but it is enough to give a flavour of the role of the inn during the war.

Chapter 7

THE RESTORATION ERA

Yea every cup is fast to others wedged.
They always double drink, they must be pledged.
He that begins, how many so'er they be,
Looks that each one do drink as much as he.

Anon

The English beer is best in all Europe it was necessary to drink two or three pots of beer during our parley: for no kind of business is transacted in England without the intervention of pots of beer.

Jarevin de Rochefort (1672)

Foreasmuch as his Highness the Lord Protector of the Commonwealth hath taken special note of the mischiefs and great disorders which are daily committed in Taverns, Inns and Alehouses . . . and the Justices of this County of Hertford are enjoyned to take special care for the effectual suppressing of all such alehouse keepers as are or shall be convicted of the prohibition of the Lord's Day by receiving into their houses any company. Or of swearing, drunkenness, suffering tippling, gaming or playing at Tables, Billiard Table, Shovel Board, Cards, Dice, Ninepins, Pigeon Holes, Trunks, or of keeping Bowling Alleys or Bowling Green or any of them, or of any other games.[1]

The austerity and suppression of the Civil War was carried on into the Commonwealth, and while many would point to the Industrial Revolution as a powerful upheaval in British cultural life that resulted in much of the past being forgotten, the Presbyterian

Ascendancy, from 1643–57, saw an unparalleled destruction of English popular culture.

> All the harmless sports, the merry gambols, dances and friscols, are now extinct. . . . Madness hath extended itself to the very vegetables, the senseless herbs and weeds are a profane estimation among them – holly, ivy, mistletoe, rosemary, bays are counted ungodly branches of superstition for your entertainment. And to roast a sirloin of beef, to touch a collar of brawn, to take a pie, to put a plum in the pottage pot, to burn a fire for your sake, master Christmas, is enough to make a man be suspected and taken for a Christian, for which he shall be apprehended for committing high parliament treason.[2]

This reference to the decision of the Long Parliament in 1644 to declare 25 December a day of prayer and fasting was written by John Taylor, the Water Poet, a landlord and an ardent Royalist. During this period – when, for example, in Shropshire only known Parliamentarians could hold licences, and, elsewhere, suspicion of Royalist sympathies was grounds for suppression – he was reluctantly forced to change the name of his alehouse from the Crown in Mourning (named after the execution of Charles I) to something less offensive to the powers that be: the Poet's Head.

> My Signe was once a Crowne, but now it is
> Changed by a sudden metamorphosis.
> The Crowne was taken downe, and in the stead
> Is placed John Taylor's or the Poet's Head.
> A painter did my picture gratis make
> And (for a signe) I hanged it for his sake.
> Now if my picture's drawing can prevayle
> I will draw my friends to me, and I'll draw ale.

Although the Commonwealth started to lose its influence on public life after 1656, the worst period of Puritan tyranny occurred during the Civil War and into the early 1650s. Apart from the above decree, and others like it, the Puritans commenced a systematic destruction of the leisure activities of the British people. In February 1643, now at war with the king, the Puritans were free

to attack those of his measures they detested, chief among which
was the *Book of Sports*. Written by James I in May 1618 under the
title *The Kinge's Majesties Declaration Concerning Lawful Sports*, it is
one of those strange examples, dotted throughout English history, of
the greater understanding that sometimes existed between the
extremes of society than existed between its lower and middle
orders. Written specifically as a recognition of the needs of the
common people with regard to recreation, it was a defence of their
leisure time against Puritan encroachment: 'And as for our good
people's lawful recreation our pleasure likewise is. That, after the
end of Divine Service our good people be not disturbed, letted, or
discouraged from any lawful recreation.'[3]

Dancing, archery, May games and poles, Whitsun ales, Morrises
and the like were all acceptable. Bear and bull baiting, miracle and
mystery plays, and bowling were forbidden on Sundays. For the
lowest orders, bowling was prohibited at any time. All these
activities either centred around the alehouse or involved communal
drinking.

As an indication of the conflict between Sabbatarianism and the
people, Charles I felt obliged to reissue the *Book of Sports* in 1633,
further incensing the Puritans, who in February 1643 outlawed it
as 'wicked prophanations of the Lord's Day'. The book was burnt
wherever it was found, along with any book or pamphlet that
contravened the fourth commandment. Also on the bonfires were
the May poles, now 'heathenish vanity, generally abused to
superstition and wickedness'. In April 1644 all those pastimes
previously defended by James and Charles were outlawed, as were
wrestling, shooting, ringing of bells for pleasure, masques, wakes,
church ales, dancing, games and other sports.

Sunday prohibition was introduced wherever Parliamentary writ
held sway, and while inns were allowed to provide food for the
itinerant poor, an act of 1650 forbade any traveller from returning
to an inn after midnight Saturday or from leaving until 1 a.m. on
Monday. All use of transport was illegal, including boats, except for
travel to and from church, without the express permission of a
justice.

For those people who attended church the Puritans had their
share of ordinances too. The Assembly of Westminster adopted
Presbyterianism as the established religion in September 1643, but
it was not until 24 November 1655 that Cromwell prohibited the

Anglican liturgy. What few organs there were at the time, as well as other musical instruments used for worship, all promptly disappeared and reappeared, as likely as not, in the alehouses, especially since from 1657 playing non-religious music within one's own house was also illegal.

> They have translated the organs out of the Churches and set them up in taverns, chanting their ditty rambics and bestial Baccanalias to the tune of those instruments which were wonted to assist them in the celebration of God's Praises.[4]

Such goes one lament from 1659, though if the Puritans had no need for the instruments they should have hardly complained if others were then to put them to good effect. Perhaps the bitterness of the complaint is a reflection that by this time Puritan power was on the wane. The rule of the Major-Generals was too much for the nation to stomach. Under Cromwell they had tended to become justices themselves, and were subsequently much keener on enforcement than many of the resident justices. This period (1655–7), for example, saw the suppression of 400 alehouses in Chester and Blackburn. Warwickshire lost one third of its alehouses and Somerset revoked all of its licences, only granting new ones at the quarter sessions.

The nation tired of such oppressive measures. The commitment of the constables frequently tailed off and evasion became easier once more. Finally, in 1656 the Second Protectorate Parliament, even without the hundred members excluded by Cromwell, showed its exasperation with the political situation in the country by refusing to sanction the actions of the Major-Generals.

Pride's Purge removed the Presbyterian majority from the Commons during December 1648, but the New Model Army remained a hotbed of religious fanaticism. The policy pursued by Cromwell and Ireton was only concluded shortly before Cromwell's death, by which time Britain was heartily sick of military governance, conscription, incessant uprisings and Parliamentary anarchy. Cromwell's funeral was an opportunity for the people to express their feelings, as he himself had prophesied they would. 'It was the joyfullest funeral I ever saw, for there were none that cried but dogs, while the soldiers hooted away with barbarous noise, drinking and taking tobacco in the streets as they went.'[5]

With the death of Cromwell the Commonwealth was spent. People did not feel the need for piety or virtue when the government was a complete shambles. Faced with a government that had no real authority, a despairing people felt free to behave as they liked.

In 1659 the greatest immortality and license prevailed in good society. Gentlemen sat and spent much of their time in ale houses. . . . In the taverns where Spanish wine was sold, the custom was so enormous that the drawers often acquired sufficient wealth to purchase estates, build fine houses, and actually buy their customers out of their possessions. In these taverns, where in other cities courtezans would hardly be vouchsafed to be entertained, ladies of high rank were habitués and there drank their 'crowned cups', roundly strained toasts through their smocks, danced after the fiddle and termed it an honourable treat.[6]

How had the inns, taverns and alehouses changed during the period between the end of the Tudor dynasty and the extravagance of Restoration England? Most notably they were larger. Suppression of houses, both illicit and licensed, lent greater legitimacy to those that remained. Their range of services was increasing too. In 1600 there were just 200 London houses retailing spirits alone. By 1673 the brewers were petitioning Parliament over the rise in spirit drinking.

Before Brandy, which has now become common and sold in every little alehouse, came to England in such quantities as it now doth, we drank good strong Beer and Ale and all laborious people their bodies requiring after hard labour, some strong drink to refurbish them, did therefore every morning and evening used to drink a pot of ale or a flagon of strong beer, which greatly helped the promotion of our own grains and is them no great prejudice. It hindreth not their work, neither did it take away their senses nor cost them much money, whereas the prohibition of brandy would . . . prevent the destruction of his majesty's subjects, many of whom have been killed by drinking thereof, it not agreeing with their constitution.[7]

However, Parliament was not disposed to hear the brewers' pleas. The Restoration's constitutional arrangements had left it permanently short of money, which was why they had likewise refused the brewers' petition of 1660 for the removal of the duties imposed during the Civil War. This was hard on the brewers since all the acts of the revolutionary governments since 1642 were now held to be invalid under the terms of the Restoration, and the continuance of wartime malt duties assisted the growth of spirit consumption.

Brewing techniques had also come on. Already at the start of the century the majority of home counties production was beer, not ale. Many factors favoured beer, not least the economies of scale to be gained. During the seventeenth century a bushel of malt would produce eight gallons of ale but eighteen gallons of beer. With regard to strength, some beers were just as powerful as the old strong ales. There was greater variety, too. These exceptionally strong beers had names like Crown and Dagger ale; Pharoah was so named because it would not let the people go. Nipitato was a slang, generic name for strong beers, while huff-cap and double-huff would have taken their names from a 'huff', a trick or trickster. However, it must not be imagined that all beers were of these superlative strengths, though there were many sound reasons to make beer and ale stronger rather than weaker. It travelled better, kept for longer, and the profit margin on strong brews was greater. In 1619 we hear of an injunction against storing beer in wine casks because of the added strength that resulted.

The mid-seventeenth century saw the beginning of the replacement of wood, earthenware and leather drinking vessels by plate and pewter. Just as the replacement of pewter by glass in the nineteenth century was to seal the fate of porter and popularise lighter Burton beers, so the introduction of pewter also induced a change in fashion towards lighter ales and beers. Beers travelled better and transport around the kingdom was improving. Popular lighter beers gained regional fame, especially those from coastal towns. York, Chester, Hull and Margate were all famous for the quality of their beer and these reputations carried far beyond the local region. It must have been a comfort to the burghers of Nottingham to find their beer admired; 200 years earlier their ale was regarded as pretty awful.

Of course, increasing the value of your drinking vessels brought its own dangers.

The Sharper calls for two pints of sundry wines, the drawer setting the wine with two cups (silver, for water) as the custom is. The Sharper tastes of one pinte, no matter which, and finds fault with the wine, saying 'Tis too hard, but rose water and sugar will send it down merrily!' – and for that purpose takes up one of the cups, telling the stranger he is well acquainted with the boy at the bar and can have two pennyworth of rose water for a penny of him, and so steps from his seate. The stranger suspects no harms because the faine guest leaves his cloak at the end of the table – but the other takes good care not to returne, and it is then founde that he hath stolen ground, and out leged the stranger more feet than he can recover in haste for the cup is heaped with him, for which the woodcock that is taken . . . must pay 50s or three pounds and with nothing but an old threadbare cloak worth not more than two groats to make amends for his losses.[8]

During the 1630s bottling beer became a viable option, creating the possibility of bright and gassy beers. Bottles were valuable items, however, and although the practice grew, early accounts of bottling would appear to suggest it was more a hobby carried out by country gentlemen.

There was little that was done to ale that was not done to beer. It did not mull so well, but Braggot became a fashionable London drink. Taking its name from Brage – the Viking god of poetry – and drunk from the Bragging Cup, it was made from warm beer and spices. On the whole, warm beverages were made of ale and wine rather than beer. In the latter half of the century buttered ale was popular as a substitute for an evening meal, being made from hop-free ale, sugar, cinnamon and butter.

Towards the end of the century the terms ale and beer ceased to have their precise meanings. Pepys's diaries refer to Margate ale, Northdown ale and Lambeth ale. These were beers. At this time ale was coming to mean the lighter, drier, bitter beers – the quality beers from Burton and Derby. Ale was by no means extinct, and in the far north of England it was still the norm, but while in 1651 the Water Poet was still able to write that 'beer is a Dutch boorish

liquour, a thing not known of in England till of late dayes, an alien
to our nation, till such times as Hops and Heresies come among us,
it is a saucy intruder in the land.'[9] He was nothing if not
reactionary, and within a few years people who wanted ale would
be asking for unhopped beer.

Another alternative beverage of the time, and one popular with
Pepys, was Mum. This was an ale brewed with wheat malt and oat
malt, and spiced with cardamom, ginger, sassafras, walnut rinds,
madder,[10] red sanders[11] and elecampane.[12] Introduced from
Brunswick, it took its name reputedly from its inventor Christian
Mummer, or from the German verb for 'to mumble', which, if Pope
is to be believed, may have been the end result of its consumption.

> The clamrous crowd is hush'd with mugs of mum,
> Till all, tuned equal, send a general hum.

Pepys drank it at the Fleece, in Leadenhall, which he tells us was a
mum house, so there were apparently certain houses which
specialised in its production. Pepys was among the last generation
able to drink metheglin, and we know that he tried it and liked it.
As a widely available drink it had been killed off by the
Reformation. Surviving on large estates, its life was temporarily
prolonged by Stuart patronage. It was a mead of Welsh origin,
spiced with rosemary, hyssop, thyme, sage and orgaine, and was a
truly ancient drink.

Tobacco was a new commodity provided by the taverns.
Fashionable after the 1630s in polite society that sought to
emulate its betters; as the price fell it was retailed by the pipe and
was said to be 'drunk'. It must have caught on fairly quickly for as
early as 1633 the Crown realised it was worthwhile taxing it.
Indeed there was widespread domestic tobacco cultivation, which
lasted until the Hanoverian monarchs restricted it in order to
stimulate the economies of the new American colonies. Imports of
tobacco by 1640 were in the region of 1.3 million lb.

The general effect of the Puritan suppression was an increase in
standards. Food was more widely available as was lodging. The
infrastructure of the inns and taverns that was to support the
great coaching era was starting to become recognisable;
Restoration England saw the first coaching routes. In the towns the
great age of the tavern was dawning.

In the countryside suppression was only effective while it was being maintained. As soon as the pressure was off or the local authorities were sympathetic, illicit houses reopened again. Throughout the seventeenth century they continued to outnumber the legal houses, though they were naturally smaller and ruder. The ever present possibility of suppression made investment in anything above the most rudimentary essentials unwise, even supposing that the landlord was able to afford any luxuries. If there was a change it was the emergence of the painted inn sign, so that by the end of the century the ale stake was completely obsolete.

Seventeenth century descriptions of the alehouse tend to focus on the activities inside rather than on physical descriptions of the commonplace, so to an extent we must deduce its physical appearance by an appreciation of how it met people's needs and of the kinds of people who frequented it. In 1602 we learn:

> If these houses have a box brush or an old post it is enough to show their profession; but if they be graced with a sign complete it is a sign of good custom! In these houses you shall see the history of Judith, Susannah, Daniel in the Lion's Den and Lazarus painted upon the wall. It may be reckoned a wonder to see or find the houses empty, for either the parson, churchwarden, or clerk, or all, are doing some church business usually in this place. They thrive best where they are the fewest. Hot weather and thunder and the want of company are the hostess's grief, for then her ale sours. Your drink usually is very young, two days old! Her chiefest wealth is seen if she can have one brewing after another. If either the hostess or her daughter or maid will kiss handsomely at parting, it is a bird line to draw the company hither again the sooner. She must be courteous to all . . . for she must entertain all good and bad, rag and tag, cut and longtail. She suspects tinkers and poor soldiers most, not that they will not drink soundly, but that they will not lustily. She must keep touch with three sorts of men, that is the maltman, the baker and the justices' clerks! She is merry and half made upon Shrove Tuesday, May Days and feastdays. A good ring of bells in the parish helps her to many a tester, and she prays the parson be not a Puritan. A bagpiper and a puppet play bring her in birds that are flush, she defies a wine tavern as

an upstart outlandish fellow and suspects the wine to be poisoned. Her ale, if new, looks like a misty morning, all thick; well if her ale be strong, her reckoning right, her house clean, her fire good, her face fair and the town great or rich, she shall seldom or never sit without the chirping birds to bear her company; and at the next churching or christening she is sure to be rid of two or three dozen of cakes and ale by gossiping neighbours.[13]

This is a respectable licensed house, probably near to, or on the road to a market town. The landlady is possibly a widow, or if not her unmentioned husband has another occupation and leaves the management of the house and the brewing to her. The fact that she is the brewster, if married, would indicate that though the town 'be great or rich' this alehouse is probably not in the town and is some distance from London. The alehouse is near the church. Clearly she counts respectability a better return than impropriety. It is decorated with religious scenes and obviously has an important function in binding together church and community. It may well be a flourishing alehouse, but it certainly has much in common with its fifteenth- and sixteenth-century ancestors.

If all alehouses were like this, the Puritans would have had little cause for complaint. and although this description was chosen as being appropriate to Victorian sensibilities there are no real reasons to believe that this particular alehouse was any more lewd than shown. Licensed houses were, after all, in the minority. What is apparent for all to see are those aspects of this alehouse, and the community it served, that did not survive the Presbyterian Ascendancy. Neither were all illicit alehouses complete hovels. Thomas Dekker gives a description of a country alehouse of 1608, preparing for a 'beggars' banquet.

I stept forward and came to the place, which was so fenced about with trees, quickset hedges and bushes, which were growne so high (that for the smoke) it was not possible to imagine how a house could there be builded. There was but one path leading to it, which (after much searching and many turnings) being found, boldly I went on and arrived at a homely cottage, the very door of it put me in mind of that poor inn of good Bauchis and Philemon . . . for it was so low. This house stood not like great men's places, always shut, but wide open, as if Bounty had been the partner, and being within, it seemed hospitality dwelt there and had given you welcome. For there was a table ready covered with fair linen, nut-brown round trenchers lay in good order, with bread and salt keeping their state in the middle of the board. The room itself was not sumptuous . . . the windows were spread with herbs, the chimney dressed up with green boughs and the floor strewed with bulrushes, as if some lass were that morn to be married.[14]

Dekker is exaggerating slightly, as the point of his story is to describe the various types of thieves that come to the banquet and illustrate the profitability of the calling. Provided we keep this in mind, we can see that in some areas a certain amount of rustic comfort was possible, where there was confidence that there would be no suppression.

As for the town, we are given an insight into a typical London tavern by means of an inventory taken at the King's Head Tavern, Leadenhall Street, in 1627.

Item in the Tavern, the Barr with the Bynnes and three shelves. Six drinking Rooms with partitions with Benches at the ends and sides of four of the rooms and the other two with benches at the sides and tables fitted to them of Elm Plank. . . . Item in the Yarde between the two buildings. Six drinking rooms covered with leade with twelve benches and six tables of Elme Plank fitted to the same, one dresser board or table of plank to scrape trenchers on, one shelf and a cupboard on it.[15]

This establishment is clearly the precursor of the chop house. It seems that it has not always provided food and has covered over the yard to provide extra seating areas either in response to competition from other taverns springing up nearby, or to satisfy and impress the magistrates. That as much space as possible has been turned over for seating suggests a healthy lunchtime trade. In the evening the upstairs rooms would have been more the focus of activity with parties drinking sack, claret or strong beer in the intimacy of the booths provided and drinking healths and toasts. There is little by way of ostentation here. Such an inventory may have been made when there was a change of owner, in which case much of the fittings may have departed with the previous landlord. What is of interest in this description is the reference to the bar. Both here and in the account of the sharper, above, the bar would have been little more than a serving hatch, through which the pot boys and drawers passed jugs, flagons, pints and bottles. The earliest reference to a bar was in 1592, and so these examples are still relatively novel. In the case of taverns the presence of a bar marked a departure from the medieval practice – and indeed requirements – of keeping casks within sight of the drinkers, and would indicate that an increasing number of premises had subterranean or dedicated cellars.

To embellish the somewhat clinical picture provided by this inventory Bishop Fade gives us, in 1629, an idea of what was going on around those elm plank tables.

It [a tavern] is a broacher of more news than hogsheads, and more jests than news, which are suckt up here by some spongy braine, and from thence squeez'd into a comedy. Men come here to make merry, but indeed to make a noise and this musicke above is answered with the clinking below. The drawers are the civilest people in it. . . . A house of sinne you may call it, but not a house of darknesse, for the candles are never out. . . . To give you the total reckoning of it, it is the busieman's recreation, the idle man's business, the melancholy man's sanctuary, the stranger's welcome, the Innes of Court man's entertainment, the scholar's kindness and the citizen's curtesy. It is the study of sparkling wits and a cup of sherry their booke, where we leave them.[16]

There were two other institutions that developed during the century as offshoots of those alehouses and taverns that decided to specialise. The first of these was the ordinary, the second was the coffee house.

An Ordinary is a handsome house, where everyday, about the hour of twelve, a good dinner is prepared by way of ordinary, composed of a variety of dishes, in season, well dressed, with all other accommodations fit for that purpose, whereby many gentlemen of great Estates and good repute make this their resort, who after dinner play a while for recreation, both moderately and commonly without deserving reproof.[17]

Strictly speaking the ordinary was a set meal around a communal table, rather than the premises, but it may be seen as a development from the alehouse. One method of conforming to the pressure for respectability was to provide food, a fact that was just as true under the Puritans in the early seventeenth century as it was under the later Temperance and the Public House Improvement lobbies.

Coffee was introduced into Britain in 1650, and the first coffee house proper at the Sign of My Own Head was opened in 1652. Ironically at the same location today one may find two of the country's remaining ordinaries – Simpson's and the George and Vulture, where Pickwick stayed during the Bardel suit, in St Michael's Alley, Cornhill. Chocolate was introduced in 1657 and tea, though very expensive, was introduced in 1660, being first retailed from Garraway's Coffee House in Change Alley whose 'narrow sound, though deep as hell' was immortalised in Swift's *South Sea Bubble*. With three new beverages there was clearly an opportunity for a new type of establishment, and while the earliest coffee houses were little more than taverns that sold coffee, they quickly developed their own character and their own clientele.

Frequently the best descriptions of a country are those by foreigners, and this, from 1669 by an Italian, provides a snapshot of the types of premises found in Restoration London and their relative standing.

Coffee houses, where coffee is sold publicly and not alone, but other beverages, such as sherbert, tea, ale, cock ale, beer etc. according to the season.

In these houses there are divers rooms and meeting places of newsmongers where one hears all that is or is thought to be news, true or false as may be. In Winter to sit round a large fire and smoke for two hours costs but two soldi. If you drink you pay besides for what you consume.

The houses that are known by the name of inn, are for the most part most noble and are all superbly furnished, so that persons of high quality, as well women as men, do not take the smallest scruple of going to them.

There are also a great number of 'ordinaries' which in France would be called *bonstructeurs* – that is to say people who provide dinners and suppers, some kept by Englishmen and some by Frenchmen, where the first gentlemen of the Court go in the morning, with the same frequency that gentlemen of Florence go to inns in the evening. . . . The difference between taverns and ordinaries is that people generally go to the first to drink, not that you cannot sometimes eat at the former or that you may never drink at the latter, but that is out of the ordinary way, and in such cases the hosts are out of their element, the matter of fact is that both one and the other are very dear.

There are an infinite number of beer shops where every sort of drink in the country is sold; of these I have counted as many as thirty-two kinds. These places are not very extravagant and they are almost to be found full downstairs, crowded with the rabble, and upstairs with every condition of man from artisan to gentleman. They differ in this point from the taverns namely that in those they drink Spanish wine which they call sack, wines of the Canaries, Malaga and Bordeaux and other valuable foreign wines, whilst in the beer shops there is nothing but ale, cock ale, butter ale, Lambeth ale and the like.[18]

What is interesting is that a clear evolutionary process is visible. At the bottom level the beerhouses are muddling along much as ever, but by now their better class patrons are retreating upstairs, indicating that the beer shops are getting larger. Our correspondent seems to pitch taverns and ordinaries at about the same level. The distinction he makes is not one of appearance, price, reputation or appointment but of function. The public at large, by their behaviour, made a distinction between the services offered by each, and while there was a high degree of duplication, people seemed to be able to distinguish between an ordinary that provided drink and a tavern that served food. The inns were by far the grandest of the establishments, but also the fewest in number. Their golden age had not yet come. Travel was still the prerogative of the rich, which accounts for the 'superb furnishings' associated with the London inns.

In 1669 the adolescent coffee houses had not fully acquired their final character. With their bay windows and long trestle tables spread with newspapers, they would appear to have had a tavern style layout and served more in the way of cheap alcoholic beverages than would have been available in their descendants.

Already we can see in this description of Restoration drinking establishments how things were to develop. The coffee houses became the gentlemen's clubs; the ordinaries became chop houses and restaurants while the taverns wilted as the upper classes abandoned them in the nineteenth century, and they and the alehouses became pubs.

The coffee houses provided a service for the city that had previously been performed by the guilds and by the trade 'quarters' of the town, and a gradual formalisation of the gossip process gave us the newspaper. However, contrary to popular belief, apart from insurance there does not seem to be much actual business going on here. Business was still taking place in the taverns.

> There accounts were settled, conveyances executed, and there attorneys sat, as at inns in the country on market days, to receive their clients. In that space near the Royal Exchange . . . the number of taverns exceeded 20, and on the site of the Bank there stood no less than four. At the Crown which was one of them it was not uncommon of a morning to draw a butt of Mountain 120 gallons, in gills.[19]

Neither were the coffee houses short of detractors. Ned Ward had a low opinion of them and their customers, regarding them as foppish and effete.

> In we went, where a pareil of muddling muckworms were as busy as so many rats in an old cheese loft; some going, some scribbling, some talking, some drinking, some smoking and the whole room stinking of tobacco, like a Dutch scoot, or a boatswain's cabin. The walls were hung round with gilt frames, as a farrier's shop with horse shoes; which contained abundance of rarities viz, Nectar and Ambrosia, May-dew, Golden Elixil, Popular Pills, Liquid Snuff, beautifying waters, dentifrices, drops and lozenges; all as infallible as the Pope. Where every one above the rest deservedly has gained the name of best;

best medicine being so Catholic it pretends to nothing else but universality. So that had my old friend not told me 'twere a Coffee House I would have taken it for Quacks' Hall, or the parlour of some eminent mountebank.[20]

The coffee house in question was Man's, a famous house, and what Ward was looking for was a method of upsetting the 'Sir Foplins' and the other 'sweet breath gentlemen who are always running their noses into the arse of a civet cat'. If Ward was in no doubt as to where his loyalties lay neither, it would seem, were the great minds of the eighteenth century. Johnson, Garrick, Goldsmith and Addison were all firmly of the opinion that the tavern was the 'throne of human felicity'.

With time, drinking healths became ever more ludicrous operations. They also became more significant. With the overthrow of James II drinking became charged with political significance, and, in a fashion, was to remain so in the eighteenth-century Mug Houses, from whence issued the becudgelled Whig gangs to quell the riotous mobs, down to the liberal generosity that rival establishments displayed to potential voters on behalf of the Buffs and the Blues at the Eatanswill election (as recorded in the papers of the Pickwick Society) until the 1867 Reform Act. Nor was this corruption thought untoward, as is demonstrated by the frankness with which one election agent of the 1760s recorded his expenses: 'To 20 strong men to be at Sir Robert's Meeting and making a noise . . . to taking 12 voters away, cost of ale, and not bringing them back in time to vote £8-13-4 . . . for secret encouragement of rioters, disbursed £40.'[21]

It was possible to overstep the mark, however, for in 1765 two justices of Corfe Castle were sent to prison for a month and fined £50 for refusing a licence to a landlord who had voted for the other party. Corruption undoubtedly made democracy a more enjoyable political system, as the electors of Horsham in 1844 would have agreed.

Every public house and beer shop in the Parish was secured by one side or other as an electioneering stronghold. At every one of them Pink or Blue flags were flying, the meaning of which could not be misunderstood. . . . If a voter wanted a drink he could go into any public house and obtain any kind of refreshment without being asked for payment. . . . The labourer whose taste was usually satisfied with small beer was now in a position to discover and indulge a palate capable of appreciating more aristocratic beverages. . . . It is not too much to say that most of the male population of Horsham were frequently drunk, many were continually drunk and some were continuously drunk for the whole six weeks preceding election day.[22]

Defoe tells us that after the Restoration the 'King's health became the distinction between a Cavalier and a Roundhead.' In 1688 it also became the distinction between a Jacobite and a supporter of the Glorious Revolution. In the case of the Jacobites they had to be very discreet, but they were also anxious to identify themselves to the initiated and avoid any ambiguity. Their cyphers and rituals developed to a Masonic level of secrets. When in a company where a loyal toast was proposed the Jacobite would hold his glass over the jug to indicate that he was drinking not to William of Orange, Queen Anne or George I, but to the 'King over the Water' – James II the old Pretender, or Bonnie Prince Charlie.

In many ways the English may have come to regret the passing of the raffish Stuarts. Charles II and James II may have been libertines, but they were temperate men compared to their father and grandfather and the nation's preferred choice, William of Orange, brought with him a substance that twice in British history threatened to bring the nation to its knees – gin.

Several factors conspired to popularise gin. First, it was constantly available. The availability of wine depended upon whom we were at war with. Since we were usually at war with either France or Spain, French or Spanish wine was often unavailable. The eighteenth century was the Port century, for Portugal was our oldest European ally. Portuguese supplies could always be relied upon, even during years like 1679–85 when French wine was prohibited. On this occasion a balance of payments deficit rather than a war was the problem, some 9,645 tuns of French wine having been imported in 1676 alone. A doggerel verse written in 1691 tells of the fruitless travels of two friends from tavern to tavern in 'Search of Claret'.

We order'd the Drawer to call from our Friend,
If a glass of good Claret to us he'd commend:

> He smil'd at our Question, and shaking his noodle,
> He told us by Yea and by Nay not a Bottle;
> But if we would call for a Glass of Red-Port,
> He'd afford us the best, or be paid nothing for't.

When relations with France were bad brandy as well as wine became unobtainable. Naturally, when William of Orange became King William III relations with France became very bad. Not only was Louis XIV funding the attempts by James II to recover the throne, but William and the House of Orange had been perpetually at war with France ever since the Thirty Years War of 1618. If brandy was unavailable or prohibited then gin was the only other spiritous liquor, the Scots only abandoning French wine – always available north of the border – in favour of Scotch in the early eighteenth century. William wasted no time at all in encouraging the gin trade.

In 1680 a Member of Parliament had remarked, 'there must be a reformation of ale, which is now so strong that it is for a groat a quart. It is strong as wine and will burn like sack.' One need do no more than imagine a beer so strong that it will burn to comprehend the awesome strength of the beers then available. Before long, however, people would look back fondly to the days when people indulgently toasted each other in strong ale, for in 1688 William III did for 'sensible' drinking once and for all. The tax on strong beer was raised to 2s 6d per barrel and to 3s in 1689. By 1692 this had risen to 5s. In 1690 the distillers lost their monopoly and a spirit duty of 2d a gallon was set, discriminating heavily against beer.

1689 – the year which saw the prohibition of imported foreign spirits – was also the peak year for seventeenth-century beer production. Some 5,134,309 barrels of strong beer were produced by the common brewers and victualling brewers, and a further 2,707,726 barrels of small beer. Comparable volumes were not produced again until 1822, and if one includes domestic production, which in 1689 was still twice as much as commercial production, comparable volumes were not brewed in England until 1864. The ratio of strong to small beer production at this time was 2:1. In 1691 the London brewers produced 1,222,764 barrels of strong and 865,831 barrels of small beer – a ratio of 1.4:1 – and by 1695 London production figures were 909,299 barrels to 813,824 as a result of further tax increases – a ratio of 1.1:1.

More alarmingly there was also a reduction in the volume of small beer produced. Small beer was a staple for the vast majority of the population, water being unsafe, and small beer was the primary source of fluid intake. Yet there was less beer brewed in 1712 than at any time since 1684, even though the population was 300,000 greater. Production did not rise again until the popularising of 'three thread' in the 1710s. The 1690s were a bad time for brewers and innkeepers. Parliament was actively trying to pursue a policy of restricting the numbers of brewers, much as Charles had wanted to do, but it was the taxes and gin that did them in. Small beer is a by-product of beer production, a final 'sparging' [washing] of the spent grains, and so output will rise as strong beer production rises. Yet because it was a staple there was a minimum demand below which demand would not fall. In a year like 1695, when the ratio of strong to small beer was 1.1:1 beer production was not profitable.

In order to offset the decline in profitability the natural reaction of the brewers was to increase prices, which, in the face of falling demand, could only be done by increasing strengths. Some ales were now matured for five years or so. An inexpensive option given overcapacity. More varieties appeared and more types of flavouring added including broom, wormwood, apricot, blackberry, cherry and china root.

To compound matters 1696 saw the recall of coinage prior to a reissue. Many alehouses were left with worthless coinage or no coins of denominations small enough for their needs. In August 1696 it was reported in Yorkshire that 'a great many alehouses . . . have given over brewing and selling of ale, because they can get no good money for the ale they shall sell.' The writer probably meant ale too, and not beer. In the period 1685–9 there were estimated to be approximately 46,000 brewing alehouses. By 1695–9 this had fallen to 37,000. To compound the situation the malt duty was raised to 6d a bushel in 1697 to finance the war with France.

Gin, on the other hand, was marching from strength to strength. In 1684 the gin on which duty was paid totalled 527,492 gallons. By 1710, the year which saw the final prohibition of any other bittering agent other than hops, and, simultaneously, the first hop duty (1d per pound English, 3d per pound Flemish), gin consumption was 2,200,271 gallons. By 1734 it was 6,074,562 gallons.

Put simply, between 1684 and 1710, as beer production fell by 12 per cent and strong beer by 22.5 per cent, gin consumption rose by 400 per cent – and that was just the legally declared quantities. Thus it is with one of those wonderful ironies beloved of history that the seventeenth century ends. The great century of religious intolerance, which throughout its course had seen strict Protestants trying to ban both Catholicism and the alehouse, succeeded in deposing the Stuarts only to have the Protestant saviour, King Billy, make the nation drunk.

Chapter 8

GIN FEVER

So quacks for cordials, filthy spirits sell,
Which soon despatch the sick to Heaven or Hell.
Not caring whether they are blessed or curs'd
Since they have picked the Patient's pocket first.

Drink has overwhelmed and drowned -
Far greater numbers on dry ground.
Of wretched mankind, one by one,
Than ever before the flood had done.

'Hudibras', Samuel Butler (1663)

William III dissolved the distiller's monopoly in 1690 and allowed anyone to start a distillery by giving ten days notice to the Excise. By 1714 there were two million distilleries in the UK and by 1735 there were five million. Of all the measures taken to promote gin the revocation of the distillers' monopoly was the most reckless and showed a callous disregard for the health of the nation. Charles I had granted the distillers their charter in 1638 at the insistence of his physician, to protect the people against the dangers of improper, inept and unscrupulous distillation. Any protection that existed was removed by William, and the mortality rates of the eighteenth century showed the consequences all too clearly.

That which William set in train Queen Anne upheld. War with France rather than the welfare of the British guided her hand, as the 1703 Distilling Act freely admits. The policies of her ministers were remarkably short-sighted. Trade with France had been prohibited since 1690, and in 1703 the Methuen Treaty – which

stayed in force till 1831 – gave trading advantages to Portugal.
Between 1704 and 1785 Portugal provided 65.4 per cent of UK
wine imports. Spain 29.3 per cent and France a mere 3.6 per cent.
This naturally led to smuggling on a huge scale. Whole
communities were engaged in it. At various times during the
eighteenth century smuggling was the largest occupation in
England.

Smuggling was incredibly sophisticated; ships had false holds,
luggers sailed at night to recover barrels sunk at predetermined
locations, labyrinthine tunnels and caves were dug. The smugglers'
tunnels which emerge in the cliff face at Kingsgate Bay in the Isle
of Thanet extend for *over two miles* inland to the village of
St Peter's. The smugglers were very well disciplined and imposed
their own discipline too. Woe betide the fool who ventured
outdoors when the 'Gentlemen were abroad'!

Smuggling naturally continued when trade with France was not
prohibited, and the Exchequer suffered accordingly. This loss of
revenue was compounded by the decline in beer production that
resulted from the large increases in the duty on strong beer, and
this decline was not being made up by revenues from gin – not just
because the duty on gin was very low, but because evasion was
very high. The number of premises retailing was so huge that duty
collection was impossible. In 1725 Middlesex magistrates reported
that London, excluding the City and Southwark, had 6,187
premises retailing spirits to a population of 700,000. The
1735 Middlesex Sessions Committee, reporting in January 1736,
estimated the number of retailers to be 7,044, but the justices
considered the figure to be an underestimation, since the returns
were compiled by the constables, half of whom were retailers
themselves. By 1739 the whole of London had 8,659 premises
retailing spirits in addition to the 5,975 existing alehouses.

The rate of expansion of the gin trade was of great concern. In
1710 duty was paid on 2,200,721 gallons. It had risen
to 3,379,695 gallons by 1722, 4,612,275 gallons by 1727,
6,074,562 gallons by 1734 and 7,049,822 gallons by 1751. If the
amount of increase in gin consumption between 1734 and 1751
appears only half that of between 1727 and 1734, this was
because duty-paid consumption peaked in 1748, since the market
was saturated, along with everyone in it. At any given time one
quarter of the population of London was completely inebriated.

This posed severe social problems. Beer had always been a universal drink, partaken of by all sectors of society. However, the upper classes had been gradually turning away from beer during the seventeenth century. So while in 1512 Lady Percy, wife of the Earl of Northumberland, had a quart of beer and a quart of wine for breakfast, and her ladies had well over a gallon of beer a day, the Percy ladies of 1712 would have been scandalised at the very thought of beer. The middle and upper classes did not drink gin, however, which only became a refined drink in the twentieth century. Respectable Victorians who harboured a taste for it invented a series of pseudonyms, even fooling themselves that labelling it 'Nig' would be sufficient to disguise its true identity from the servants.

The difference between beer and gin, as Hogarth's famous prints 'Gin Lane' and 'Beer Street' illustrated so well at the time, was that, although many beers were of a mightily powerful strength, beer and ale were foods of considerable nutritional value and had been a central part of the nation's diet for a thousand years. Gin was not only not a food but a poison which rendered its victims incapable of labour and directly led to the impoverishment and premature death of tens of thousands of people.

The famous dram shop sign:

> Drunk for a penny,
> Dead drunk for two,
> Clean straw for free.

was not a joke. Hardly less notorious was the 1736 description of a dram shop in East Smithfield where people 'laid together in heaps promiscuously, men, women and children, till they recover their senses, when they proceed to drink on, or, having spent all they had, go out to find there wherewithal to return to the same drunken pursuits and how they acquire more money the sessions paper too often acquits.'[1]

It is no exaggeration to say that every other shop in London was a dram shop. The proceedings of the Peace for the City of London and County of Middlesex are full of testaments to this fact. The evidence of Mary Till in the case against Sarah Robinson, indicted for stealing a ring on 15 August 1732, commences: 'I keep a Chandler's Shop in Scotland Yard, and this good Woman that

Pick'd my pocket is Servant to Mr Vanbritton, and so as I was suckling my Child, she comes in and asks for a dram . . . and so says I, Pray, Mrs Robinson, be pleased to serve *yourself*; and so she took a dram.'[2] A frequent question posed by the court throughout proceedings at this time was: 'Was not the prisoner drunk?'

One house in seven from Hermitage to Bell Wharf was a gin shop. Of the 17,000 houses in Westminster there were 1,300 licensed premises and a further 900 unlicensed, whereas in 1750 St Giles had 2,000 dwellings, 506 gin shops and 82 temporary houses of 'the greatest infamy, where gin is the principle liquor drunk'.

If they were not drinking gin the poor were increasingly drinking something else that did nothing to alleviate their lot – tea. Having been very heavily taxed until the early eighteenth century, its spread prompted hostility on a scale that seems incomprehensible by today's standards. In 1757 Jonas Hanway, prison reformer and pioneer of the umbrella, called tea an 'epidemical disease', adding, 'You may see labourers who are mending the road drinking their tea . . . it is ever . . . sold out of cups to haymakers. . . . Were they the sons of tea-sippers who won the fields of Crecy and Agincourt or dyed the Danube's shores with Gallic blood.'[3]

This objection was sustained well into the nineteenth century. Tea did nothing for the strength of either people or agriculture. Henry Brougham denounced tea on these terms, as did William Cobbett who famously remarked that while it was possible to raise a family of pigs on the waste from domestic beer production, the only thing that could be raised on tea was sleepless nights.

If the health of the working classes in the towns was under assault from gin and tea, the drinking establishments themselves were a third threat. Most people had little guarantee that they were drinking gin. Adulteration of beer had always been a problem and was to remain so until the beginning of the twentieth century. The adulteration of gin was a more serious problem, because of the concentration of the ingredients and the types of adulterants involved. One quack recipe included 'oil of vitriol, oil of almond, oil of turpentine, spirits of wine, lump sugar, lime water, rose water, alum and salt of tartar'. No small wonder mortality rates soared.

One anecdote may speak more eloquently than a mass of statistics. If the story is not itself incredible then the commonplaceness of its reporting illustrates how the national consciousness had become immune to the excesses of gin fever. An issue of the *Gentleman's Magazine* for 1748 reports that: 'At a christening in Beddington in Surrey, the nurse was so intoxicated that after she had undressed the child, instead of laying it in the cradle, she put it behind a large fire, which burnt it to death in a few minutes. She was examined before a magistrate and said she was quite stupid and senseless, so that she took the child for a log of wood, on which she was discharged.'4

The situation was rapidly becoming intolerable and unsustainable. Gin was not so widely drunk out of the towns, but the amount of drunkenness and crime it provoked were a grave threat to society and the nation. The authorities having let the gin Djinn out of the bottle could not get it back in. It was with some alarm, therefore, that Corbyn Morris in 1751 drew attention to:

The diminution of births set out from the time that the consumption of these liquors by the common people become enormous. . . . As this consumption hath been continually increasing since that time, the amount of the births hath been continuously diminishing. Can it be necessary to add to this shocking loss. . . the sickly state of such infants as are born, who with difficulty pass through the first stages of life and live very few of them to years of manhood? Enquire from the several hospitals in this city, whether any increase of patients and what sort, are daily brought under their care? They will all declare, increasing multitudes of dropsical and consumptive people arising from the effects of spiritous liquours.5

Between 1749 and 1751 the population of London was estimated to have fallen by over 9,300 as a result of gin consumption, confirming the prescience of those fears expressed around the turn of the century: 'Tis a growing vice among the common people and may in time prevail as much as Opium with the Turks, to which many attribute the scarcity of people in the East.'6

In 1750 a Committee of the House of Commons heard:

That the increase of patients in all the [London] hospitals from 1704 to 1718, the total increase was from 5,612 to 8,819, which was above one third; but that from 1734 to 1749 the total increase was from 12,710 to 28,147, which was near three times the number. Being asked his opinion, where he apprehended so great an increase could arise, he [a physician] answered, 'from the melancholy consequences of gin drinking principally'.[7]

The fall in population was a result of a high death rate accompanying a low birth rate. Yet at the time there were no major outbreaks of disease, the London population density was falling and people's diet was improving as corn prices were low and there were few bad harvests. Meat was fairly cheap and there was a rapid expansion in the market garden industry. There were also improvements in the sanitary facilities in the metropolis. All should have conspired to produce a boom in population. The fact that the population did not increase, but actually fell, can be laid squarely at the door of gin.

The first serious attempt to tackle the problem was the 1729 Gin Act. The act prohibited street sales, raised the spirit duty on gin to 5s per gallon and required retailers to pay £20 per annum for a licence to sell. However, it was a failure and was repealed in 1733. People stopped selling 'gin' and started selling 'Old Tom', 'Parliament Brandy' and the same foul concoctions under a variety of aliases.

It was not until 1736 that a second attempt was made to tackle the question, by which time legal consumption had risen by over 30 per cent. History is said to repeat itself, the first time as tragedy, the second as farce. Nothing could have been truer of the two gin acts. The 1736 act pompously acknowledged:

The drinking of spiritous liquours and strong waters is becoming very common, especially among the people of lower or inferior rank, the constant and excessive use thereof tends greatly to the destruction of their health, rendering them unfit for labour and business, debauching their morals and inciting them to perpetrate all manner of vices, and the ill consequences of such liquors are not confined to the present generation but extend to future years and tend to the destruction of the Kingdom.[8]

The act required retailers to buy a £50 licence, on pain of £100 fine, and imposed a heavy 20s per gallon duty on the retail trade.

It was, however, ill conceived and badly publicised. There was quite a gap between the passing of the act and its coming into effect on 29 September 1736. It also made provision for payment of informers and created the category of brandy shop, either as a sop to the brandy-drinking middle classes or in the hope that some revenue could be clawed back from the fruits of smuggling.

The act was a failure. Popular ballads hawked on the streets spread the idea that after 29 September gin would be permanently unobtainable. Riots resulted and suspected informers were murdered. In the run up to the twenty-ninth there was an orgy of bingeing and people pawned everything they owned for a final dram.

In London the *Daily Gazette* reported that:

It was observed that Monday, Tuesday and Wednesday [27–29 September] several retailers' shops were well crowded, some tippling on the spot, whilst others were carrying it off from a pint to a gallon, and one of these shops had such a good trade that it put every cask they had upon the stoop, and the owner, with sorrowful sighs said, 'Is this not a barbarous and cruel thing, that I must not be permitted to fill them again!' . . . Such has been the lamentations that on Wednesday night her [Mother Gin's] funeral obsequies were performed with formality in several parishes and some of the votaries appeared in ragged clothes, some without, and others with one stocking. . . . We hear from Bath that Mother Gin has been lamented in that city in much the same manner.[9]

Statistics initially indicate that the act was partially successful. In 1736 duty was paid on 6,116,437 gallons (actual consumption in England and Wales was nearer 14 million gallons); in 1737 duty was only paid on 4,250,399 gallons. This figure is more instructive as a guide to the loss to the Exchequer than indicative of people's drinking habits. The immediate result was, on the one hand, to add another item of contraband to the smugglers' list – it has been estimated that in 1782 annual imports of Holland's gin were approximately 2.5 million gallons of which the vast bulk was smuggled – and on the other, to increase the amount of illicit and dangerous distilling.

The ingenuity applied to the task of evading the act was a display of resourcefulness at its best. Distillers took out wine licences and sold spiced gin and wine-laced gin. Brandy shops and others simply renamed the product Sangaree – from the Spanish Sangria, literally *bleeding* – to disguise it as mere spiced wine. Other new names included Tom Row, Cuckold's Comfort, Lost Shift, Ladies Delight, Make Shift, The Baulk, King Theodore of Corsica, or Colic Waters.

Some outlets styled themselves as chemists, coloured the gin, bottled it and labelled the bottles with such instructions as 'Take 2 or 3 spoonfuls of this 4 or 5 times a day, or as often as the fit takes you.' When arraigned in court these 'chemists' would argue that 'the late act had given many people the colic, and was the reason they had so many patients.'

The act was universally detested, especially since between 1736 and 1738 12,000 people were convicted of breaking it, and only two licences were ever taken out. Despite the seemingly large numbers of convictions it was unenforceable. In London in 1739 there were 95,980 houses sheltering a population of 725,900. Of those houses 15,288 sold drink in some form, giving a ratio of outlets to houses to people of 1:6:47. In poorer areas of town this ratio was as low as one in four houses.

The salutary affects of the act were very short-lived. Consumption soon rose after the dip in 1737, so that duty-paid production stood at 7,160,000 gallons by 1742 and 8,203,430 gallons by 1743 when the act was repealed.

The reason for the act's failure was summed up by Lord Carteret. 'Since the populace saw they could evade the law they openly and avowedly transgressed it, and the transgressions were so numerous that they even set the Government itself at defiance. No private man, no under officer durst inform, no magistrate durst punish, without being De-Witted by the mob as he passed by the street.'[10]

The bulk of gin produced must have been pretty disgusting, though relief from misery, not flavour, was what its devotees were seeking.

It charms the unactive desperate and crafty of either sex, and makes the starving sot behold his rags and nakedness with stupid indulgence, or banter both in senseless laughter and more insipid jests. It is a fiery lake that sets the brain in flames, burns up the entrails and scorches every part within, and at the same time a getter of oblivion, in which the wretch immersed, drowns his most pinching cares, and with his reason all anxious reflection on children that for food, hard winter, frost and horrid empty hours.[11]

By 1743 things were getting desperate, and a further gin act received Royal Assent. Drafted by a Kentish distiller, it passed through the Commons virtually without debate. It recommended the replacement of the £50 fee with a sum that was realistically within the reach of retailers – £1 – and stipulated that the mechanism for enforcement should be at the magisterial level with taxes on spirit manufacture. Sadly, the act was hotly opposed in the Lords, and especially by the bishops, who saw it as a relaxation on the prohibition of gin consumption. A speech by Lord Lonsdale illustrates the concern felt at the horror of the gin fever.

In every part of this great metropolis whoever shall pass along the streets will find wretchedness stretched along the pavement, insensible and motionless, and only removed by the charity of passengers from the danger of being crushed by carriages or trampled by horses, or strangled by filth in the common sewers, and others, less helpless perhaps, but more dangerous, who have drunk too much to fear punishment but not enough to hinder them provoking it. . . . These liquors not only infatuate the mind but poison the body, they not only fill our streets with madmen and our prisons with criminals, but our hospitals with cripples. . . . The use of distilled liquors impairs the fecundity of the human race, and hinders that increase which providence has ordained for the support of the world. Those women who riot in this poisonous debauchery are quickly disabled from bearing children, or, what is more destructive to general happiness, produce children diseased from their birth, and, who, therefore, are an additional burden, and must be supported through a miserable life by that labour which they cannot share, and must be protected by the community to which they cannot contribute to the defence.[12]

This picture was very true. Babies not killed through starvation and neglect were frequently poisoned through their mother's milk. As Hogarth illustrated, only the pawnbroker got fat.

The 1743 act was largely ineffective. It mitigated the unpopularity of the 1736 act and halted the upward rise in gin consumption, but did little to lower it. It was, however, an adventurous measure that recognised that prohibition and punitive action were not solutions, and as such was fairly enlightened.

At best it could be said that things were not getting worse. Crime and drunkenness continued to be the norm for huge numbers of people and the avoidance of crime and drunkenness was the endeavour of the remainder. In 1751 Henry Fielding wrote in 'An Enquiry into the Causes of the Late Increase in Robbers',

> Wretches are often brought before me, charged with theft and robbery, whom I am forced to confine before they are in a condition to be examined; and when they have afterwards become sober, I have plainly perceived from the state of the case that the gin alone was the cause of the transgression, and have sometimes been sorry that I was obliged to commit them to prison. Gin is the principal sustenance (if it may be so called) for more than 100,000 people in this metropolis. Many of those wretches there are who swallow pints of this poison within 24 hours, the dreadful effects of which I have the misfortune every day to see, and to smell too.[13]

In the same year, when of the 12,000 quarters of wheat traded in London each week 7,000 were distilled, the bubble was finally burst. The Gin Act of 1751 placed an extra duty of £7 7s per tun on grain spirits. It prohibited distillers from selling to retailers unable to show a licence and made drinking debts irrecoverable at law. This last measure had the effect of undermining credit, upon which so much gin consumption was founded.

Gin consumption fell markedly, and between 1760 and 1782 remained at around the same level it had reached during the 1720s. The genie could never be put back in the bottle, but its mellifluous influence could, at least, be contained. In 1756 a crop failure led to a prohibition on the distillation of domestic grain. Rum was encouraged as less damaging than gin. It had never had much of a chance to become popular in the face of competition from smuggled spirits, only establishing a foothold with the introduction of bonded warehouses in 1736 and gaining popularity after its adoption by the navy in the 1740s.

In 1760 distilling was permitted once more, but with a duty of £24 10s per tun; and of the thirty major distilleries in London in 1750 only twelve were still functioning in 1760. Further increases in duty of £4 18s per tun on grain spirit and £6 16s 6d on molasses spirit were imposed in 1762. Increases again were made in 1779, 1781 and 1782 so that tax per tun stood at £61 19s 9d for gin and £81 6s 6d for rum, which was widely used in the production of cordials.

The effects of increases in tax were intended to reduce the consumption of gin, but each increase in duty led to an increase in smuggling rather than a decrease in gin drinking. The worst excesses of the 1740s had been beaten off, however, although the evil spirit was not defeated and lived to strike again in the early nineteenth century.

If, after such an orgy of self-destruction it was necessary to suffer a hangover, then there *was* a hangover of sorts. The opposition to the 1743 bill, focused as it was on the charge that its aim was the maximisation of revenue rather than the reduction of gin drinking, prompted a resurgence of Puritanism that lasted well into the nineteenth century.

Much of this frustration with the 1743 act was with the power it gave to magistrates, who in the eyes of the disaffected were no longer the firebrand Presbyterians of the seventeenth century, but according to the Bishop of Salisbury, were people who 'Never do refuse a licence to anyone that is willing and able to pay for it. Are there not now many notorious rude houses licensed as coffee houses or alehouses? Do not we know that when such houses become a nuisance to the whole neighbourhood it is with the utmost difficulty that the honest neighbours can prevail upon the Justices to take away the licence.'[14]

In truth, the 1743 act did not give the magistrates enough powers. Their decisions were subject to appeal, and many were overturned. Their constables were unreliable (frequently it was only agents of the gin sellers that actively sought the post) and often the dram shop owners conjoined for their mutual protection. Such facts were no mitigation for the Puritan elements, however, and we gradually see a return to the language of the seventeenth century, as evidence in a statement in 1759 that 'in many parts of the metropolis, particularly in Chelsea, every house comparatively speaking, is a public house.'[15] The notion of granting an alehouse

living as a means of keeping people off the poor rate had crept
back into favour during the century, but opponents of gin and beer
imagined that this led to a proliferation in the number of
alehouses, which in the eighteenth century tended to rise in line
with demographic trends. True, the dram shops proliferated; but
most alehouses did not sell spirits and were only forced to by the
second gin fever of the nineteenth century.

Various minor reforms subsequent to the 1743 act gradually
strengthened the magistrates' hand, just as the magistrates were
becoming more radical once more. These reforms included a
formalisation of brewster sessions; the disbarment of brewing and
distilling magistrates from sitting on the licensing bench; an
increase in stamp duty; no distiller to be a licensee; only houses
paying the poor rate to retail spirits; licensees liable for sureties and
magistrates given powers of search and discovery.

These measures helped contribute to the success of the 1751
act, but they also paved the way for a new wave of suppression
that occurred in the 1780s, and the alehouse was like as not
the victim. In 1782 Lancashire Quarter Sessions prohibited cock
fighting. In 1787 Horseley, in Gloucestershire, reduced the number
of alehouses from ten to three. The Speen division of Berkshire
refused seventeen licences, without compensation, as superfluous,
i.e. no charge of disorder was laid against the landlord. A division
of Wiltshire likewise suppressed fifteen licences and Newcastle
alehouses were issued with a rule book. On 20 September 1787
Sheffield Brewster Sessions suppressed all dram shops. Berkshire
introduced Sunday closing. Some areas made a licence dependent
upon the consent of the members of the parish vestry, and at
Brampton, Oxfordshire, this principle was, in 1787, extended to
renewals, while many benches started to impose conditions to
licences that were strictly outside their powers. The period between
1787 and 1790 saw 3,825 spirit licences disappear, and a further
2,800 went by 1799, though hardly any went in London where
relations between the bench and the trade were more cordial.

Much of the swing towards Puritan-type repression was the
result of the Industrial Revolution and the change in social values
that accompanied it. A sober workforce was necessary for the
emerging order – though the failure to provide for that workforce
led to a resurgence in gin drinking. Even so, people still found ways
around the new regulations. Where sureties and recognisances

were demanded a black market soon developed, and in Durham it was reported that blank licences were made out in advance to be filled in at the 'discretion' of the Clerk of the Peace.

It does not really matter that the Puritan fervour that closed the eighteenth century was not so much religious as Utilitarian. That something needed to be done there was no doubt. The fervour grew after the problem had been largely dealt with, and, as is the nature of such energies, it was indiscriminate. There was to be no distinction between the alehouse and the dram shop, even though their histories in the eighteenth century had been entirely different.

Chapter 9

THE ALEHOUSE IN THE EIGHTEENTH CENTURY

Stingo! To thy bar room skip,
Make a foaming mug of Flip;
Make it our country's staple,
Rum New England, Sugar-Maple,
Beer that's brewed from hops and Pumpkin,
Grateful to the thirsty Bumkin.
Hark! I hear thy poker fizzle,
And o'er the mug the liquor drizzle;
All against the earthern mug,
I hear the horn-spoon's cheerful dub:
I see thee Stingo, take the Flip,
And sling thy cud from under lip,
Then pour more rum, and, bottle stopping,
Stir it again, and sear 'tis topping.

R. Tyler (1757–1826)

The eighteenth century saw many changes in the nature of the alehouse. It could not remain entirely unchanged in the face of the gin fever, let alone the social, economic and scientific changes that were occurring. At the end of the seventeenth century the alehouse was little altered in character from its fifteenth century antecedents; a little less rough at the edges perhaps, a few more comforts, as befitted the time, but still basically 'cakes and ale'. However, by the end of the eighteenth century the alehouse was virtually a thing of the past, having given away to the beer shop and the public house.

Brewing had been a commercial activity for 300 years. The sixteenth and seventeenth centuries saw various attempts to concentrate the brewing industry, a trend which accelerated in the eighteenth with the rise of the porter brewers and the beerage and which continues to this day. Alehouses were not run on good commercial lines, however. Primarily their functions were community serving, petty victualling, provision of credit, leisure and the basic alleviation of want. The century of Adam Smith saw the commercialisation of leisure provision and the realisation that the humble alehouse could be a rewarding investment opportunity. As the century progressed it became more common to see purpose-built public houses and to find speculators buying into houses in the same way they would speculate on the level of the hop duty.

One of the quirks of the English language is the passion for calling things what they are not. The alehouse – a domestic dwelling thrown open for people to drink in the kitchen or parlour – gives way to a building purpose-built for retail liquor selling, with specialist rooms set aside for different purposes and different classes. This was called the public house.

With the transition from alehouse to pub the basic character of the alehouse changed too. England was becoming a more class-conscious society. There was an increasing drag upwards to 'respectability', and the very top echelons of society turned their backs on pursuits they had previously shared with others. Taverns and inns all aspired to be more upmarket, which became ever more important for commercial survival. For example we hear that, in 1704, Quakers Tavern in Finch Lane had 'acquired a singular reputation among the staggering zealots of that sober fraternity' – respectability indeed! Life was becoming harder for the illicit house. The alehouse could either be made more respectable by magistrates and ape the taverns and inns, or could chuck in the towel and side with the dram shops that were draining their custom, and retail the demon gin.

That choice may have been outside the landlord's control, location being a crucial determinant of the prosperity of any alehouse or pub. The traditional location of illicit houses around the periphery of a town was ended, especially after 1750, with the increasing urbanisation of towns and the new tendency for wealthier people to move to the edges and leave the centre to the growing urban poor.

Many factors contrived to alter the character of the alehouse during the eighteenth century. A revival of Puritan attitudes in the

1780s, a growing tendency to associate alehouses with crime, other inevitable side effects of the war against gin, the Industrial Revolution, more effective and better enforced legislation, the rise in porter brewing, the introduction of beer engines in the late 1790s, the growth of the brewery 'tie' and changes in brewing science all had their own profound impacts.

This is not to say that all was changed. Alehouses, such as the ones described by Timothy Nouse in 1706, were not just suited to bygone days, but would last long into the eighteenth century.

> The superfluous number of such petty inns and alehouses seems to proceed from these two causes; the first is from the application which is made frequently on behalf of some broken, half-starved merchant or idle fellow, who rather than beg or stand and be hang'd, or at best become chargeable to the Parish, hopes to get a subsistence by the little cheatings and degenerate shifts of ale selling. The other course is much of the same figure, it being commonly no other than sordid interest of some mean spirited Justice who to maintain a superfluous or indigent member of his Family, or Acquaintance, is tempted easily to license alehouses for the sake of fees.[1]

It has been mentioned several times that over the centuries the toleration of alehouses for this reason, and Nouse's recognition of it is as a common practice, indicates how 'traditional' a means of alleviating poverty it had become. In 1698 it was even suggested that poor relief be distributed, in kind, from alehouses. The reorganisation of the Petty and Quarter Sessions in the 1750s strengthened the authorities' hand as licensing mechanisms became more efficient. In 1749 an illicit Berkshire tippler, Dennis Hacker, declared that without tippling he was unable to support his family; he was suppressed.

What is of interest in Nouse's complaint is the entirely subjective use of the word 'superfluous', for his 'superfluity' arises out of his anti-alehouse prejudices. If by the granting of a licence a man and his family might make a living and be kept off the poor rate, the alehouse can hardly be said to be superfluous, but to have pointed this out in the eighteenth century would have made one few friends. A sympathetic ally of the alehouse might possibly have been found in the form of Ned Ward – the London Spy – who was less interested in passing judgement than in recording what he saw, and who was contemptuous of the conceit and bigotry behind the 'informed' opinion of the time.

Ward understood the lower classes and was able to describe them without condescension. In 1704 he records a visit to a very inferior Billingsgate alehouse.

> In a narrow lane, as dark as a Burial-Vault, which stunk of Stale Spirits, piss and Sir-reverance, we groped around like a couple of thieves in a coal-hole, to find the entrance to that nocturnal theatre in whose delightful scenes we proposed to terminate the night's felicity. At last we stumbled upon the threshold of a gloomy cavern. . . .
>
> We no sooner entered but heard such a number of female tongues so promiscuously engaged in a mess of tittle-tattle, that had a waterman knocked down his wife with his stretcher, and been tried for the fact by a Parliament of fishwomen they could not have exercised their nimble instruments with more impatience.
>
> We turned ourselves into the smoky boozing den among them; where round the fire sat a tattered assembly of motherly flat-caps, with their fish baskets hanging upon their heads . . . with everyone her nipperkin of warm ale and brandy. . . .
>
> The one looking over her shoulder and spying me behind her accosts me after this manner. 'God save you honest master, will you pledge me?' 'Aye, Dame,' said I, 'with all my heart.' 'Why then,' says she, 'here's a health to mine arse and a fart for those that owe no money,' . . . 'Come, come away,' says my friend, 'these saucy tong'd old whores will tease us to death.' Which unhappy words one of them over-heard, and starting up like a fury, thus gives her lungs a breathing. 'You white livered son of a Fleet Street bumsitter, begot upon a chair at noonday between Ludgate and Temple Bar. You puppily offspring of a mangy night walker, who was forced to play the whore an hour before she cried out, to pay the bawd her midwife, for bringing you, you bastard, into the world, who is it that you call whore?'[2]

Ward managed to rescue his friend before the fishwives had him gutted and filleted. Although a coarse alehouse, it was not small and appears to have had several rooms. After leaving the fishwives with their nipperkins – quarter pints – they wandered through to a room where some watermen were eating a rude meal of boiled herrings, bread, cheese and onions. A drunken sailor returned and had to be helped upstairs to his bed, and his progress upstairs was punctuated by curses as his stumbling climb brought shins and stairs into contact.

> After these bolted in two seamen with a little crooked fiddler before them, short pipes in their mouths, oaken truncheons in their hands, thrumcaps on their heads and canvas trunks on their arses. The two lousie subjects to the pickled God Neptune having washed off their brine with a plentiful dose of freshwater ale began to be as brisk as a town rake, that had shaked off his poverty. In their frolicks they happened to espy a hook drove into the mantle-tree which they immediately converted to a very comical use, laying violent hands on the fiddler and by the hind slit of his breeches hung him on the tenter, who being sorely affrighted at this unexpected elevation shot that into his trousers, which made the crooked vermin out stink a pole-cat. In this condition . . . he hung sprawling, begging with humble submission to be set on Terra Firma. All the time dripping his guts upon the hearth like a roasting wood cock; till at last, by wriggling he broke the strings of his breeches and came down our broiled scraper into his own sauce.[3]

Ned Ward is not affronted but delighted by the earthy scenes confronting him, and it would seem to have been a highly entertaining evening. Yet the fishwives are drinking brandy not gin. The gin fever has not yet taken grip, and Ward did not return in twenty years to see whether they had foresaken their brandy and if their cheeks were still 'plump like an infant's buttocks.'

Houses like that visited by Ward are resilient. It would have been possible to find similar houses in London until the 1860s, and the gin shop was effectively the eighteenth-century counterpart of the seventeenth-century illicit alehouse, but it was becoming harder to be a small house. The intention was to bar smaller, less reputable houses, and already the mentality that was to produce the 'fewer and better' policy of the twentieth century was starting to bring its influence to bear. Indeed, in recognition of the rise in importance of alehouses as 'respectable' commercial centres there was an increase in sheriff's officers, justices' clerks, constables and bailiffs as landlords.

The 1750s was a watershed decade when effectual regulation came into being. Justices' Clerks and Clerks of the Peace had a direct profit incentive to enforce the regulations, though incentives naturally led to abuses.

> On every day of licensing the Clerk of the Peace or his deputy attends the meeting of the Justices of the Peace, and upon a large scroll takes a recognisance of the alehouse keeper, who produces any securities without enquiry being made into circumstances upon oath, and for this he, the Clerk of the Peace, receives 12*d*, which I am sorry to say is the only advantage [that] arises to anyone from these recognisances, and then the roll is carried to the Clerk of the Peace's offices and never heard of after.[4]

As licensing regulations came into effect controls on maximum prices fell by the wayside and market forces played a greater role in determining price, though these were very static for most of the century. This is not necessarily to say that free market forces were at work. The retail end of the beer trade may have been a free market, but the manufacturing and wholesale end was controlled by a handful of brewers and distributors who were increasingly prepared to act as a cartel.

One of the major differences, therefore, between the eighteenth century and earlier centuries was that while previously it had been in the interests of the ruling elites to ensure that the price of ale was kept as low as possible, commensurate with the state of the harvest, the ruling elite was now either indifferent to the issue or keen to raise the price to the maximum profit that could be sustained by the market. Perhaps more than anything else this change of pricing policy ties the eighteenth century to the modern age. It may be objected, at this point, that the eighteenth century was a period of unprecedented price stability. This is true, yet price stability was a result of the increased competition that arose during the century. The brewers' hold on the market was not yet complete enough, in the days before advertising and product differentiation, to switch competition from quality to price. Indeed, competition was fierce enough to ensure that the extra costs associated with fluctuating harvests were shouldered by the brewer and not the drinker.

The early part of the eighteenth century was one of increasing national prosperity, shared even by the agricultural labouring classes. It had a corresponding effect on the alehouse, in as much as people expected an increase in standards, which the more commercially-minded landlords were able to provide. In 1751 a writer on the *Gentleman's Magazine* was able to report that he lived 'in a country village and we have six common stews or alehouses, they brew 130 quarter of malt in the year. Our farmers drink but little, our day labourers drink less, the consumption is chiefly by our weavers and combers.' The farmers and day labourers would have brewed their own ale or beer, while the annual production of the six alehouses would have been between 2,000 and 2,400 gallons of beer depending on the strength of the brew and the sophistication of the brewing.

Of course, it is difficult to paint a simple picture since town and country alehouses varied as did practices in the north and south, east and west. On the whole we can say that while in the 1690s the average size of the alehouse keeper's family was slightly below the national average, by 1745 it was slightly above, indicating an increase in wealth among alehouse keepers and even the emergence of the ability, in places, to retain domestic servants. A characteristic of the medieval and Tudor alehouse was its comparatively short lifespan. It was now much more likely that an alehouse keeper would stay in one location for much longer periods and if and when he or she moved on it was again more likely that he would move on to another alehouse or inn, rather than to a primary occupation. Alehouse keeping was beginning to be seen as a profession and not as a secondary source of income or a respite during a period of unemployment. Fledgling trade unions tended to make alehouses their meeting places, first floor rooms often being made over for their use. The landlord frequently became the club treasurer, either because he was impartial or because he had a strongbox or safe. The London Corresponding Society first met in the Bell, Exeter Street, in 1791. So started the long association between organised labour and the alehouse, which led to the formation of working men's clubs, the CIU and co-operative breweries. By the nineteenth century this association was traditional enough to attract the attention of at least one group of confused and slightly hysterical temperance campaigners.

But ⁹⁄₁₀ of the tyranny and violence of Trades Unions which sometimes exhibit themselves in overt acts, but are more frequently suffered in silence by individuals, arises from the intemperance of those who are in many cases more prominent members, and from the facilities afforded by the present iniquitous system for hatching secret plots over a glass of grog or a pot of beer in the public house.[5]

Just as organised labour met in alehouses, political parties also developed their own alehouse-based clubs. The Whigs organised in the Mug Houses with the aim of suppressing any Tory-inspired Jacobinism. The Mug Clubs had their own character, as can be seen from the Mug House Club in Long Acre.

They have a grave old gentleman, in his own grey hairs, not within a few months of 90 years old, who is their President, and sits in an arm'd chair some steps higher than the rest of the company, to keep the whole room [in] order. A harp plays all the time at the lower end of the room; and every now and then one or other of the company rises and entertains the rest with a song. . . . Here nothing is drunk but ale, and every gentleman hath his separate mug which he chalks on the table where he sits as it is brought in, and everyone retires when he pleases as from a coffee house.[6]

The Mug Houses were often decorated with mugs on the exterior to represent the members' mugs suspended on the inside. They were a relatively short-lived phenomenon during the early years of the century, as, political hothouses, they rapidly got out of control. The Salisbury Court Mug House – the last of its kind – was pulled down at the instigation of Parliament, and several Mug House members were executed. A Tory bastion was the October Club, which met at the Bell in King Street, Westminster, and which could claim Jonathan Swift as a member. It was so called because of the strong October Ale drunk, and was a direct response to the Mug Houses. Tory alehouses also frequently displayed a punchbowl.

While many premises, especially beer shops, continued to be domestic residencies converted to beer retailing until well into the nineteenth century, purpose-built premises were an inevitability once magistrates indicated their preference for larger houses. On occasion they often insisted on the provision of stables at alehouses, which had formerly been the sign of an inn, but was now an emblem of respectability for a prosperous house. During the reign of George II tavern-style partitions started to appear in alehouses. In 1730 Sarah Kiddington, of Stamford, was reported to have 'a great room with drinking booths'. These booths were occasionally referred to as 'modesties' and were the forerunner of the 'snug', which was so much a feature of Victorian public houses. The expansion of the alehouse also added to its versatility. They frequently doubled as prisons or temporary places of confinement, excise offices, meeting places for local authorities, mortuaries and coroners' courts.

As an indicator of the general increase in respectability of many alehouses there was an increase in the number of female proprietors. There had been a gradual increase in female alehouse keepers since the 1640s; most alehouse labour was female and many women ran houses that were licensed in their husband's name, hence the high incidence of widows being permitted to run houses. It should also be pointed out that a quarter of dram shop proprietors were female.

Alehouses had always been seen as being frequented by criminals but also as being in league with criminals. Now they experienced a smartening up of their reputation in this area too. In time when petty crime was a necessity for survival for much of the population, the association with crime was inevitable. Obvious footpads, cutpurses, setters, biters, lifters, budgies, droopers, crossbyters and sharpers decamped to the gin shops or poor country alehouses, while the alehouses' criminal patronage moved upmarket. Since so many people relied on crime, the highwaymen and smugglers – the criminal aristocracy – were popular heroes. Jack Shepherd, who escaped from Newgate three times before he was finally hanged in 1724, aged twenty-two, became an early Tussaud exhibit. Dick Turpin, who was born in an alehouse – the Crown, Hempstead, Essex – was a lot less pleasant than popular legend suggests, but his body was carried in triumph by a mob after he was hanged at York in 1739. Jonathan Swift wrote, in 1727, of the execution at Tyburn of Tom Cox, who he renamed Tom Clinch.

As clever Tom Clinch, while the rabble were bawling,
Rode Stately through Holborn to die at his calling,
He stopt at the 'Bowl' for a bottle of Sack,
And promised to pay for it when he came back.
His waistcoat and stockings and breeches were white,
His cap had a new cherry ribbon to tie't.
The maids to the doors and the balconies ran,
And said 'lack-a-day', he's a proper young man,
And as at the windows the ladies he spied,
Like a beau in a box he bowed low on each side,
And when his last speech the loud hawkers did cry,
He swore from the cart it was all a damn lie.
The hangman for pardon fell down on his knee,
Tom gave him a kick in the guts for his fee;
Then said 'I must speak to the people a little,
But I'll see you all damned before I will whittle.
My honest Will Long, he long held his place,
He lengthened my life with a whole year of grace,
Take courage dear comrades, and be not afraid,
Nor Skip this occasion to follow your trade;
My conscience is clear, and my spirits are calm,
And thus I go off without prayer book or psalm;
Then follow the practise of clever Tom Clinch,
Who hung like a hero and never would flinch.

Tyburn was 'That most celebrated place/ Where angry justice shows her awful face/ Where little villains must submit to fate/ That great ones may enjoy the world in state.' It was situated, originally, on the eastern fork of a 'burn' or stream, roughly where Oxford Street meets Strafford Place. Gradually it moved westwards until, at the modern-day site of Marble Arch, it was midway between the Tybourne and the other half of the stream at Westbourne Grove, where it stayed until 1783. The nearby taverns and alehouses did a roaring trade, both at Tyburn and all along the tumbril route from Newgate, as did alehouses all over England on such occasions until 1868, when public executions were ended.

The traditional last drink was customary and the condemned man who failed the obligatory joke about paying for it on his return was thought to be a bad sport, for it was as *de rigueur* for the mob as was a music hall comedian's catchphrase. Like many customs it was not without sound foundation. In the days before the final drink was taken at the Bowl, which was situated at the corner of Endell Street and Broad Street, but was taken at the hospital of Matilda at St Giles, a man had refused a final drink with the result that the procession proceeded directly to Tyburn, where he was hanged just in advance of the arrival of his reprieve. Subsequent visitors to Tyburn were, therefore, anxious not be hanged 'for leaving their liquor'.

The condemned man aside, however, a reprieve was bad news. It meant bad business for the hawkers, who, as Swift points out, made money by selling handbills of the condemned man's last speech. That these had been printed in advance of his saying anything did not seem to concern the large mobs who turned out for the occasion. Better off spectators had a permanent grandstand at Tyburn, and when in 1758 the notorious fraudster Dr Hennesy was reprieved the outraged mob destroyed the seating.

The link between tavern and Tyburn was a strong one.

An Ordinary serves as a nursery for Tyburn, for if any one will put himself to the trouble of observation, he shall find that there is seldom a year wherein there are not some of a gang hung as precious jewels in the ear of Tyburn. Look back and you will find a great many done already. God knows how many there are to follow.[7]

Thomas Witherington, executed in 1635, stopped the executioner's cart on Holborn Hill protesting that,

I owe a small matter at the Three Cups Inn a little further on, and I am afraid I shall be arrested for debt as I go by the door. So I shall be much obliged if you will be pleased to carry me down Shoe Lane and bring me up Drury Lane, so we don't pass it and perhaps lose my appointment at Tyburn.[8]

In 1732 William Manley, landlord of the Rose and Crown on Lickey Hill, near Bromsgrove, was finally unmasked as the ringleader of a notorious gang of highwaymen and thieves who had been operating over four counties, with an extensive, inn-based intelligence network, including the Swan, Birmingham; the Swan, Hinckley, Leicestershire; the Cock, Stourton,

Staffordshire; the Cock, Meriden, Warwickshire; the Fox and Goose, Bromsgrove, and the Fox and Goose, Redditch. Manley used to fence the gang's takings to a pretended jockey who travelled up from London. Manley was hanged in Stafford that year.

A far more gruesome landlord, in the previous century, was the owner of the Ostrich at Putloe, Gloucestershire, whose inn unaccountably prospered in spite of its disadvantageous location. So well did the landlord and his wife thrive that they were eventually able to move to a more favourable inn, whereupon they leased the Ostrich to a blacksmith, who in the course of time decided to erect a shed in the yard. He was not long in this endeavour when he came across a corpse buried in a shallow grave. Upon further investigation, seven other bodies were unearthed, and one was found to be sporting one of the previous innkeeper's knives in his chest. The landlord and his wife had systematically been robbing their guests for years, and those who had become suspicious had been summarily dealt with. Both landlord and wife were executed in 1675.

While the eighteenth century saw many changes in the alehouse – often as a result of greater prosperity, a search for greater respectability and the appropriation by gin shops of many of the worst traditional aspects of alehouse life – much remained unchanged. Industrialisation reduced the number of itinerant poor in the countryside and in certain years meant greater rural prosperity. There were still poor country inns, just as there were still rough town alehouses competing with neighbouring dram shops. Lean years, such as the 1740s, saw a rise in middle-class and Puritan paranoia about the 'evil of petty alehouses'. People were convinced that there was an increasing number of alehouses, when in fact the per capita number was falling in most areas, especially in the south.

Few people wished to hear such facts, and Adam Smith made few friends when he inconveniently exploded many prejudices with the publication of The Wealth of Nations in 1776, in which he stated: 'It is not the multitude of alehouses . . . that occasions a great disposition to drunkenness among the common people, but that disposition arising from other causes, necessarily gives employment to a multitude of alehouses.'

Such words went unheeded, and the 1780s saw yet another period of concerted clampdown on public houses that lasted till the

end of the century. This is not to suggest that the clampdown was
not entirely unwarranted.

> The magistrates of Bow Street have done one laudable act,
> which if followed up, will go a great way in restoring the police
> of Westminster to the power of discharging the offices for which
> the police in general is established. There is a house in Russell St
> – late a public house, known by the sign of the Sun, which is
> frequented by a gang of thieves, who used to meet there for the
> purposes of planning their nocturnal measures. The magistrates
> have taken away the licences from the publicans who kept the
> house; but if they do not form a resolution to take away all
> licenses from all persons suspected of entertaining dishonest
> company, the shutting up of one house will be of little effect,
> while so many others remain for reception of thieves and
> prostitutes.[9]

At this time there was a profound change in the national mood
following the loss of the American colonies. Not only was there an
economic impact, but there was a deep-felt sense of humiliation.
There was also a heartfelt duty to restore national dignity, and
national sobriety was one aspect of this process. With the successes
achieved in the war against gin in the 1750s and 1760s, the
alehouse once again became the public villain. This was reinforced
by the demands for a disciplined labour force that accompanied the
Industrial Revolution, and since much of the labour migration
associated with early industrialisation took people out of areas
with large numbers of gin shops, towards new conurbations where
there were few or none, the alehouse was seen to blame for
society's woes until the gin shops caught up again.

In June 1787 there was issued a Royal Proclamation Against
Vice, which was an official nod to the justices that they were free
to crack down on the alehouses as they saw fit. This hit smaller
alehouses disproportionately. Different areas took different
measures: some tried to impose closing times, others interfered
with the layout of an alehouse, trying to find structural reasons
why a licence should be denied. Curbs on music, dancing, singing,
gaming, cockfighting and baiting were tried. Prohibitions on
paying wages in pubs, discrimination against smaller premises
and greater scrutiny of publicans were further measures

variously applied. In general the main thrust of policy was to refuse to license premises. In Cambridge the increase in population between 1792 and 1814 would have justified an extra 200 public houses, just to maintain a per capita parity. In fact the numbers of licences issued fell by twenty-two, while in the same year (1814) beer duty rose by 10s a barrel. So zealous were the justices in their suppression of houses that in 1790 the Excise was forced to complain of the losses it was suffering as a result.

The mood in England during the Napoleonic Wars was not particularly liberal. In 1792 City of London magistrates withdrew licences from all premises allowing meetings of radicals. In 1795 the Sale of Beer Act stated that anyone convicted twice for selling beer without a licence could be barred from selling beer for life. All such measures as these were ineffectual, since, in those days, there was no statutory body responsible for prosecuting those who offended against such legislation. The initiative was left to voluntary bodies. The tally for proceedings pursued by the Society of the Reformation of Manners for 1718 shows that there were many 'concerned citizens'.

Prosecuted for lewd and disorderly practices	1,253
Keeping of bawdy and disorderly house	31
Exercising their trades and calling on the Lord's Day	492
Profane swearing and cursing	202
Drunkenness	12
Keeping common gaming houses	8

The point here is that law enforcement was being left to highly partisan interests. Publicans had no effective mechanism for countering the activities of such bodies and the late eighteenth century saw their rapid proliferation. The inauguration of the Proclamation – from the 1787 Proclamation – was in 1788. The Society for the Bettering of the Conditions of the Poor was founded in 1797. The Society for the Suppression of Vice, whose aim was to prosecute publicans who sold liquor during Divine Service, saw the light in 1802 and the grandly named Society for the Suppression of Mendacity was founded in 1819.

All these societies had one thing in common. They refused to accept Adam Smith's explanation of the root cause of the number of alehouses. They were not interested in ameliorating the conditions of the working class, other than by insisting that they would be better off if they did not drink. Their analysis did not extend to the consideration of why people drank, unless it were to prove that it was because of alehouses. What offended the sensibilities of the members of these societies was that people were able to drink and swear during Divine Service. The religious sentiments of the people in the alehouses were not a consideration.

Religion and the working class during the Industrial Revolution were perhaps best summed up by Dickens in *Hard Times*.

> No. Coketown did not come out of its own furnaces, in all respects like gold that had stood the fire. First the perplexing mystery of the place was, who belonged to the eighteen denominations? Because, whoever did, the labouring people did not. It was very strange to walk through the streets on a Sunday morning and note how few of *them* the barbarous jangling of bells that was driving the sick and nervous mad, called away from their own quarter, from their close rooms, from the corners of the streets, where they lounged listlessly, gazing at the church and chapel going, as at a thing with which they had no manner of concern. Nor was it merely the stranger who noticed this, because there was a native organisation in Coketown itself, whose members were to be heard in the House of Commons every session, indignantly petitioning for Acts of Parliament that should make these people religious by main force. Then came the Teetotal Society, who complained that these same people would get drunk, and showed in tabular statements that they did get drunk, and proved at tea parties that no inducement, human or divine (except a medal), would induce them to forgo their custom of getting drunk.

With the demon gin raising its head again during the early nineteenth century, largely as a result of ill-aimed attacks on the alehouse and other short-sighted government policies, this kind of repressive mood conspired to ensure that the persecution of the pub continued and the opposition to the public house of the late eighteenth century developed into the temperance movement of the nineteenth. However, by the nineteenth century the drink trade was better able to deal with the threat of anti-drink militants. It was now better organised, and it was organised because it was concentrated – a result of the rise of the porter brewers.

Chapter 10

PORTER

Brewers from their tuns and coolers
Arose to be our sovereign rulers,
And still to their immortal praise
Build coaches daily out of drays.

In 1598 Stow reported on the 'Great Brewers' clustered along the banks of the Thames. It was at this time that many of these breweries were sinking their own wells. This required considerable private capital. The common brewers had always been encouraged and, while they were very few in the north and west of the country, the seventeenth century saw a rise in their fortunes. Common brewing automatically led to a concentration of the industry, and in the face of a growing demand and a growing population concentration meant profits.

If, as has been suggested, the period after 1660 was a turning point after which the status of the alehouse keeper was no longer measured in terms of poverty, but gradually came to be measured in terms of wealth, then the common brewers played a considerable part in this transition, since they had, for over a century, made substantial profits, and nothing changes popular conceptions of an activity quite like success. In 1686 a Commissioners of Excise report spoke of alehouse landlords, 'most of them being in debt to the brewers and living on their stocks'. The conditions were clearly becoming ripe for the establishment of a tie, though one or two changes in the industry structure were needed before the tie could develop apace. The introduction of porter was to trigger these changes and to provide the right conditions for the development of a recognisably modern industry.

Brewing had been the nation's largest industry since the sixteenth century. Concentration was gradual and confined to the south-east. In 1699 there were 194 common brewers in London, while during the seventeenth century brewers had come to the fore of the provincial bourgeoisie. In 1700 six brewers supplied Salisbury with its beer. A concentration of the industry meant it was easier to apply pressure on brewers not to sell to unlicensed houses, and as such was not resisted by the authorities, but exercising this policy gave great local influence to brewers. Poor, illicit houses had to brew their own liquor, but by this time the difference in quality between commercial brewing and the output of the brewing victuallers and private houses – still a huge source of production – was sufficient to convince many to quit brewing. Porter accelerated this trend, so much so that by 1821 William Cobbett, the great champion of the rural poor, was lamenting that 'In former times to set about to show to Englishmen that it was good for them to brew beer in their houses would have been so impertinent as gravely to insist that they ought to endeavour not to lose their breaths, for in those times to have a house and not to brew were a rare thing indeed.'[1] Since a tie is founded on debt it requires considerable capital to maintain, more capital than was prudent to venture at the turn of the eighteenth century without further concentration of the industry. Porter provided both the means of concentration and the surplus capital.

The pro-gin measures adopted by William III had a profound effect upon beer-drinking habits. One response of the brewers was to increase the strength of their beer. A major response by drinkers was to match their taste to their pockets. The fashion was to mix beer from each of the two strengths brewed by the town brewers, with a third measure of pale beer brewed by the country brewers. The price of the strongest beer was diluted, while the strength of the weakest beer was fortified. The result was popularly called 'three-threads'.

Unlike today's barstaff, who have the benefit of beer engines to raise the beer, the pot boys of the eighteenth century found the taste for three-threads effectively tripled their carrying duties. In addition, producing a blend from three separate barrels trebled the possibility of an inconsistent product, making it hard to satisfy permanently, and so keep custom.

What was needed was a beer that had all the characteristics of three-threads in one brew. It would simplify the cellar and would enable the town brewers to encroach upon the barrelage of the country brewers. It was in 1722 that Ralph Harwood of the Bell Brewery, Shoreditch, perfected a recipe for three-threads, which was first served up at the Blue Last public house. Later that same year a malt was produced allowing anyone to brew the popular drink, which now went under the name of 'mild beer' or 'entire'. The name 'porter' did not catch on until the 1740s as a result of the favour it found with London's market porters.

Porter was always London's own. The nature of London water lent itself to the production of porter, just as the strongly gypsum-bearing waters of Burton lent themselves to the production of the lighter, 'bitter' ales that later earned the area international fame. Yet such was the power of porter that even the Burton brewers brewed it. A porter brewery was opened in Sheffield in 1744, Dublin in 1759 and Glasgow in 1775, but universally the drink was hailed as 'London porter', and the great brewing dynasties that grew up on its back were London porter brewers.

Porter was extremely lucrative. It had to be, because it was very capital intensive. Between 1730–1750 the porter brewery of Ralph Thrale doubled its capital valuation. In 1747 the *London Tradesman* noted that more capital was required to set up as a porter brewer than for any other trade except banking.

An idea of the extent of the capital tied up in a porter brewery can be gained by an examination of just one brewery. Meux, at Gray's Inn Lane, prided themselves on the size of their fermenting vessels. At the end of the eighteenth century Meux installed twenty-four vats with a combined capacity of 35,000 barrels (8,400,000 pints). One vat alone contained 1,296,000 pints. This was small beer compared with what was to come later. In 1795 Meux subsequently installed a vat with a capacity of 20,000 barrels or 5,760,000 pints. It was 30 ft deep, 70 ft in diameter, and was bound with iron hoops each weighing three tons and costing £300 each. The whole vessel cost £10,000. A vessel of similar capacity once hosted a banquet wherein 200 people sat down to eat. Indeed, no royal state visit was complete without a visit to a London porter brewery. Fortunately, this monster was not the vessel which burst in October 1814 at a Meux site. This vat was a mere 22 ft high and contained only a modest 3,555 barrels of porter, or 1,045,840 pints. Eight people died in the deluge, either drowned in their basements or overcome by the fumes. Several houses were demolished by the flood.

Although porter brewing was capital intensive there were huge economies of scale to be derived, as witnessed by the relative price stability obtained from 1722 until the Seven Years War of 1760 forced a price rise of ½d per quart to 3½d.

Porter was very robust and was less susceptible to rough handling. Its principal advantage was that, although it required much longer to mature than other beers, it could be stored in bulk. The bigger the size of the vessel, the smaller the ratio of surface area to volume, and the chances of the beer being spoiled were greatly reduced. Porter was made of cheaper materials than the lighter, clearer beers. Much of London's porter malt came from Hertfordshire, while finer grades of pale malt came from further afield. Porter could be mashed to a higher degree of extraction. This meant it could compete with bright beers on both a price and strength footing, for at similar rates of extraction bright beers would have suffered clouding from starchiness and would have required greater concentrations of hops to offset sweetness from unfermentable sugars.

One final advantage was crucial from the businessman's point of view. A high level of capital outlay is perfectly proper, provided the rate of return on capital is sufficient. The rate of return is partly determined by the rate of exploitation of the capital, and, here too, porter brewing had an absolute advantge over its rivals, for porter could be brewed for more months of the year. It was not until the 1740s that bulk maturation came into vogue and the huge porter profits started to appear. At the same time there occured other peripheral changes which were to help shape the modern industry. In a century that saw the population double, the number of common brewers also rose from around 750 at its outset to around 1,400 at its conclusion. Over the same period the number of brewing victuallers fell from around 40,000 to 24,000. Brewing was becoming a profession, and although the Brewers' Company had existed since 1437, it had never shared the same privileges as other trade guilds and livery companies, since it could never prohibit anyone from brewing. In the mid-eighteenth century the situation changed, and it became very difficult to become apprenticed to a common brewer. Apprenticeship now cost money, and traditional apprentices now found themselves as brewery labourers. Now that the brewers' profits were increasing, they took the inevitable step of all 'professions' and set about erecting barriers to entry.

At this time there was a concentration of the industry and not just a displacement of production from victuallers to brewers. For although a number of common brewers established themselves in parts of the country where they had not existed before, most of them were not porter brewers. Therefore, they had to find less capital to set up, but the eighteenth century was a period of growing capital availability. Much of this venture capital was generated by speculation on the hop market. In 1781 we know of profits of £1,000 p.a. on a hop holding at Martley Rectory in Worcestershire. In the heart of hop country, at Canterbury, smallholders frequently tended hop gardens of half an acre which could yield as much as 5.5-6 cwt of hops. In a good year an acre of hop garden could yield as much as 50 acres of arable land, and thus could provide a very lucrative income.

An indictor of the value of the hop industry can be seen in Borough High Street, London, at the Hop Exchange. Its magnificent interior testifies to the predominance of Kent as the principal centre of hop production, although fourteen counties in all produced hops. What is remarkable about this display of wealth is that the hop trade was completely indigenous. Demand for hops was outstripping supply, even in the seventeenth century, so that none of the wealth was a result of a trade surplus from abroad. It is entirely due to the central position of the hop in England as a traded commodity.

Speculation was so keen that after 1774, when an act required the labelling of hop pockets with the year, place of origin and grower's name, it became necessary to carefully load the pockets onto the wagons bound for Southwark in order that no labels were to be seen. This would ensure that no intelligence could be garnered from the sight of a wagon of hops that might be advantageous to traders. In Kent these pocket labels were rather plain, while the Hampshire pocket designs were rather more ornate, especially those from the Surrey enclave of Farnham.

Of the 1,914 London common brewers operating in 1700 only 127 were in business in 1808. This is just what we might expect if we were to examine the eighteenth century from the viewpoint of

capitalist development. Not only was brewing the largest industry
in the country, it was intrinsically and umbilically linked with
the evolution of capitalism. Brewing shared many of the
characteristics associated with modern industrial capitalism, as
opposed to its mercantilist and cottage-based progenitors. First,
there is the question of the capital intensity of the brewing
process. The inventions of the eighteenth and nineteenth centuries
that enabled and powered the Industrial Revolution were to require
capital investment on unparalleled levels. The porter brewing firm
of Samuel Whitbread installed a Boulton and Watt steam engine in
1775, the installation of which was supervised by Rennie, the
builder of the London, Southwark and Waterloo bridges, while
John Smeaton, of Eddystone Lighthouse fame, designed the
brewery's six underground cisterns, the largest of which held
3,600 barrels of porter. The steam engine was the talk of London,
and was the pride of the brewery.

> Last summer we set up a steam engine for the purpose of
> grinding our malt, and we also raise our liquor with it. It is built
> in the place where the mill-houses used to stand with the malt
> loft over it. . . . Our wheel required six horses to turn it, but we
> ordered our engine the power of ten, and the work it does
> we think is equal to fourteen horses, for we grind with all our
> four mills about 40 qtrs an hour, besides raising the liquor. We
> began this session's work with it, and have now ground about
> 28,000 qtrs without accident or interruption. Its great uses and
> advantages give us all great satisfaction and are daily pointed
> out afresh to us. We put aside now by it full 24 horses, which to
> keep and feed did not cost less per annum than £40 a head. The
> expense of erection was about £1,000. It consumes only a
> bushel of coals an hour.[2]

Brewing required relatively little labour in relation to capital, and
from any perspective the elimination of labour from the production
equation vastly increases the profit-making potential of a concern.
    The design of the brewery, once an easily recognisable feature of
every small town in the country, was a direct result of the
elimination of labour. The whole layout of the brewery was
designed to ensure that gravity provided the motive force wherever
possible. The raw materials were hoisted to the top of the brewery,

from where everything flowed downwards under the control of the brewer and his staff. Physical labour was not required again in the production process – the cleaning of vessels apart – until the filling, manhandling and distribution of the barrels.

In the words of Sydney Smith (1771–1845), an eighteenth-century cleric and wit, 'what two ideas are more inseparable than Beer and Britannia.' This characteristic of omnipresence required the brewers to keep accurate records in order to keep track of their stock. This required the development of accounting techniques, bureaucracy and management hierarchies of a complexity that had hitherto only existed inside the Admiralty. Unlike the Admiralty the brewers were commercially minded. Their bureaucracies were not particularly labour intensive either. The focal points of managerial activity were the great leather-bound ledgers of the brewers, called rest books. The rest was the brief summer period when brewing ceased, when inventories were taken, accounts drawn up and the profits from the year's brewing were assessed. These new management accounting techniques enabled the brewers to calculate their worth to the last half-penny and provided the asset of most value to the capitalist – information. The information supplied by the rest books enabled investment decisions to be made, rates of return to be calculated, projections of capacity to be monitored, demand to be recorded, sales strategy to be planned and all the other tasks and considerations that were, and are, necessary for management then and now to be undertaken. These first generations of 'managers' put their information to excellent use.

In 1741 Truman's porter breweries were valued at £23,340. In 1760 they were valued at £92,320, a threefold increase during a period when the price of porter, unlike the price of malt and hops, remain unchanged. In 1780 the value had again almost doubled to £171,860, and by 1790 Truman's was valued at £271,240, the country's fourth largest producer of porter, with an annual output in the region of 100,000 barrels.

The number one position was held by Samuel Whitbread, the archetypal beer baron. Born in 1720 in Cardington, near Bedford, he was apprenticed to a brewer at fourteen by his widowed mother. Eight years later he set up as a brewer with brothers Godfrey and Thomas Shewell as partners. By the time he was thirty he had purchased the King's Head Brewery at Chiswell Street where the Whitbread brewery was to remain for over 200 years. By 1761 both of the brothers had resigned from the partnership, leaving Samuel as sole proprietor. From modest beginnings and with a small source of external finance the business gradually grew, assisted by Whitbread's readiness to adopt new technologies and techniques. By 1768 Whitbread had been elected MP for Bedford, campaigning against the slave trade. By 1787, the year when King George III and Queen Charlotte chose to visit the now famous brewery with its huge steam engine, the brewery's output was 150,280 barrels per annum. By 1796, the year Samuel Whitbread died aged seventy-six, output was 202,006 barrels per annum. In 1762 Whitbread's were worth £116,000; in 1783, £178,770 and in 1790 they were valued at £271,240.

The brewery managers were also powerful men. Some of those employed by Whitbread had their portraits painted by Thomas Gainsborough and George Romney. The rewards for these men could be great too. The slow rate of diffusion of porter brewing outside London was not entirely due to the peculiarities of London water or any inherent economies of scale to be derived from London's size. The jealously guarded nature of the secrets of porter brewing was also a factor. So, although Perkins, later of Barclay Perkins, started out as a manager in a brewery, brewers prudently realised that such men were worth keeping.

These men were good planners too. They understood that efficiency was a function of their scale of operations. Implicit in this was an understanding of the distribution process. The large brewers understood that an efficient distribution system had to correspond to proposed increases in capacity, and that it was a precondition of expansion, and that expansion meant profits. This had profound effects for the future of the pub after the 1760s. The *Gentleman's Magazine* in 1760 noted that beer was, 'mostly fetched from the brewhouse by the customers and paid for in ready money so that the brewer was entertained by few servants and had no stock of beer and ale before by him, but a trifling quantity of cash and his money returned before he paid either his duty or his malt.'[3] This practice was about to change. Already the larger brewers were using drays to deliver beer, indicating the changing relations between the brewers and the publicans during the eighteenth century.

The latter half of the eighteenth century, while on the one hand seeing the emergence of the great porter brewers and the conscious efforts to derive economies of scale and improvements in brewing technology (the introduction of isinglass finings in 1758 and the saccherometer in the 1760s), also saw the renewal of the policy of alehouse suppression and increases in malt duty brought on by the Seven Years War with France. In 1760 malt duty rose to 9½d, in 1780 it was 1s 4½d and by 1802 it was 2s 5d, rising to 4s 5¾d the following year. The duty did not fall to its 1802 level until the defeat of Napoleon and peace between England and France.

The increase in malt duty caused a rise in price of ½d per quart to 3½d and reduced the publican's profit by approximately 1s to 12s a barrel. It must be remembered that the price of porter had not changed since 1722 and was the benchmark against which other beers took their measure, so that prices had not changed for many people's entire lives and were, not surprisingly, seen as 'traditional'. The malt duty hit private brewers as well as commercial brewers, with the result that yet another nail was driven into the coffin of brewing victualling.

The brewer was stuck between two stools. Increased output to maximise profits and return on capital was being confounded by increased competition to supply a falling number of outlets at a time of rising prices. The relative balance of power was temporarily swinging in favour of the publican. The publican could now force the brewer to bring the ale to him, and his economic strength at this time meant that the 3d in the pound discount for prompt payment became standard. In addition, the publican was emerging in his modern guise, not the owner of the beer, as the brewing victualler had been, but the brewer's agent. As his agent the alehouse keeper declined to take full responsibility for the brewer's beer. Sales made were the alehouse keeper's concern. Ullage and unsaleable beer was now the concern of the brewer, with the corollary that brewers' Rest books regarded 'beer in publicans' cellars' as an asset of the brewery.

Once having got his beer into a publican's cellar, the brewer had to keep it there. Much of this responsibility fell on the draymen, who not only had to deliver the beer but, as 'abroad coopers', also supervised the 'fining' of the beer and ensured that the landlord was proficient in the art of cellarmanship, which was by no means assured in the century which saw the decline of the brewing victualler.

Clearly the brewer was 'exposed'. Devourers of capital and equipped with an expensive distribution structure, they were vulnerable at the point of retail. This vulnerability was compounded as the century drew on, since the alehouse suppressors grew in number and boldness. Competition for outlets, when prices were rising, ran into a further problem which increasingly placed the brewers in a bind and which, by the 1790s, was reaching endemic proportions – adulteration.

For centuries adulteration of beer and ale was strictly prohibited by law. The population at large regarded adulteration as an especially heinous crime, for which, temporally, the ducking-stool and, spiritually, purgatory were the fitting punishments. Beer sellers seem to have survived the worst excesses of the gin fever without overly aping the temptations to adulterate, to which the dram shops succumbed. The price rises of the 1760s sapped any resistance the beer retailers may have felt, and as their margins fell the tendency to adulterate grew, so that by the 1790s it threatened the well-being of the brewers.

At the root of the problem again was gin. The Industrial Revolution created social discord, upheaval and urban squalor on an unprecedented scale; social bonds were dissolving, and the agricultural rhythms that had been the faintly perceptible heartbeat of England were choking in the belching smog of mills and furnaces. The malignant gin demon seized the opportunity of the Industrial Revolution, and its fragile prison was rudely smashed by the harsh reality of the misery of back-to-back slums. The Industrial Revolution, having released the gin Djinn, was not about to control it. Thus a second gin fever gripped the nation until it was finally contained in the 1830s when, coincidentally, the Industrial Revolution is commonly regarded to have exhausted itself.

Faced with the added competition from gin, the problem of beer adulteration grew in direct proportion. The most popular adulterant during the late eighteenth century was Cocculus Indicus (India Berry) a highly poisonous plant related to Deadly Nightshade used in India to stupefy fish to facilitate their capture, and, as such, not something one would expect to find in a pint of London porter.

As time passed, and techniques became more sophisticated, common adulterants came to include tobacco, Grains of Paradise, chillies, caramel, coriander seeds, quassia, sulphuric acid, salt, extract of aloes, liquorice and sulphate of iron. Not a few of these were straight imports from the gin adulterators' pharmacopoeia; others were the result of experimentation to reproduce or stretch out the flavour of porter. One wonders how desperate people must have been before they decided to see whether chillies or sulphate of iron would be likely to produce the desired result.

Clearly for the brewers there had to be some form of defensive action. As rational capitalists the answer was to extend their influence over the distribution process. The result was the loan-tie. Initially the brewers did not wish to initiate the form of tied system that so dictated the modern pub landscape up to 1990. They were almost reluctant to take on the responsibility of a full tie, even if they were happy to see publicans in their debt. In 1746 Whitbread had only thirteen tied houses; in 1780 there were twenty-four and in 1800 there were eighty. However, one-off informal arrangements became more frequent, and once a pattern emerged and the industry recognised the full implications of having a loan-tied estate, the gradual move to tied houses became a stampede. In a contracting market place it very quickly became necessary to establish a tie, or lose your retail outlets altogether. Once the supply of tied houses dried up – a process that took over a century – there then came the next logical progression of capitalist development: the cartel.

The January edition of the *Monthly Review* for 1773 complained that brewers,

> not contented with such trade and gain as might spontaneously arise . . . but where known to buy up paltry little houses and settle retainers in every little parish, as well as every little town and city, and for fear there should be a place in the kingdom exempt from their advantage, we have scarce a village without some of their cottages and huts, where servants and labourers, inferior tradesmen and handicraftsmen, young people and old, are secreted and allowed by various sports, pastimes and fooleries, till intoxicated with every mixture that can tempt their palate or drain the pocket, they swallow in like swine the filth of debauchery, and are a disgrace to our laws and reproach to human nature.[4]

It may have been the case that part of the initial impetus for the tie came from the non-porter brewers. Alarmed at the meteoric rise of their porter-brewing rivals and unable to achieve the savings in malt that the long maturation period of porter brewing allowed, they first took to the tie as a means of self-defence against porter and rising prices. If this were the case, the above extract would make more sense if the process were viewed piecemeal. The porter brewers did not resort to this defensive type of loan-tie at such an early juncture, and the London market remained free for many decades after loan-tied estates were being assembled elsewhere in the country.

What cannot be stressed too strongly in this history is the Londonocentric nature of the drink industry; innovations were introduced in London and diffused gradually throughout the nation. In the eighteenth century, therefore, it would have been the case that common brewers were establishing tied houses, while in remote parts of the north medieval-style victuallers were still the norm. As the Industrial Revolution had its main sway in the north, this was also a period when the rate of technological diffusion accelerated, and with technological change came changes in the structure of the industry, so that the indebtedness of brewing victuallers to maltsters that existed in areas away from London was gradually replaced by indebtedness to brewers, and with that came the tie.

An example of the process can be seen in the gradual ending of the position of aleconner. In 1758 the aleconners of Woodstock were redesignated 'clerks of the market', at a time when, in London, markets and mobile barrows were starting to give way to permanent shops, the fixed premises that enabled Napoleon to label us the 'Nation of Shopkeepers', and assisted the transition from alehouse to public house by removing many of the trading functions of the alehouse from medieval to modern establishment. Such trends, of course, by divesting both publican and brewer from wider responsibilities to what had been the 'community', assisted the public house to be ever more a commercial venture and to move further away from its humble origins.

The price rises that were a result of war with France in the 1760s gave way to further price rises that were a result of war with America in the 1770s. Despite the advances in productivity that characterised the industry from the 1760s and the rapid mechanisation of the industry that followed (notably the introduction of steam), it was not sufficient to save them from the effects of restrictive licensing in the 1780s, the bad harvests of the 1790s and the war taxes of the Napoleonic era, all of which militated in favour of greater adulteration of beer and the extension of the tie.

Originally brewers were reluctant to embark upon the establishment of a tied estate, but once spurred into action they quickly discovered the advantages of a tie. It was a defence against adulteration, which they disliked since it reduced their profits and ruined the reputations of their beers, and it ensured the quality of the product and simplified the distribution process and accounting methods. It helped formalise the debt system by which houses fell under the tie, thus helping the brewers reduce their financial exposure. At a time of a falling number of licences in per capita terms, which meant more competition between alehouses and busier alehouses, it allowed the brewers to assist in direct investment in a property so as to maintain an advantage over proximate rivals and, of course, the benefit was not all one way. The publican was in a fairly strong bargaining position, provided he could not be publicly accused of adulteration. The brewery had to humour him to some extent, the full weight of the tie not yet extending itself to the evicting of tenants. The scarcity of premises gave rise to the concept of 'goodwill', a sum paid to outgoing landlords, which naturally made buying into a property that much more expensive. This practice soon became universally recognised, and while it benefited the brewers by enhancing the respectability of the premises – so marginally reducing the chances of suppression – it also enhanced their role as brokers of capital, so that new landlords would be in their debt before they had even drawn a pint (a situation that reached crisis levels in the 1890s and is again causing problems at the start of the twenty-first century).

The brewers faced little competition once they had embarked on their course of action. The distillers never sought to establish tied estates, though they shared a tie on a few occasions. The race for the brewery tie was underway before the distillers enjoyed the gin-drinking renaissance of the early eighteenth century; they seem to have been disinclined to feel the need for it and indeed managed perfectly well without.

The late eighteenth and early nineteenth centuries seem to have been, for the brewers if not for many more of the nascent capitalist class, a period where the rule 'heads, the big cats win – tails, the big cats win' started to apply, and has ever since.

As mentioned, it was the smaller brewers who rushed into the tie. These smaller firms snapped up the inner city sites, mostly by buying them outright and then leasing them. The properties they bought were those they could afford, and in general were in the older parts of town. Although, for a while at least, the Middlesex magistrates worked on the principles of 'once a public house, always a public house', and 'bricks and mortar commit no sin', this was not always the case. Elsewhere magistrates were more frequently disposed to add riders to licences, which naturally fell hardest on the oldest premises. In 1792 the Tower Hamlets magistrates suppressed the eighty-seven worst alehouses and beer shops of the 1,000 within the borough, and many others had to comply with the conditions attached to their licences to secure renewal. This made the financial investments of the brewery firms very uncertain and costly. The larger firms preferred loans to leases. Loans could be swapped, and while a weaker form of the tie, they were at least less vulnerable. By positively adopting a loans policy they were more attractive to licensees in newer parts of London, where expansion opportunities existed, who wished to retain a degree of independence and choice. As a result, the larger companies retained a larger amount of the free trade. A company like Meux – ninth largest by output in 1787 – was in 1808 supplying 48.1 per cent of its output to loan tied houses, only 26.6 per cent to leased houses and not much less, 25.3 per cent, to the free trade.

Other influences were at work, the fluctuations in the building market being one. Years of little property development saw a preference for leases and more rigid ties. Years of rapid building saw a preference for loans, especially in the post-1815 peacetime boom and populist libertarian air.

The policy of the Middlesex magistrates must also be seen in context. To an extent they were pursuing a policy of 'drowning out gin', but it should not be assumed that there was much overall let up in the repressive attitudes of the time, even allowing for regional variations. The policy of the 1780s and 1790s favoured the bigger firms. At the end of the Napoleonic War the reversal of popular attitudes also favoured the bigger firms.

The justices who had been so persistently suppressing alehouses for thirty years or more suddenly found themselves portrayed as assailants of the freedoms of Englishmen, and it was felt that it was a pernicious evil that they should be allowed to deprive a man of his livelihood on a whim. In their defence it must be pointed out that they were not unaffected by the popular mood. In 1816 the Berkshire Division of Newbury announced its intention to favour untied licences, while in the following year the Marlborough bench, 'refused to grant licences to those who held their houses of common brewers, unless such brewers first declared that they were not bound to take their beer of their respective landlords, except it was good and such as was generally approved of,' and, 'informed those persons who held public houses under brewers that in case their landlords give them notice to quit their houses in consequence of taking beer from other brewers, they would authorise them to remove their licence to any other house and never license such brewer's houses in future.'[5]

The Marlborough magistrates were acknowledging a shift in the trade that had occurred during the eighteenth century, that from licensing an individual to licensing a house – a change that had taken on considerably more weight with the growth of the tie, since the property was now of greater importance as surety against bad debt.

The porter bubble burst quite suddenly, just like the hoops on Meux's giant vat, and at roughly the same time. The reasons were many and intricate, but change was quite dramatic. A rapid growth was replaced by a rapid decline. This can be easily illustrated by looking at the volumes brewed, and the industry dominance of the big twelve porter brewers.

Year	Total Brewed 1,000 brls	Big 12 %	Barclay's 1,000 brls	Truman's 1,000 brls
1748	915.5	41.9	35.3	39.5
1760	1114.5	47.1	32.6	55.5
1780	1319.5	52.8	105.5	95.5
1815	1768.5	77.7	337.6	172.2
1830	1441.5	85	231.3	150.3

Source: The Brewing Industry in England 1700–1830

It was not a case of outgrowing the market but of the market becoming more concentrated. The big twelve, of course, were not the first to suffer. Even though the volume of London porter brewed declined by 327,000 barrels between 1815 and 1830, the big twelve increased their dominance to 85 per cent of output and many firms must have gone to the wall. Indeed, between 1808 and 1822 the number of London brewing firms declined by twenty-nine. Prices fell and firms had to take losses in order to defend surplus capacity; Barclay's production slumped by almost one-third in fifteen years.

The reasons why porter declined are intricate, but simply expressed. One might point to a loss of confidence caused by persistent adulteration; competition from gin; increased Temperance sentiment, fuelled by such things as the 1787 Royal Proclamation against Vice and Immorality; rising prices due to war and the rising cost of the tie. All of these were undoubtedly factors. There had been a petition on beer quality in 1814, signed by 14,000 Londoners complaining of adulteration and high prices. The brewers were certainly going through a period of unpopularity. Free-traders and Whigs formed vocal political opposition to the brewers and the, by then, Tory beerage, but the brewers did not adulterate their own beer. The best defence against adulteration was the tie, and the tie infuriated the free-traders. The big brewers also tried to resist price rises while small brewers constantly agitated for them, but so long as the big brewers could use their surplus capacity to keep prices down, and force smaller brewers to the wall, they did so. This helped stem the upward pressure on prices; it also meant that adulteration continued and brewers were forced to supply known adulterators in order to safeguard their outlets.

Underlying all these contributory factors was a more fundamental reason for the decline of porter. Porter was a fuel of the Industrial Revolution. It had been a necessary precondition of that revolution, a cheap, sustaining, nutritious beverage every bit as vital to its success as waterwheels or coal. The England of the post-Napoleonic era was, however, very different from that which had existed before the revolution in America. Mechanisation had transformed society; beam engines not only raised malt to the top of the brewery and pumped the liquor into the mash tun, but in 101 other industries steam power replaced human effort. Just as in the early eighteenth century coal replaced wood as the fuel used for brewing, so coal replaced porter as the fuel powering the nation.

Not only this, but porter failed to capture the post-Napoleonic mood. The new lighter Burton beers were making inroads into the London market. The Burton brewers operated a similar cartel to the London brewers; they too competed on quality rather than price, but they did not burden themselves with London estates. Their lighter beers won popular acclaim by a public tired of suspect dark beers.

All this was not to say that porter died a sudden death. It was still an immensely important commodity, just as there was still much exhausting physical labour being performed. It was, however, in decline. London brewers started to diversify and brew other types of beer. The big brewers were not going to be unduly worried by the decline of porter. It was still the major London drink throughout the nineteenth century, even if some drinkers preferred bitter or pale ale and others preferred stout or Guinness, which was to appear on the scene increasingly during the century.

Perhaps the final nail in the coffin of porter was the replacement of pewter with glass as the main material for drinking vessels. In a glass it was easier to see the quality and condition of lighter beers than thick, dark porter. With the introduction of glass came the decline of the quart as a measure. The weight of glass needed to make a vessel large enough and robust enough to hold a quart was uneconomic and cumbersome. The pint of beer gradually did for the pot of porter.

All things exist within the framework of their own timescale, and do not exist terribly well outside them. Porter is available today, indeed is making a comeback, but it is drunk out of curiosity and nostalgia. We enjoy it and savour its fullness, but we also understand that it is from another time, when food was coarse, transport meant going on foot or on horseback, exposed and cold; when an open fire was bliss at the end of a frozen day; when clothes were heavy and rough; when cities were filthy and close; before sewers, or gas, or drains, or trains, or electricity, or piped water; from the days of tuberculosis, typhoid, cholera, diphtheria, polio and smallpox.

Something else died at this time and it died for many of the same reasons as porter. Its death was more sudden, but then its time and place in history was to run much faster. That something was the stagecoach, and when it died so did the great temples to the English way of life – the coaching inns.

Chapter 11

ENGLAND'S GOLDEN AGE: THE COACHING ERA

> Whoe'er has travelled life's dull round,
> Where'er his stages may have been,
> May sigh to think he still has found,
> The warmest welcome at an inn.
>
> William Shenstone (1714–63)

A BRIEF HISTORY OF COACHING

All those desirous to pass from London to Bath, or any other place on their road, let them repair to the Belle Savage on Ludgate Hill in London and the White Lion at Bath, at both which places they may be received in a Stage Coach every Monday, Wednesday and Friday, which performs the whole journey in three days (if God permits) and sets forth at five in the morning. Passengers to pay £1–5s each, who are allowed to carry 14 lbs of weight – for all above to pay 3½d per pound.

So proclaimed the handbill of the 'Flying Machine' in 1667. A miserable three-day journey, it was one of the earlier routes ushering in the new coaching era: the golden age of the inn and, in the popular mind, the golden age of England.

The vast majority of pubs and hotels have stagecoach scenes yellowing gradually in at least one corner, and just as hand pumps seem traditionally to depict scenes of the hunt, scenes of the coaching era of the eighteenth and nineteenth centuries are part of the uniform the pub wears. It was the pastoral champion William Cobbett who wrote that 'next to a foxhunt the finest sight in England is a stagecoach. A sentiment that seems to have defied dissent. Even with the demise of the coaching age the coach and coaching inn acquired an almost mythological status within living memory. In 1866 George Eliot completed *Felix Holt*, the opening paragraph of which illustrates the fond feeling the Victorians attached to their recent past. The fact that she was writing about events within the memory of many of her readers, and was able to do so without being seen to be sugary or romantic, testifies to the popular place coaching held in the national psyche.

> Five-and-thirty years ago the glory had not yet departed from the old coach-roads; the great roadside inns were still brilliant with well polished tankards, the smiling glances of pretty barmaids, and the repartees of jocose ostlers; the mail still announced itself by the merry notes of the horn; the hedge-cutter or the rick thatcher might still know the exact hour by the unfailing yet otherwise meteoric apparition of the pea green. Tally-Ho or the yellow Independent; and elderly gentlemen in post-chaises, quartering nervously to make way for the rolling, swinging, swiftness, had not ceased to remark that times were finely changed since they used to see the packhorses and hear the tinkling of their bells on their very highway.[1]

A list of the painters who made stagecoaches and inns their subjects at some point during the eighteenth and nineteenth centuries will, perhaps, provide an insight into the importance in which coaching was held.

Hogarth is known to have painted an inn sign – 'A man burdened with mischief' (his wife and a monkey) – and also helped to organise an exhibition of the Harp Alley, Shoe Lane, sign painters' inn signs in 1762 as a rival to a more stuffy, establishment art exhibition. Less well known is the fact that J.M.W. Turner was also responsible for an inn sign in Dartford High Street. Apart from painting inn scenes, other academicians and artists often painted inn signs, usually to settle a debt. A David Cox inn sign is preserved in the Royal Oak at Betws-y-Coed, and he also painted a Blue Bowl at Bristol. Old Crome painted a Jolly Sailor, Yarmouth, and a Top Sawyers, Three Cranes, Lame Dog, Lamb and Maid's Head, Norwich. The academicians Hodgson and Leslie painted the George and Dragon, Wargreave, in 1876, doing a side each as a wager. Leslie also painted the Row Barge at Wallingford and the King John's Head at Southwark Street. Princess Louise, herself the subject of several inn signs, was supposed to have painted the Ferry, Roseneath. The list could go on. The artist most closely associated with inns and alehouses has to be George Morland, largely because he was often to be found in one. His favourite haunt was the Bull, North Hill, Highgate, though in a Paddington alehouse he recorded his intake for one day.

Hollands Gin, Porter, Hollands, Ale, Bottled Porter, Ale, Gin and Water, Rum and Milk, Bottled Porter, Porter, Hollands and Water, Port Wine (dinner), Opium and Water, Shrub, Coffee, Punch, Shrub, Port and Ginger, Porter, Port (supper), Rum (for bed).

That could have been the Paddington alehouse where he painted the sign of the White Lion, and where he often used to retire with his friends Rathbone and Ibbetson, who also painted the sign of a house at Troutbeck. Morland also painted the Goat in Boots in the Fulham Road, and the Cricketers at Chelsea Bridge. For his efforts, Morland had a brewery named after him, not undeservingly, which only ceased brewing in 1999.

Artists concerned more with painting inns rather than drinking in them include James Pollard and T. Hosner Shepherd, though a more comprehensive list would include names like Alken, Rowlandson, Du Maurier, Wenceslaus Hollar, J.C. Buckler, J.B. Payne, G. Shepherd, W.B. Redfren, H. Mottram, T.J. Watson Hart, J. Brittan, Hanslip Fletcher, G. Scharf, C.J. Richardson, Robert Smirke, Richard Wilson and more.

Much of what is left of pub 'furniture' comes from this era. The highly polished copper pots, bed pans, lamps, ale mullers, measures and jugs that are suspended from countless beamed ceilings all conjure up the bustle, variety and duties of the coaching inn. As a nation we have collectively decided that this is how we wish to preserve our drinking heritage – outside the town, at least. In part this may be because of all the elderly public houses that survive, most are genuinely from the coaching era, most are outside towns, and so they are less vulnerable to the ravages of war, car, or urban development. For a nation of predominantly urban dwellers, the preservation of the coaching-inn mythology of our country pubs, with their bogus horse brasses and framed prints of horses drawn out of proportion, provides a comforting link with a rural past that, subconsciously, we are aware of having lost.

The 'Flying Machine' was not the first coach route by any means. In 1657 a regular three-times-a-week service was operating between London and Chester, a trip that would cost the traveller 35s 6d for a four day journey, and is reckoned to be the first proper coaching route. What is of interest is the choice of departure point. La Belle Sauvage was a well-established and famous inn in the sixteenth century. In the 1590s the Belle Savage was the favourite pitch of a travelling entertainer, named Banks, who was famous throughout London on account of his dancing horse. An intelligent beast, it could count as well as dance and delighted the populace wherever it appeared. On one occasion Banks and horse arrived at the Belle Savage to find their usual place occupied by a clown who refused to give way. Banks's horse ended the argument by picking up the clown in his teeth, bodily carrying him off and dumping him on the ground, to the delight of all. Banks decided that greater fame and fortune lay abroad and took his amazing horse to the Continent where, accused of harbouring a demon, both he and horse were arrested and burnt at the stake by the Inquisition in Rome.

The Belle Savage dated back to at least 1453, when it was known as the Bell on the Hoop, and supposedly took its later name from its first landlady Isabella or Arabella Savage, who may have been related to the William Savage who owned the site as early as 1380. Its sign, a pun on her name, was a bell within a hoop, though in later centuries its tavern tokens depicted an Amazon maiden with either a bow or a bell. The Belle Savage survived as one of the most famous inns in England until its demolition in 1873.

It was destroyed during the great fire in 1666 and was probably expanded and refitted during reconstruction. Its most famous resident during this period was Grinling Gibbons (1648–1721), the mason and carver. Whether the reconstructed Belle Savage benefited from his attentions is unknown, though he apparently did use his time there to carve a pot of flowers, which stood on his windowsill. So delicate were the flowers that they were said to have rustled in the breeze. The Belle Savage could clearly be a windy place. During the noted storm of 26 November 1703, a Mr Hempson was blown out of an upper window of the inn, in the midst of his slumbers, and remained oblivious of the fact until he awoke the next morning to find himself and his bed located on Ludgate Hill.

Other London inns and taverns had Grinling Gibbons's signs over their portals, notably the Cock and Bottle in Fleet Street where the story goes that, during the 1655 plague, the landlord wishing to close his house in an honest fashion, advertised for all holding his tokens to repair to the Cock and Bottle in order to receive their sterling equivalent. Pepys, Kipp and Mrs Pierce travelled there by water from the Temple to celebrate Charles II's coronation on St George's Day, 1661. In 1768 the Cock and Bottle was still going strong.

> Nor think the Cock with these not on a par,
> The celebrated Cock of Temple Bar
> Whose Porter best of all bespeaks its praise,
> Porter that's worthy of the Poet's lays.

Later still, Tennyson wrote lines on the 'plump headed waiter at the Cock'.

The Belle Savage was also the inn from which Sam Weller's father, the sagacious coachman Tony Weller, operated, though for the purposes of a part of Dickens's tale Weller starts for Ipswich with the Pickwickians from the Bull Inn, Whitechapel. This is an odd coincidence because at the time the Bull was owned by a Mrs Ann Nelson, mother of Robert Nelson, the proprietor of the Belle Savage. By Pickwick's time there was not only the Chester coach operating from the Belle Savage, which then bounded the Fleet Debtors' Prison, but also a Bath coach. The Star took the Cambridge run, while further coaches made the inn their terminus from Bristol, Exeter, Plymouth, Gloucester, Coventry, Nottingham and Manchester. Running a service from London to Chester or Bath three times a week would have meant a minimum of eight coaches, not allowing for any to be out of service. The inn yard must have been substantial.

Until the early seventeenth century wheeled traffic on English roads consisted entirely of agricultural or mercantile vehicles, the baggage trains of armies, and heavy wagons engaged in trade or moving the valuables and furniture of royalty and nobility as they progressed around the nation. People travelled either on foot or horseback or, if exhausted, elderly, or infirm, in a litter. Not until the reign of James I were private coaches to be found, and these were monstrous affairs requiring six or eight horses to drag them through the mud. In London it was slowly becoming possible to hire a coach in the seventeenth century, but then London was the only part of the kingdom with paved streets.

The London–Chester coach and the Flying Machine, of 1657 and 1667, were among the pioneers of extended travel within the realm. Under the Commonwealth England had had her first standing army, which had been fairly mobile, and coupled with the administrative skills of the Commonwealth it produced an improvement in the nation's arterial routes. It is significant that by 1660, the year of the Restoration, there was a coaching route between Royalist Oxford and Parliamentarian London, a two-day journey with an overnight stay at Beaconsfield.

An improvement in roads accompanied an improvement in trade. Restoration England, indulging in the profligate euphoria of the restoration of the king and stability, underwent an economic boom, requiring merchants and bankers, lawyers and speculators to travel as never before. Merchants had been travelling England's highways and byways for several hundred years without the benefits of coaches, and so we must not assume there was a sudden headlong rush into this new form of transport, but the attractions soon became manifest. On 26 April 1669 the Flying Coach left All Souls, Oxford, with a complement of six passengers, paying 12s apiece, and arriving in London a mere thirteen hours later.

Naturally, advances in stage coaching were slow, the speeds possible being determined by the construction of the coaches and the state of the roads, which were, in turn, determined by the volume and nature of the traffic. Early eighteenth-century coaches were low-slung, springless, solid affairs, with leather-bound exteriors, picked out in relief by brass nails, and with heavy baize or leather curtains. In shape they resembled large sedan chairs on wheels, for essentially that was what they were. The best surviving example is undoubtedly that belonging to the Speaker of the House of Commons.

The Turnpike Trusts appeared in 1663, enabling a gradual improvement in some roads, and in 1665 steel springs were first used in coaches to reduce the weight and the nauseating swinging of coaches suspended on leather straps, and glass windows were

132 AN INEBRIATED HISTORY OF BRITAIN

introduced in 1650. In 1665 Pepys tried out several new designs of
coach, finding 'one did prove mighty easy . . . it is very fine and
likely to take. This design attaching the body of the coach by
means of leather straps to two curved springs.' By 1669 Pepys had
his own coach and was driving 'through the town with our new
liveries of serge, and the horses' manes and tails tied up with red
ribbons and new green reins.'

Road technology progressed very slowly. In 1621 four-wheeled
vehicles and loads in excess of one ton were banned. In 1629
teams of more than five horses were banned. In 1651 all carts and
wagons were to have wheels of at least nine inches in width.
In 1664 tolls were waived on all vehicles with sixteen-inch wheels.
Outside passengers started to appear during the 1760s, and in
1768 we hear of a coach travelling with eight inside passengers,
paying 1s per five miles, with a further ten on top, plus driver and
guard.

It was the introduction of the mail coaches that really provided
the spur for the coaching era, since the mails set the standard
against which all other coaching services had to compete. The Post
Office at the time favoured a system of mounted couriers or
post boys. This system was slow. The post boys were ill paid, poorly
mounted and corrupt. The service on the Great West Road was so
notoriously bad that it was said that 'every common traveller
passes the King's Mail on the first road in the Kingdom.'
To improve upon this sorry state of affairs a Bath theatre manager,
John Palmer, despatched the first mail coach to London on Monday
2 August 1784. It took sixteen hours to do the journey and
established the new coaches as a safer and cheaper method of
transporting the mail. The Bristol Mail always remained the senior
service among the mails until the last run in 1841, and it no
doubt benefited from the very good Bath road provided by Beau
Nash in 1754 in his attempts to popularise the town. John
Palmer's idea caught on and he was amply rewarded. His portrait
was painted by Gainsborough. He became Lord Mayor of Bath and
MP for the town. Ironically, John Palmer was the alias adopted by
Dick Turpin prior to his capture in York.

The mail coaches changed horses every seven to ten miles and
carried only four passengers inside and four out, being smaller
than commercial coaches. The coachman was an employee of the
coaching company from which the coach was leased, and took his

instructions from the guard who was an employee of the Post Office and identified by his scarlet livery. They were a trusted and respected body of men. They were equipped with a brace of pistols, a musket, a sealed timepiece and a horn to announce their arrival so that turnpike gates and tolls should be opened for their passage, since they paid no tolls. The firearms were all too necessary. Highway robbery was an everyday occurrence on English roads. The punctuality of the mails was legendary, and tradition has it many local villagers and townsfolk set their clocks by the passage of the mails. Thomas De Quincey (1785–1859) – the Opium Eater – wrote of two coaches that started simultaneously 200 miles apart and 'met almost constantly at a particular bridge that bisected the total distance.'

By the nineteenth century the organisation of the mails was phenomenal. The posting stage was now down to four miles on the fastest routes, and a complete team of horses could be removed from the traces and replaced within a minute. Of course the mails, distinguished by their maroon, scarlet and gold livery, were not by any means the only or the most colourful coaches on the road. The mails left in the evening and travelled by night as much as possible. During the day the Bath road, for example, resounded to the clatter of hooves and horns of the Blue, the Shamrock, the Regent, the Regulator, the Emerald and the Chronometer, all with their distinctive and colourful liveries. These coaches were much larger and carried more passengers. They were not prohibited from galloping, as were the mails, and rivalry was intense, races were common, accidents frequent and speed the watchword. In 1811 the average speed from London to Towcester was 7.2 mph; by 1837 the speed was up to 9.8 mph.

In 1830 the *Coventry Chronical* for 8 May reported: 'Saturday se'night, being May Day the usual competition took place between London Coaches. The Independent Tally-Ho running between Birmingham and London, performed a feat unparalleled in the annals of coaching, having travelled the distance of 109 miles in seven hours and 39 minutes.' The Independent Tally-Ho, one of the famous Tally-Ho line, notched up an impressive average speed of 14 mph. This was made possible only because of Thomas Telford's road. His major contribution was to smooth out the gradients that had been the curse of so many coachmen and the death of so many horses.

In 1836 the roads of England were home to over 3,000 coaches, drawn by over 150,000 horses. Hyde Park, which 150 years earlier had been on the edge of London, from which fearful travellers passed through the highwaymen's resorts of Kensington Village and Hounslow Heath, was then the departure point for no less than 300 coaches by day and a further 28 mails by night. In 1837, 52 new mail guards were appointed. They little knew that the 1838 mail coach parade, which was held annually on the king's birthday with the liveried guards and drivers toasting William IV's health in porter outside St James's Palace, would be the last such parade, and London would never again turn out to see such a fine sight. In 1843 only one new mail guard was appointed; most others were now looking for jobs on the railways. The coaching age was over.

A Brief History of the Inn

Amid all this coaching activity there was the inn. Food was of vital importance; people had to keep warm, and eating to keep warm was as important as wrapping up warmly. It was not uncommon, in winter, for outside passengers to freeze to death in the course of their journey. Such an unfortunate fatality was rather more common than the fate of the woman passenger decapitated by a coach entering a yard through a low arch, as related by Mr Jingle at the Golden Cross, Charing Cross.

> Terrible place – dangerous work – other day – five children – mother – tall lady, eating sandwiches – forgot the arch – crash – knock – children look round – mother's head off – sandwich in hand – no mouth to put it in – head of family off – shocking – shocking.[2]

Such an event actually occurred, hence Dickens's decision to relate it. Whether it happened at the Golden Cross is uncertain. Nineteenth-century pictures of it would seem to indicate plenty of headspace. However, in the days before outside passengers, archways were built much lower and it is possible that such an accident could have occurred at an inn built before 1750 and not at the time converted to take taller coaches.

The Golden Cross was a lucky survivor, since it had attracted the venom of the Puritans in 1643 who ordered that it be demolished as 'superstitious and idolatrous', as indeed they subsequently deemed the stone Eleanor Cross that gave Charing Cross its name. The Golden Cross was restored along with the king, and in 1757 coaches were leaving there for Brighthelmstone, better known as Brighton, the fare being 13s – children in laps and outside passengers half price. By 1821 forty coaches a day left through its arches, for besides the famous Comet and Regent coaches to Brighton, there were coaches to Exeter, Salisbury, Bridport, Dorchester, Blandford, Hastings, Tunbridge Wells, Cambridge, Cheltenham, Dover, Norwich, Portsmouth and the famous Tally-Ho to Birmingham that set the speed record on May Day 1830. The building Canaletto painted was rebuilt in 1811 and then demolished to make way for Trafalgar Square in 1827. In the same year the building Charles Dickens described in both the *Pickwick Papers* and *David Copperfield* – Copperfield meets Steerforth there – was erected, so we may deduce that the unfortunate decapitee was not entering the Golden Cross opposite the soon-to-be-built Charing Cross station.

It would appear that the English took a lot of pride in their inns. Much money was needed to equip an inn, purely from the point of view of ostling facilities and providing for changes of horses, not to mention the costs associated with the needs of passengers. Not surprisingly, national pride tended to gloss over a number of less than wonderful establishments.

My sheets were so damp and the blankets so dirty and stinking, and the room so smelling of putridity that I slept little, though I took off the sheets and employed all the brandy, nearly a pint, in purifying the room and sprinkling the quilt and blankets. Glad I was to rise, tho' with a headache and gloomy as the day. . . . This, our Rugby charge for one night, two meals and three horses 11s 7d, will prove touring to be a very extravagant pleasure.[3]

This was penned in the 1780s by John Byng, Viscount Torrington, when the coaching era was in full swing. Prices were coming down, mail-coach routes were opening up and competition was fierce. Coaching passengers were no longer exclusively of the better sort and, more to the point, once out of town they were a captive market. Many seasoned travellers took their own linen with them, and a famous Gilray cartoon depicts a long-suffering passenger climbing out of his damp bed in order to wreak bloody havoc upon the innkeeper.

Inns were still elite drinking establishments, though they were not without their own forms of sharping. Ostlers were particularly suspect. The name originally came from the French *hostelier*, but for many it was merely a derivation of 'oat stealer'. Frequently the traveller would ensure that the ostler had attended to his task before they would look to their own creature comforts. The ostler was often regarded as no better than a highwayman's agent, whose trick it was to appear eager to assist with luggage or saddlebags in order that their weight might be gauged and any valuables therein surmised. Writing in prison in 1627, John Clavel, a reformed highwayman, gave advice to travellers, in which he warned them of some of the practices they were likely to come across.

> Oft in your clothier's and your grazier's inn,
> You shall have chamberlains that there have been
> Plac'd purposely by thieves, or else consenting
> By their large bribes, and by their often tempting;
> That mark your purse drawn, and give a guess
> What's there, within a little more or less.
> Then will they grip your cloak-bags, feel their weight.
> There's likewise in mine host sometimes deceit.
> If it he left in charge with him all night,
> Unto his roaring guests he gives a light,
> Who spend full thrice in wine and beer
> As you in those and all your other cheer.[4]

Nothing really changes, and whether it be the eighteenth century or 1563 the following was always prudent advice.

> Some think it a gay matter at their coming to commit their budgets to the goodman of the house. For albeit monie be safe for the time it is in his hands (for you shall not hear that a man is robbed at his inn), yet after their departure the host can make no warranty of the same and there cannot be any surer token unto such as pry and watch for those booties than to see any guest deliver his cupcase in such a manner.[5]

Inside the inn there were various con tricks also. At the popular staging centre of Stoney Stratford a coach's log tells that having arrived at 1.47 it departed, dinner and all, at 2.12 sharp. These rigorous schedules provided scope for fraud. Dickens describes how such tricks were played, even in such great inns as the Golden Cross.

> It strikes 5.15 as you trudge down Waterloo Place on your way to the 'Golden Cross', and you discover for the first time that you were called an hour too early . . . the coach is in the yard, and will be brought round in about 15 minutes. . . . You retire to the tap-room for the purpose of procuring some brandy and hot water, which you do – when the kettle boils, an event which occurs exactly two and a half minutes before the time fixed for the starting of the coach. The first stroke peals from St Martin's steeple as you take the first sip of the boiling liquid. You find yourself in the booking office in two seconds, and the tap waiter finds himself much comforted by your brandy and water in about the same period.[6]

Certainly many inns were as bad as John Byng described.

> The innkeepers are insolent, the hostelers are sulky, the chambermaids are pert, the waiters are impertinent, the meat is tough, the wine is foul, the beer is hard, the sheets are wet, the linen is dirty, and the knives are never cleaned. . . . I look upon the inn as the seat of all roguery, profanes and debauchery; and sicken of them every day. . . . For the sake of hasty gain innkeepers hire horrid servants and buy bad provisions and poisonous liquors.[7]

Some remote inns were obviously fairly poor, and the frequency of trade may not have been sufficient to provide adequate finance to maintain all the facilities that it was necessary for an inn to provide. In *Barnaby Rudge* the Maypole is such an inn. It has plenty of ale and victuals and is a clean and wholesome inn, as suited Dickens's purpose, but it is remote, not apparently on any regular coaching route (being set in 1780), more likely catering for the wagoning trade, and not so busy that it requires an expensive army of domestic servants.

On the whole, inns tended to be suited to the station of their clientele. This means that there was a wide range of establishments falling under the generic term 'inn'. In the towns many of the inns, as the equivalent of the modern hotels or the railway termini, would have been rather grand. Elsewhere they would have varied, depending upon their location, how busy the road was, how affluent a route it was, whether or not they were on a 'stage', a convenient end-of-day location.

Thus some inns, such as the Maypole, were little better than alehouses. Pastor Moritz, who gives us many valuable descriptions of England during the early years of the Industrial Revolution, provides just such an insight to an inn of this kind in the Potteries.

At last I came to another Inn, where there was written on the sign 'The Navigation Inn', because it is the depot, or warehouse, of all the colliers of the Trent. A rougher, or ruder, kind of people I never saw than these colliers, whom I here met assembled in the kitchens, and in whose company I was obliged to spend the evening.

Their language, their dress, their manners were all of them singularly vulgar and disagreeable, and their expressions still more so, for they hardly spoke a word without an oath, and thus cursing, quarrelling, drinking, singing and fighting, they seemed to be pleased and to enjoy the evening. I must do them justice and to add that none of them, however, molested me. On the contrary, everyone again and again drank my health, and I took care not to forget theirs in return. . . . And so as often as I drank, I never omitted saying, 'Your healthes Gentleman all'.[8]

Not all inns were coaching inns. The coaching traffic was composed of the middle and upper classes, and coaching inns tended to cater for middle- and upper-class comforts. This had always been largely true, so the eighteenth-century traveller would have understood much of this description of a sixteenth-century inn.

Those towns that we call thoroughfares have great and sumptuous inns for such travellers and strangers to pass to and fro. The manner of harbouring is not like that of some other countries, in which the host or goodman doth charge a lordlie authority over his guests; here in England every man may use his inne as his owne house, and have for his monie, how great or little variety of victuals, and what other service hisself shall think expedient to call for. Our inns are also with naperie, for beside the linen that is used at the tables, which is commonly washed daily, is such as belongeth to the estate and calling of the guest. Each comer is sure to be in cleaner sheets, if the traveller have an horse his bed doth cost him nothing, but if he go on foot he is sure to pay a penny for the same. If his chamber be appointed he may carry the keys with him. . . . The horse is attended by the hostelers or hired servants appointed at the charge of the goodman of the horse, who in hopes of extracting reward will deal very diligently after outward of appearance in this their calling.[9]

Although there was an expansion in the numbers of inns between the above description, from 1577, and the experiences of Pastor Moritz in 1782, there had also been an increase in the numbers of rich people and the amount of travelling each one undertook. The inns then regarded themselves as catering for the elite and as such were the elite of the victualling trade.

This was a period of great social mobility. The towns were demanding ever more labour and the countryside was emptying of people for whom the inn had little meaning. It offered no shelter and promised no alleviation from hunger. The country alehouse was able to perform its traditional role in this respect, but these were being suppressed, and, as William Cobbett pointed out in his *Rural Rides*, once the countryside was denuded of its population the alehouse itself could not survive.

Travel was therefore taking on a class emphasis as Pastor Moritz discovered. His friends declared him to be mad when he announced his intention to view England on foot, and he soon came to understand their reaction. In Trollope's *Last Chronicle of Barset* the peripatetic trip of Mr Crawley to the bishop is remarkable enough for servants to note he 'footed it all the way, and he's a gentleman, too.' Moritz was not exaggerating when he explained that,

In England a person undertaking so long a journey on foot is sure to be looked upon and considered as either a beggar or vagabond. . . . It is impossible . . . to approve of a system that confines all of the pleasures and benefits of travel to the rich. A poor peripatetic is hardly allowed the honour of being honest.[10]

Moritz had elected to stand outside his station, and expressed surprise when others failed to recognise his position.

His arrival in Nettlebed is a scene that would look at home on any pub wall: an inn to the left of the main street with an impressive gallows sign across the thoroughfare. This specimen would appear to have been unusual, for although of the pendulous size then fashionable, the sign merely bears the name of the proprietor rather than the name of the inn. This may indicate that the inn had some pretensions towards being a coffee house, or may, as was not uncommon among provincial alehouses and inns, have made some light affectations to what is supposed a London coffee house was like. Remember that most of the people who passed under the sign would have been illiterate.

In all other respects, however, it is a very typical English inn, and the general impression is one of rosy propriety, as can be deduced by the number of staff and the powdered wigs of the waiters, indicating that the inn was making the effort to provide its own livery. The innkeeper was a portly, prosperous fellow, a direct descendant of Boniface, his medieval progenitor. It was not just that this was the popular perception, but it was likely to be the case. The coaching inn was a positive larder of 'honest' English rustic fare, the adopted home of the 'groaning board'.

As we drove into the great gateway of the inn, I saw on one side the light of a rousing kitchen fire beaming through a window. I entered and admired for the hundredth time that picture of convenience, neatness, and broad honest enjoyment, the Kitchen of an English inn. . . . Hams, tongues and flitches of bacon were suspended from the ceiling; a smoke-jack made its ceaseless clanking beside the fireplace, and a clock ticked in one corner. A well-scoured deal table extended along one side of the kitchen, with a cold round of beef and other hearty viands upon it over which two foaming tankards of ale seemed mounting guard. Travellers of inferior order were preparing to attack this stout repast, while others sat smoking, or gossiping over their ale, on two high-backed settles under the direction of a fresh bustling landlady, but still seizing an occasional moment to exchange a flippant word, and have a rallying laugh with the group around the fire.[11]

All that needs to be added to this scene is snow and a troupe of carol singers with cherubic faces protruding from tightly wrapped scarves, glowing in the orange light spilling from their lantern, as they peer in through the frostsy window and the popular image would be complete, all ready for packaging on countless Christmas cards.

The Victorians revelled in this image of the inn. To them it was an emblem of national wealth and identity. The *Pickwick Papers* is a rich progression from one inn to another. Mr Pickwick's first encounter with Sam Weller, the 'boots' at the ancient White Hart in the Borough, is one of the best-known passages in English literature. Dickens was as lavish in his praise of what he liked as he was scathing of what he did not; but he was not romanticising the inns he immortalised; the Bull, Rochester; the Leather Bottle, Cobham; the Angel, Bury St Edmunds; the Great White Horse, Ipswich; the Golden Cross, Charing Cross; the Fox Under the Hill, Thameside; the Blue Boar, Leadenhall Market; the Hop Pole, Tewkesbury; the Marquis of Granby, Dorking; the Black Boy, Chelmsford; the Magpie and Stump, Whitechapel; the Old Royal, Birmingham; the Saracen's Head, Towcester; not to mention the further fictional inns based on real public houses and inns he was familiar with. *Pickwick* was completed in 1837, when the coaching era was at its height. The railway was starting to make itself felt, but it was not then apparent that the coaching day was done, for in some ways it was not. In 1844 a new London to Cambridge service was established, and although the 1840s and 1850s saw the eclipse of the golden age by steam, the last commercial coaching run – Amersham to London – survived until 1894, only being killed off by the opening of the Metropolitan Underground Railway.

Nor do we have to rely solely on Dickens for confirmation of this popular image of the inn. In 1847 Disraeli wrote *Tancred*, which contains the following description of a coaching dinner.

'Tis a delightful sound. And what a Dinner! What a profusion of substantial delicacies! What mighty and iris-tinted rounds of beef!

What vast and marble-veined ribs! What gelatinous veal pies! What colossal ham! Those are evidently prize cheeses! And how invigorating is the perfume of those various and variegated pickles! Then the bustle emulating the plenty; the ringing of bells, the clash of thoroughfare, the summoning of ubiquitous waiters, and the all pervading feeling of omnipotence from the guests who order what they please to the landlords who can produce and execute everything they can desire. 'Tis a wondrous sight.

With wigs and bells, waiters instead of footmen, stagecoaches instead of landaus and phaetons, the model of many larger inns was clearly the country house. Indeed, many of the later inns resembled the houses of the gentry, such as the Angel, Bury St Edmunds, while others resembled their town houses, like the White Hart, Bath, the Bull, Rochester, or the Old Royal, Birmingham.

On the whole, however, the inns of the eighteenth century can be divided into four types.

Poor country inns

Likely not on major roads, and popular with highwaymen, among these would have been the inns of Highgate and also the Spaniards Inn, Hampstead. The Spaniards, associated with Dick Turpin, gained further notoriety during the Gordon Riots of 1780, when the rioters, having torched Lord Mansfield's house, proceeded to the Lord Chief Justice's country seat, but were forestalled by the landlord of the Spaniards, who threw open his cellars to the rioters, which bought time enough to send for the Horse Guards.

By its notoriety and proximity to encroaching London the Spaniards, like many inns of its ilk, gradually ceased to be a purely rural inn.

Country coaching inns

Often old country inns were rebuilt or enlarged as a result of the prosperity that accompanied the general agricultural expansion of the latter half of the eighteenth century and increased coaching traffic. Such an inn would have been the Jolly Farmer at Farnham, the birthplace, in 1762, of William Cobbett. Identifying these inns can be difficult, unless the original age is known, for remodelling and extension tend to confuse them with later inns. For example, the Cross Keys, St Neots; the Sun, Hitchin; the White Hart, Lewes; the Lion, Shrewsbury; the George, Rye, and the Dolphin, Southampton, where Jane Austen wintered in 1808, were all rebuilt between 1730 and 1780.

Interestingly, in a list of fairly randomly selected seventeenth-century inns at least four have names of some heraldic significance, which we may use to try to deduce some facts about the history of these inns. For example the Cross Keys is the symbol of St Peter and also the papacy. As such it was a name that declined rather than grew in popularity over time. Its survival will be strongly indicative of an association with a religious house dedicated to St Peter. St Neots is within the diocese of Peterborough, where there was a tenth-century Benedictine Abbey until 1539. The Cross Keys was a common choice of name among church reformers at that time as an acceptable downgrading of a more objectionably Catholic title, usually the St Peter's Finger, evocative of a Papal blessing.

Other Catholic signs to receive similar treatment include the Catherine Wheel, commemorating the martyrdom of St Catherine in AD 375. This was frequently changed to the Cat and Wheel, or, as in Bristol, the Clock Wheel. The Salutation survived the Reformation only to fall foul of the Commonwealth. Occasionally it was changed to the Soldier and Citizen, otherwise it survived by fortuitous repainting of the sign to give it a purely secular meaning. Likewise the Angel, a very common sign, and, like the Salutation, derived from the Annunciation, survived by removing all reference to the Virgin, even though the Angel frequently was seen to retain his scroll, which contained the papist words *Ave Maria, gratia plena, Dominus tecum*.

The purpose-built coaching inn

These must be split between those found en route and those found at the London or provincial termini. The last kind developed a style all of their own; the Angel, Bury St Edmunds, has already been mentioned. In the same class can be found the White Hart, Salisbury; the Swan, Bedford; the Royal, Plymouth; the Cups, Lyme Regis; the Royal, Falmouth. With their classical columns they became samplers of provincial wealth and pride, meeting places for the local well-to-do and social focal points in their own right. In a more Regency style can be found the Regent, Leamington Spa; the Queens, Cheltenham; the Old Ship, Brighton, the Antelope and the Kings Arms, Dorchester.

The first kind of these inns, the en-route inns, can still be seen in many towns today, some retaining a country-inn look, while others in the market towns often have a more Regency feel about them. The Bull, Rochester, is a fine surviving example and is typical of many that have made the transition from inn to hotel without too much difficulty. Others in the mould include the White Hart, Southall; the Lion, Hartford Bridge; the White Hart, Hook; the Rutland Arms, Newmarket; the Old George Aylesbury; the Bell, Barnaby Moor; the White Hart, Launceston; the White Lion, Cobham; the Sugar Loaf, Dunstable and the Bull, Redborn.

The great coaching inns

These are the inns that for the most part are no longer with us. Their complete *raison d'être* was coaching, and as such derived no benefit of location, with the advent of rail, which enabled them to survive. Most were in London, since they were the starting point for several destinations. In the provinces their counterpart termini have often survived, less pressured for space and often fortuitously located to become railway hotels.

One such great inn was the George and Blue Boar, Holborn; the starting point of the Glasgow coach. The last of the traditional stopping places of the condemned on their way to Tyburn, it contained an impressive forty bedrooms, stabling for fifty-two horses, seven coach houses and, to facilitate the movement of the bustle within its gates, a driveway a full seventy yards long.

Some, like the Angel, St Clements-in-the-Strand, were medieval inns that enjoyed a renaissance. In January 1555 Bishop Hooper was detained at the Angel before he was transported to Gloucester to be burnt at the stake during the Marian persecution. Before its great days as a coaching inn a Mr Owen, who was residing at the Angel, advertising the forthcoming auction of an eleven-year-old black girl on 28 March 1769. By 1821 the Angel was the departure point for the Salisbury Post Coach which, leaving sharply at 7 a.m. pulled up in front of the White Hart at 7.30 p.m.

At the same time the Bell and Crown, Holborn, was the departure point for three coach services. At 6.15 a.m. the Post Coach would leave for the Black Horse, Salisbury, taking a mere twelve hours. The 'Old Coach' took the same route at a more sedate pace, leaving at 3.30 p.m. and arriving at 7 p.m. while the Royal Auxiliary Mail left at 5.15 p.m. for the New London Inn, Exeter, due to arrive at 7 p.m. the following evening.

Archbishop Leighton once said that if he were to choose a place to die in, 'it should be an inn it looking like a pilgrim's going home, to whom his world was all an inn and who was weary of the noise and confusion in it.' He had his wish granted, for in 1684 he died in the Bell, in Newgate Street.

THE INN AND THE MARKET TOWN

Many books have been written on coaching, coaching inns and travels along the coaching roads, and accordingly, one cannot expect to condense the whole nature of the subject within a history of drinking and do it with full justice. The problem is essentially one of the huge diversity of the inns that existed within a relatively short period of history but across a wide area of countryside.

Many substantial communities grew up in the eighteenth century purely as a result of their staging situation. Most famous perhaps is Stoney Stratford, Warwickshire, which had no fewer than eleven inns in a town that was not much larger than the high street along which they were lined. Near Towcester can be found Foster's Booth, which had not existed as a settlement prior to the arrival of its cluster of inns, its only structure having been the forester's booth in the woods from which it takes its name. Rochester grew fashionable and wealthy as a result of its convenient Dover road staging location, aided by the patronage of George I and George II who liked to stay there en route to and from Hanover. The principal inn in the town was originally built in 1708 as a private residence and subsequently converted into an inn – the Rose – repeating the process by which several notable inns had come into being in the fifteenth and sixteenth centuries. It was renamed the Royal Victoria in 1825 after Princess Victoria stayed there. Her patronage, and the association of Dickens with Rochester, was not enough to save the inn from the railways and only the King's Head and the Bull survived from among several majestic Rochester inns, though the King's Head was bombed in the Second World War.

Some of the great Tudor inns and their Stuart progeny also benefited from an extra lease of life as a result of their locations, which, in any case, tended not to be accidental. The Haycock at Wansford, the George at Stamford and the Angel at Grantham – which sported an inn yard several hundred feet long from High Street to Swinegate – were not only on the Great North Road, but were also at the crucial thirty-mile stage. The George is an aristocrat of English inns. The daughter of one of its fifteenth-century proprietors married into the powerful Cecil family and her grandson became Viscount Burghley – a social mobility undreamt of in the victualling trade. Charles I stayed there during August 1645 en route between Newark and Huntingdon during the campaigning season of that year, though the inns where he and his son stayed are so numerous that this is no great pedigree. A more interesting anecdote concerns a man named Bolton, who was either landlord or tapster of the inn. In 1714 he was accused of Jacobite sympathies and obliged to drink a health to the late Queen Anne. As he did so he was run through by a dragoon's sabre.

Other inns in this group include the Saracen's Head, Towcester (now the Pomfret Arms); the Salutation Inn, Topsham; and the Black Lion, St Michaels, St Albans. Unusually far east to be a reference to 'the black lion of Powys' – Owen Glendower (c.1350–1415) – it is probably a reference to Queen Philippa of Hainault, the wife of Edward III, who interceded on behalf of the Calais Burghers. There are also the Griffin and the Swan, Amersham; the George, Pangbourne; the George, Buckden and many others.

Off the Great North Road and on the Manchester Road the large coaching towns located at roughly equal distances were Dunstable, Market Harborough, Northampton, Loughborough, Leicester, Derby, Ashbourne and Buxton. Three of these towns are county towns and much may be learned from the study of one of them – Northampton.

By particular desire of several of our customers, we are to acquaint the public that the Berlin will set out at 6 o'clock and it is humbly hoped that no one will take amiss if, after this notice, they should lose their earnest . . . in case they are not ready in time . . . for so much time is lost in going about the town, and those whom we have taken up first are so much displeased at being carried about and at sitting to wait for others who too often are not ready that everyone is now desired, for the general good, to walk down to the George or Red Lion, a little before six, a porter shall be sent to each person's house to give proper warning.[12]

The almost apologetic nature of this advertisement placed in the *Northampton Mercury* in August 1752 borders on the quaint. The deferential tone gives a clue as to the relative position within the provincial social hierarchy of the passengers. The tone is very much at variance with the strident and boastful terms of later coaching firm advertisements. Competition will have stiffened in the subsequent decades, but the Northamptonshire 'Flying Berlins' had an average speed of 5.5 mph, which was quite creditable, though barely faster than a brisk walk.

By the 1760s Northampton's inns could cater for 3,500 horses, and this does not include extra capacity at alehouses and other premises. The population at the time was little over 5,000. Clearly not all these animals were required for coaching purposes. The inns, then, were providing facilities for beasts employed in other activities, and obviously most of them were agricultural. Even assuming that such capacity was only required on market days and fetes, it would still imply huge traffic congestion. Most squares in English market towns are no larger than an acre, and Northampton is no exception. To fill that space with horses, carts and wagons would require a fraction of the number of horses available from the town's stabling capacity.

Northampton was fortunate that a fire in the town in 1675 had permitted road widening as rebuilding took place, but traffic was, as in most market towns, a severe problem, without adding sheep and cattle to the horse problem. Many inns spread themselves out around the town. This was as a reaction to the traffic problem, but also because the greater the distance between themselves and rival inns the greater the influence they could wield and the more facilities they could offer.

In Canterbury, the Falstaff, outside the narrow west gates of the city, became popular with drovers. The fifteenth-century inn could provide pens and pasture in the fields behind its yard, and once it became established as a meeting place it became unnecessary to persist in driving sheep through the narrow and crowded streets on market day.

In Northampton and other towns the same principle applied. Different inns became associated with different trades. In a way this was nothing new. The famous George at Norton St Philip, mentioned previously, was already associated with the wool trade in the fifteenth century, while York was forbidding 'foreign' poulterers from selling in inns in 1389. In 1492 'foreign' cloth was being traded in York inns, and in 1537 the city's inns had a capacity of 1,000 beds and stabling for 1,700 horses, a useful indicator of its economic importance. At that time Northampton had fewer than 15 inns; by the 1760s it had 62.

Obviously these inns varied immensely in size and importance. Those that fronted the market square in the eighteenth century retained their pre-eminence even when other inns colonised the suburbs. In Northampton one of the 3 principal inns was the Red Lion in Horsemarket. With 41 rooms it was slightly more modest than its rival the George. Its rooms were named rather than numbered, the principal room being called the Queen's Head Chamber, containing over 90 yards of tapestry, a mahogany dining table, Chinese wallpapers, Japanese tea tables and Virginian chairs. In 1743 the inn had in excess of £200 worth of silverware. An inventory also listed 16 dozen plates, 13 dozen soup plates and 160 other dishes, as well as 10 roasting spits. In addition it also sported a coffee room where the London papers could be perused. The Peacock, which had a frontage onto the square 11 arches, or bays, long, as was the architectural style of the time, was 200 feet in depth to the rear of the inn, while another, the Rose and Crown, had an even larger frontage. Defoe remarked on the principal inn of the town, the George, that with 40 odd bedrooms it was 'more like a palace than an inn.' The best room at the George was also called the Queen's Head Chamber. When the landlord of the George, Henry Lyon, died in 1698, his estate was valued at £800, a large sum for the time. The furnishings of the inn were valued in excess of £500, while the linen, brass and pewter alone were worth in excess of £80.

Crops, of course, can be examined in samples. This had the advantage that the transport of large amounts of goods into the centre of town was not necessary. The inns were, therefore, ideal market places. Traders and growers could come into the town, stay in an inn overnight and conduct their business under the same roof. In Northampton the hop trade was centred on the Woolpack Inn, which was also the home of the turnip-seed trade, as was the Hind Inn, which, with its entrances in Sheep Street and Market Square, was already an old coaching inn in the 1740s and was popular with gentlemen travelling with their families. It must not be forgotten that the turnip was much more of a staple than it is today. Clover seed was traded at the Old Goat in Gold Street as well as the Chequer, on the Square, which was also the home to traders in trefoil and grass seed generally.

Market day may have been a regular event, but various crops and commodities came into and went out of season, so the activity at various inns would also adopt a seasonal character. As a result farmers throughout the county would keep an eye open for advertisements in the local papers announcing when merchants would arrive in town, and at which inn they would be staying.

In Northampton part of the phenomenal stabling capacity was explained by the fact that the town was a centre for the horse trade, which was also carried out at the inns, the most famous being the King's Head. A further proportion of the stabling capacity would be taken up by the carrying trade, for which Northampton was a local centre, and for which inns were the principal agents and operators. Given the nature of the goods being traded and the volumes being moved, larger inns offered storage facilities. Inns in many parts of the country provided corn silos, such as the Fleece and the Chequer in Northampton.

The Chequer, centrally located, was a focal point for the grass and seed corn trade for the county. It was an important building in the town, built on an impressive scale, with a long, narrow yard, a couple of hundred feet long, lined either side with stables, coach houses and warehouses. Such a picture would have been common in many market and country towns. Shaftesbury had no fewer than six of these types of inn around its square – the Raven, the Lamb, the George, the Bush, the New Inn and the Lion and Star.

To this picture we must add regional variations, the specialisation so beloved of Adam Smith, that made the trade that supported these magnificent inns so attractive. In Northampton the

specialism was in the leather and shoe industries. It was the
demand for boots during the Napoleonic wars that trebled
the town's population and firmly established the long association
between Northampton and shoes. Up until 1723 the leather
industry's base had been the Star Inn, on the market square.
When the inn was sold the wealthier tanners and dealers wanted
to move the trade to the Talbot, outside the square. The
shoemakers, the tanners' poorer cousins, objected, fearing a loss of
status and a depreciation of their standing within the coveted
hierarchy of Northamptonshire society, and they declined to leave
the square. The dispute dragged on for several months, until a
meeting of the general trade unanimously decided, on 11 May
1724, that the leather 'fairs and markets be for the time to come
kept at the Peacock Inn in Northampton, where all tanners are
desired to meet their chapmen'.

Inns were where the trade was to be done and, as such, where
money was to be found. People did not come to town just to trade,
for having done their business they were then at liberty to
purchase the necessities and luxuries they needed and wanted,
and since many came to town infrequently, they often had very
large shopping lists to fill and many tasks to attend to. For the
ancillary trades – peddlers of luxuries and professional services –
in the days before shops, offices and fixed premises, the logical
thing was to go where the money was. The demise of the assizes
is still within living memory, and these were still days, as they had
been since the conquest, when the assize operated on a circuit.
The law patronised the inns, just like any other trade. Fortunate
was the inn favoured by the circuit and its retinue. The circuit
was wealthy, endowed prestige and frequently appointed its own
wine stewards to ensure that they were supplied with quality
wines on their processes, so augmenting the cellars of many a
provincial inn. Inns acted as auction houses and general bazaars.
Anything was purchasable there: books, silver, jewellery, furniture,
glass, carpets, upholstery, linen, clocks, spices. All these
commodities had to be transported, if not by the merchants
themselves, who stayed at the inns, then by wagoners who
operated from the inns, and since the inns had the secure
warehousing to safeguard the goods it seemed pointless to
transport them to yet further premises for the purpose of retail.
The system was so beautifully simple that it was only the

permanently established traders – the butcher, the baker and the candlestick maker – who did not operate from the inn.

All this activity made the proprietors of these premises powerful and wealthy men. Since so much money changed hands under their roofs they frequently acted as bankers, just as medieval gold and silversmiths had found that their credit notes became acceptable paper. As highwaymen were a problem – Rockingham Forest in Northamptonshire was as notorious as Hounslow Heath or Shooters Hill in London – money was often deposited with innkeepers. As inns specialised in specific trades, information was readily available. Anyone's credit worthiness in a particular business could be readily ascertained, and so the risk to the innkeeper was minimised. The innkeeper was a fixed star in a moving sky. Different merchants and growers, farmers, traders, producers and craftsmen would come and go, but as they all stayed with him, he quickly became an expert in the markets. The innkeeper was in an enviably advantageous position, and as such it was through innkeeping alone that these men were able to make their fortunes.

Innkeepers grew to be wealthy citizens in many of these towns. Innkeeping was one means of achieving social mobility in a provincial society that was, if anything, more rigidly class-conscious than urban society. It was not uncommon for an innkeeper to sell an inn only to reappear in a grander one. As a result of the advantages of social mobility that the trade conferred, there grew up a fraternal attitude among the innkeepers, who were jealously suspicious of new entrants. As a true mark of how far innkeeping had come since its humble and lowly medieval origins, the eighteenth century saw the establishment of innkeeping dynasties. For example, in Nottingham in the early part of the eighteenth century, both the George and the Red Lion were held by members of the Lyon family. Innkeepers became civic figures, aldermen, mayors and MPs. In Northampton, Sloswick Carr, who moved from the Goat to the Red Lion in 1743, became mayor in 1750. In 1739 he had been a newcomer to the town. Carr died in 1751, mayor, magistrate and owner of a pack of beagles. His wife took over the management of the inn, from where the Flying Berlins left for London. Defoe tells us that in Doncaster in the early part of the eighteenth century the landlord at the Post House was not only postmaster but also mayor and capable of the not inconsiderable expense of hounds. Sloswick Carr's was not, therefore, an isolated career. Indeed social mobility among innkeepers did not go unnoticed at the time.

> They among them their distinctions know,
> And when a thriving landlord aims so high,
> As to exchange the Chequer for the Pye,
> Or from the Duke of William to the Dog repairs,
> He takes a fiercer coat and finer airs.[13]

Opportunities were there to be had. Information travelled along the coaching routes, and just as innkeepers moved from inn to inn so did employees. In 1629 Northampton was expressing concern at the influx of new innkeepers to the town, but in part this was a failure to appreciate the effects of their own success and of the prosperity of the time. In the early eighteenth century John Earle was a drawer at the Peacock in Northampton, from where he moved to a position at the Ship Inn at Wellingborough. By 1759 he was innkeeper of the Swan Inn, Wellingborough. This degree of social mobility was open to very few professions. As inns of the first rank were few, expensive and sought after, movement between inns of the third rank of drovers and carriers inns was more common. In 1736 Joseph Cook, of the Sun in Northampton, took over the Fleece, while Joseph Williams took over the Sun by vacating the Raven. Within three years Williams was following in Cook's steps and, in 1739, also moved from the Sun to the Fleece. In 1744 Williams was on the move again, upwards this time, to the Goat, when its landlord, Sloswick Carr, moved to the prestigious Red Lion.

In such a class-conscious society, awareness of hierarchy extended to hierarchy within the trade. As is the way of class, the pecking order was unspoken but implicitly understood. Provincial society was very close knit as well as being clearly defined. The inn was not just a trading centre but a social and recreational centre as well. Different inns would offer different forms of entertainment as befitting their standing in the town. A clear example of this is given in Thomas Hardy's *Mayor of Casterbridge*, where there is a clear division between the clientele of the King's Arms and the Three Mariners. Cockfighting and pugilism, football and skittles at one end of the social order would gradually move towards concerts, lectures, recitals, exhibitions, readings, galleries and flower shows and dances, balls and dinners. In 1759, 119 people sat down to dinner at the George, Northampton, upon the election of Frederick Montague to the House of Commons. In 1770, 200 people dined at the White Hart in Leicester, where eighteen years later the centenary of the Glorious Revolution was celebrated with a banquet, with 627 people sitting to dine in three different inns.

Assembly rooms and ballrooms became fashionable additions to the inn as the Industrial Revolution expanded the ranks of the gentry and leisured classes. These were the provincial alternatives to the Tea Gardens of London, popular during the Regency and early Victorian eras, which were, of course, unnecessary in the countryside. They were also ahead of London, in as much as the addition of the saloons and ballrooms to the larger London pubs only took place during the latter half of the nineteenth century. Ironically, these London venues were emulating the splendour of the inns, which by that time had all but gone.

The Blackamore's Head, in Northampton, would certainly have had a ballroom, for that was the 'seat' of the Northamptonshire aristocracy, who could not be without their own inn but, of course, could not be associated with 'trade'. As such, the Blackamore's Head was never one of the town's 'great' inns. Elsewhere the same things were happening. The Lion, Shrewsbury, entertained the Duke of Clarence, soon to be William IV, in 1807; Madame Tussaud exhibited there in 1830 and Paganini performed there the following year.

Nor were the political parties without their respective homes. Just as the London taverns were frequently split along political lines, so the politically-minded hung together in Northampton, the Whigs to the Swan, the Tories to the Goat, from which vantage points they hurtled invective at each other, oblivious of the fate awaiting the inn.

The steam train was a novel invention of which the Victorians were fiercely proud. Few of the inns' occupants could foresee the havoc that the iron horse would wreak upon them. Within twenty years steam would destroy a way of life that had taken over 200 years to evolve. In front of the Juggernaut's grinding wheels, history and tradition, civic pride or a colourful livery would be as just another jet of steam to evaporate before the eyes.

Chapter 12

TAVERNS

The Gentry to the King's Head
The Nobles to the Crown
The Knights unto the Golden Fleece,
And to the Plough the Clowne.
The Churchman to the Mitre,
The Shepherd to the Star,
The Gardener Hies him to the Rose,
To the Drum the Man of War.
The Huntsman to the White Hart,
To the Ship the Merchants Goe,
But you that do the Muses Love
The Sign callede River Po.
The Banquout to the World's End,
The Fool to the Fortune hie.
Unto the Mouth the Oyster Wife,
The Fiddler to the Pie.
The Rogue unto the Cockatrice,
The Drunkard to the Vine,
The Beggar to the Bank, there meet,
And with Duke Humphrey dine.
          'The Rape of Lucrece', Thomas Heywood (1608)

There is no private house in which people can enjoy themselves
so well as at a capital tavern. Let there be ever so great a plenty
of good things, ever so much grandeur, ever so much elegance,
ever so much desire that everybody should be easy, in the
nature of things it cannot be; there must always be some
degree of care and anxiety. The master of the house is anxious

to entertain his guests; the guests are anxious to be agreeable to him and no man but a very impudent dog indeed can freely command what is another man's house as if it were a tavern, there is a general freedom from anxiety. You are sure you are welcome; and the more noise you make, the more trouble you give, the more good things you call for, the welcomer you are. No servants will attend you with the alacrity with which waiters do, who are incited by the prospect of an immediate reward in proportion as they please. No, Sir there is nothing which has yet been contrived by man by which so much happiness is produced, as by a good tavern or inn.[1]

Johnson's eulogy aptly describes the difference between the inn and alehouse, on the one hand, and the tavern, on the other. The inns and alehouses provided useful services and fulfilled economic needs as well as social ones, whereas the tavern satisfied wants rather than needs and was, as such, more of a bourgeois luxury. Its patrons were not looking for rude shelter or escape through alcohol from their miserable lot. They were not en route from town to town. They did not call into the tavern to take shelter from bad weather on the road, to change horses, dry wet clothes in front of the fire, or meet to trade.

The tavern was an urban phenomenon. What the inn was to the mercantile classes and provincial society, so the tavern was to the professional classes and urban male society. The principal figures of tavern society may, like Ben Jonson at the start of the heyday of the tavern, or like Dr Johnson in its Indian Summer, may have been hard workers of a prodigious output or, like Pepys, have acquired wealth through their diligence or, like Garrick, enjoyed success through talent, or, like Goldsmith, been admired though never free from money worries. But after them came ranks of others, men from the legal profession and the emerging 'professions' in general, city gentlemen, Members of Parliament, actors, writers, government officials; people absorbed with urban life, fully in accord with Johnson's maxim 'When a man is tired of London he is tired of life.' It is no coincidence that the only location where genuine taverns have survived and retained even a fraction of their character is the City of London. However, none of the City's coaching inns have survived.

Behind this rank of tavern customer came the ranks of the sinecured, whose numbers were at their height during the eighteenth century and who, along with the pensioned, Cobbett liked to refer to as the 'Dead Weight'. With them, as with the literary figures and wits who so stamped their own personalities on the taverns, came bands of acolytes and sycophants.

There were also the great public figures of the day, along with the gentlemanly clientele of the coffee houses and the membership of the newly emerging clubs who, in those drunken times, preferred to finish their evenings off in a tavern booth.

> Men of all ages drink abominably. Fox drinks what I should call a great deal, though he is not reckoned to do so by his superiors. Sheridan excessively and Grey more than any of them, but it is in a much more gentlemanly way than our Scotch drunkards, and is always accompanied with lively, clever conversation on subjects of importance. Pitt I am told drinks as much as anybody.[2]

Sir Gilbert Elliot's testimony is supported by the cartoonists' lampooning caricatures of these people. Gilray lambasted Pitt's drinking in May and November 1795 and Sheridan's in February 1797, while the previous year he had lampooned the irony of the raising of the wine duty by a minister whose drinking was notorious throughout London.

A fashionable accompaniment to heavy drinking at the time was heavy gambling, which was prevalent among both sexes, the eighteenth century being a period where female participation in tavern life was acceptable and commonplace. Gambling was endemic in all levels of society, even to the extent of betting on ratting contests (how many rats a terrier could despatch against the clock), but heavy drinking, since it took more time than moderate drinking, meant heavier gambling, and vice versa. Charles James Fox was not unknown to sit at the card table for twenty-four hours at a time and was reported to have, on one occasion, lost £500 per hour.

The important point to remember is that there was nothing disgraceful about drunkenness at that time, indeed drinking prowess was much admired. ('They tell me that you like a glass of wine?' 'Those who have informed Your Majesty have done one a great injustice, they should have said a bottle.' Such is George III's Chancellor, Northington, supposed to have replied to his monarch's questioning.) Dr Johnson is supposed to have remarked on one occasion that, 'All the decent people of Lichfield get drunk every night and were not the worse thought of.'[3]

During the reign of the taverns, therefore, heavy drinking was the order of the day. The writer of *Ebrietatis Encomium* was, in all seriousness, able to argue that, 'So far is drunkenness from prejudicing our health that, on the contrary, it highly preserves it. . . . Everyone knows that Hippocrates, the Prince of Physicians, prescribes getting Drunk once a month as a thing very necessary for the Conservation of Health.'[4]

Apart from the respectable figures enjoying respectable overindulgence, there were respectable figures enjoying indefensible indulgence. This is a reference, of course, to the sons of aristocracy, the beaus and dandies, who used to pour forth from the taverns and engage in wholesale vandalism and terrorism with absolute impunity, and who would terrorise the watch and sedan chairmen and late night travellers. There are reported cases of murder committed by the sons of the aristocracy, where the courts have dismissed the cases merely on the basis of the identity of the culprits. For a brief period the aristocracy had the right to murder in all but name.

Finally, the taverns were the haunt of many and varied types of people of indeterminate positions: the arrivistes, lechers, confidence tricksters, opportunists – the kinds of people who add colour and danger to all places and all times. Their faces leer out at us from the eighteenth century in Hogarth's prints of the *Rake's Progress* and the *Harlot's Progress*. The tavern, therefore, was the preserve of the 'non-productive classes', the wits and sages, poets and actors, playwrights and writers, aesthetes and politicians. The inns and alehouses – on the whole – were not.

As ever, such distinctions and divisions within a society are best observed through the eyes of foreigners. Don Manuel Gonzales, writing in 1731, observed:

The principal taverns are large handsome edifices, made as commodious for the entertaining of a variety of company as can be contrived, with some spacious rooms for the accommodation of numerous assemblies. Here a stranger may be furnished with wines, and excellent foods of all kinds, dressed after the best manner; each company and every particular man, if he pleases, has a room to himself, and a good fire, if it be wintertime, for which he pays nothing, and is not to be disturbed or turned out of his room by any other man of what quality so over, till he thinks fit to leave it.[5]

The tavern has a kind of privacy that may be enjoyed singly in a feet-up manner or boisterously in an away-from-prying eyes fashion. It was more aloof than the alehouse, with better quality fare, but not as stuffy as the club, where standards had to be observed. Few standards had to be observed in the tavern, regardless of who you were.

Don Gonzales did not regard the alehouses as quite so decadent.

And though the taverns are very numerous yet alehouses are much more so, being visited by the inferior tradesmen, mechanics, journeymen, porters, coachmen, carmen, servants and others whose pockets will not reach a glass of wine. There they sit promiscuously in common dirty rooms, with large fires, and clouds of tobacco, where one that is not used to them can scarce breathe or see; but as they are a busy sort of people they seldom stay long, returning to their several employments, and are succeeded by fresh sets of people of the same rank of men at their leisure hours all day long.[6]

The alehouse was not a glamorous place. It could be base, dirty and crowded, and it was not a leisured scene, as was the tavern. Men used it for refreshment for the brief time before they returned to their occupations. Admittedly, while there they might indulge themselves to a great extent. Benjamin Franklin, while travelling in England in the eighteenth century, noted how English printers frequently consumed twelve pints during the course of a working day. In the sugar industry, where the immense heat involved in the production of loaf sugar resulted in a mortality rate higher than in any other industry, workers were free to drink limitless quantities of free beer.

To Johnson, however, we leave the final opinion of a tavern, as something different – a haven and a relaxation not intended for, or open to, the multitude.

As soon as I enter the door of a tavern, I experience an oblivion of care, and a freedom from solicitude; when I am seated, I find

the master courteous and the servants obsequious to my call,
anxious to know and ready to supply my wants; wine there
exhilarates my spirits and prompts me to free conversation, and
an interchange of discourse with those whom I must love;
I dogmatise and am contradicted; and in this conflict of opinions
and sentiments I find delight.[7]

The golden age of the tavern was rather longer than that of the
inn, though it ended somewhat earlier. In many respects it was
more of a victim of gin than the alehouses.

The tavern was at its height from roughly the Elizabethan
period until around the time of the death of Dr Johnson and the
French Revolution (1783–89). In 1660 Pepys could still be a full-
time civil servant, able to spend his evenings in lascivious and
intemperate behaviour with no imputation on his position, or
even a raised eyebrow. The wholesale drunkenness unwittingly
unleashed by the policies of the Whigs, who drank to the good
riddance of James II, had the effect of gradually making
drunkenness less acceptable in upper-class circles. Fox, Pitt and
Sheridan may well have been big drinkers, but by the 1790s their
drinking was starting to become worthy of comment by members
of their own social class who obviously did not share their
indulgence.

With the emergence in Elizabethan England of mercantile
classes, arising from the rapid expansion of foreign trade, rivalry
with the Dutch, and exploitation of the New World, there was
bound to be some visible expression of the enjoyment of this
national wealth and confidence. This expression was manifest in
the rapid expansion in the numbers and popularity of taverns.

Wine was very cheap at 4d per quart, at a time when a capon
was 3s and beef 2s a stone. More wine was imported into England
during the reign of Elizabeth I than during the reign of Victoria.
This was partly due to the fact that bottled wine was unknown and
it quickly went off. The wine could never mature and so had to be
drunk young. This and wine's low price helped shape the character
of the tavern, which was to remain largely unchanged for nearly
200 years. Many of the characteristics of tavern life originated in
the late sixteenth century, such as the habit of sending wine into
the rooms of gentlemen in the taverns by way of greeting and
introduction.

> Sir John, there's one Master Brook below would fain speak with
> you and be acquainted with you; and hath sent your worship a
> morning's draught of Sack.
>
> *Merry Wives of Windsor*, Act II, Scene I

Any reader of Shakespeare will sooner or later come across sack.
This was probably the most important and widely drunk wine of
the period. A Spanish wine, its name is a corruption of sec, or dry,
but how dry it actually was is a bit of a mystery. Falstaff is seen
sweetening his sack – although there is no reference to sack in
England before 1532, so in fact Falstaff would never have heard of
it. Sweet wines were available, so why sweeten a dry wine? It
would make sense to sweeten a sweet wine that was still not sweet
enough, bearing in mind that the Elizabethan tooth was a very
sweet tooth indeed. It is likely that its sweetness varied greatly
according to the area of its origin, since it was shipped from Cadiz,
Malaga, Alicante and Jerez. Those from Jerez were often called
sherris sack, from which we get the term sherry, and although
sherries are fortified wines they too vary greatly in sweetness.

Wine's importance probably declined during the seventeenth
century with the gradual opening up of internal trade and the
greater transport of beer around Britain. It was certainly never
again as cheap as it had been under Queen Elizabeth, but by the
accession of James I the tavern was established as the drinking
place of the upper classes. It was under James I that cork was
introduced, and who, as the first Stuart, ensured that the taverns
would be centres of political intrigue for the next century, and his
heirs would set the fashions that would be aped in so many tavern
rooms, whose improprieties would be much debated, and whose
courts would be the subject of so much tavern gossip and biting
jests. Even when the Stuarts were no more, their legacy would
continue to dominate the taverns. It would not be until the end of
the English Renaissance, the demise of the playwrights and wits,
that the tavern's golden age would draw to a close. For as all ages
have their own places and all places have their own age, there was
to be no place for the tavern in the age that followed.

The Industrial Revolution had profound effects upon the social
composition of society, the new money and 'new men' were not
the same breed as the tavern dwellers, while the alehouses,
squeezed by the new antipathetic mood of the ruling classes,

sought respectability by more closely emulating the taverns. The remnants of tavern society sought to maintain their distance and so debunked to the clubs.

A perennial problem of the taverns during the eighteenth century was one of supply. The shortage of claret that came fairly rapidly upon the heels of William III has already been mentioned, and the extent of the smuggling trade was the nation's way of expressing its opinion of the government's policies. In the early part of the eighteenth century, although approximately 42 per cent of legally imported wines came from Portugal, these were not what we call Port (which did not come into vogue until the advent of the cylindrical bottle that allowed wine to be binned). Portuguese wine was just a type of quaffing wine; this meant that much Bordeaux could enter the country as Oporto. The Methuen Treaty of 1704, which gave Portugal preferential trading arrangements, saw a decline in the amount of wine legally imported of some 22,000 tuns between 1704 and 1708. As with all attempts at drink regulation, it was not successful. Primarily aimed at reducing the consumption of French wine by displacing it with Portuguese, it actually resulted in a fall of Portuguese wine imported. In 1693 13,000 pipes of Oporto were legally imported into Britain. Between 1703 and 1712 the average annual amount shipped was only 8,111 pipes. This huge decline led, as with gin and beer when authority interfered with supply, to adulteration, and the period from 1704 until the end of the Spanish War of Succession was one of notable adulteration of wine. Naturally, the taverns suffered most.

Ned Ward pulls no punches in denouncing two known wine adulterators.

> Let B-ks and H-r vend their cloudy wines,
> In Wapping Brothels, and in Country Inns;
> And furnish Midnight Cellars in By Streets,
> For Roaring Bullies, Punks and Sodomites,
> And by the trusty Help, of Chip and Dusk;
> Fill every dusky hole with liquid trash:
> Squeez'd from the berry on which Elder Grows,
> Lengthen'd with cyder, and made rough with Sloes
> That Sweetners, when they've played some villains Trick,
> With City Cull, Raw Youth or Country Hick,

And Preached the Parson with a Harmless face,
Or us'd the Rug and Leather with success;
May to some Midnight dark house made this way
Where B & H justly bear the sway,
There share their ill got booty e'er they part,
O'er damaged Dregs and their flatcap whores,
Swear, drink, debauch and squabble on all fours.
Till poisoned by bad wines, with which they're pleased,
They reel away drunk droughty and diseased.[8]

There was one positive benefit from the shortage of quality wine that afflicted the early decades of the eighteenth century: the development of fortified wine. Demand for wine was greater than supply, and the best Portuguese wine area, Minho, was producing at capacity. To increase output grapes from the Douro region were also 'pressed' into service, but these fermented too quickly. A solution was to halt the fermentation by the addition of brandy distilled from the preceding year's vintage. The new fortified wine was an immediate success, and with the advent of the binnable bottle made its entrance into Britain between 1727 and 1730, and thus started the long association between British families and the Port producing areas of Portugal.

All these factors gradually conspired to sap the strength of the tavern, but perhaps the simplest reason for its demise was that it had lost its *raison d'être*, its monopoly on the sale of wines. Wines could be got at ordinaries, coffee houses, inns, gentlemen's clubs and the wine merchant. If wine was becoming universally available to those who wanted it, the remaining advantage of the tavern was that it was a place where one could drink in convivial surroundings, in privacy and to excess without attracting opprobrium, but this was no longer as fashionable as it had once been.

The taverns' laudatory hero, Dr Johnson, was, if anything, rather better known among his contemporaries for his prodigious tea drinking than for his alcohol consumption. James Boswell may well have been a drunkard, but Johnson frequently became abstemious for long periods, and would in no way have approved of the drinking party where a small boy was employed to sit under the table and loosen the cravats of those who, through inebriation, found themselves down at his level. By the start of the nineteenth century, very few others would have approved either.

Chapter 13

TEMPLES OF THE WORST PASSION: MORE GIN

Gin! Cursed fiend with fury fraught,
Makes human race a prey,
It enters by a deadly draught,
And steals our life away.

Beer! Happy produce of our isle,
Can sinewy strength impart,
And, wearied with fatigue and toil,
Can cheer each manly heart.

Revd J. Townley

The early nineteenth century was a hotch-potch of influences and changes. So many different forces were at work within society that trends and patterns must be heavily qualified. Society's institutions were changing, declining, reforming and moulding themselves to the new industrial age. The coaching age reached its zenith, and like a glorious old soldier, faded away, leaving haunting memories of distant post horns. The railways came and changed society with concepts of immediate travel. The Victorians marvelled at the seemingly endless engineering feats that were accomplished in the service of the iron road; society rethought its values in the light of industrial experience, replacing old ways with industrial concepts and mechanical metaphors. Commerce was the order of the day. David Ricardo and Adam Smith shaped economic thought, replacing Rousseau, Hobbes and Locke. The division of labour in pin manufacture would exercise minds more than theoretical abstractions on the nature of the 'noble savage'. Writers like Thomas Paine would appeal to those concerned at where cold, calculating pin counting would lead mankind, while Bentham, Smiles and James Mill sought to elevate pin counting into a series of incontrovertible laws and maxims. A welter of writers and thinkers, increasingly influenced by the industrial process, attempted to resolve the seeming incompatibility of industrial organisation and liberty, from Burke and Carlyle to Marx.

Marx's contribution to the historical development of the public house in the nineteenth century was limited to that of customer. He and Engels are reported to have, more than once, helped each other down the Old Kent Road – with or without trousers – after having put the world to rights over a pot or several in a public bar, in the time-honoured fashion.

The public house was buffeted by many storms during the nineteenth century. Some were a result of the social turmoil occasioned by the colossal effects of urbanisation and industrialisation, the changing patterns of the distribution of wealth within society, and the changing composition of class this engendered. Demographic changes were not without impact, as were, more crucially, the varying policies of brewers, magistrates, governments, rival political parties, temperance agitators, urban planning policies and even the dominant economic ideology.

While publicans and dram shop owners reacted to the hundred and one pressures, fashions and influences that manifested themselves in a society emerging from the turmoil of the Industrial Revolution, they also had to adjust to the specific strictures of legislation addressed directly at them. In this respect, the nineteenth century resembled the eighteenth very closely. That this should be so is not that surprising when one considers the propensity of men to forget the lessons of previous errors, and in England, their attachment to a legislative machinery that encourages repeated compounding of errors.

At the risk of oversimplification, the eighteenth and nineteenth centuries may be summarised as follows. An initial unpopularity of magistrates combined with propitious economic circumstances and political actions to produce an explosion of gin drinking. Various measures were tried to curb the much condemned use of gin, largely by relying on the substitution of gin by beer. Some actions did more harm than good, but drinking excesses were gradually brought under control. There followed a period when moral campaigners dominated the arena. In both centuries they rode on the back of the hysteria generated by the excess of gin drinking, and were at their most vocal after the worst excesses had been curbed. The climate engendered by the moralists, who had little success 'on the ground', coincided with economic factors to produce an era of alehouse or public house suppression and tighter regulation, the net effect of which was to further enhance the brewery tie, reduce competition and penalise small brewers and publicans while enhancing the wealth and prestige of the larger ones. Both epochs concluded with periods of war; the Napoleonic Wars in the first instance, the First World War in the second, the disciplines of which far more effectively curbed drink abuse than either the peacetime efforts of governments or the agitations of Puritan or temperance-minded campaigners.

> Disbursed at the most enormous rate of profit, you will see these temples for the gratification of the worst passions, giving shelter to the houseless poor, merely while they spend the product of their latest pledge, or that portion of their hard earned gains their children possibly require elsewhere – erected in many cases without regard to expense, and property invested in the most costly appearances to lure the wary and entrap the passers by, casks of the largest dimensions, so placed above the windows to be easily seen from the streets, domes, occupying the usual situation of first floors – and plate glass in prodigious quantities, prodigally spread over with brass rods to heighten and add to the general effect.[1]

The conclusion of the Napoleonic Wars had several internal domestic effects in England. As the victor and the world's most advanced industrial nation, Britain was the most powerful nation in the world. A rapidly expanding empire provided her with cheap raw materials, ready markets for finished goods, a rapidly growing population and increases in agricultural productivity. All these factors favoured an expansion in trade which produced tangibly appreciable wealth, so that Free Traders carried the day and the dominant economic ideology of the century was born – *laissez-faire*.

Domestically, this popular infatuation with the principles of free trade sat uneasily with the composition and practices of the drink trade, which had begun to attract the increasing attention of

Free Traders during the early years of the century as a result of the tie and endemic adulteration. On the one hand, the very concept of the tie was unpopular. By 1805, 82 per cent of the outlets serviced by Whitbread were in some way tied to them. On the other hand, a simple cause and effect that could enable accusing fingers to be pointed at the brewers was elusive. In 1816 a House of Commons Committee examined the question of the tie. The composition of the committee was biased in favour of the Free Traders, but it still managed to lay the blame for the fact that 50 per cent of London pubs were tied by brewers as either owners, purchasers or equitable mortgagors on the magistrates rather than the brewers.

The magistrates wanted a reduction in the number of premises, which initially forced brewers to acquire sites defensively. The magistrates' predilection for larger houses meant that larger brewers could outbid smaller producers, with the result that by the early nineteenth century the twelve largest brewers controlled 75 per cent of the London market. So far the brewers were acting as any rational capitalist would to defend market share in adverse times. However, they did not stop there. Frequently the brewers and magistrates colluded to their mutual advantage.

The magistrate would grant a licence on the condition that a publican took his beer from a certain brewer. If the publican subsequently changed his supplier the magistrate would revoke the licence. The brewer, for his part, undertook to starve the illicit trade of supplies. Naturally this part of the bargain did not work so well. Since the magistrates did not treat all brewers equally there were plenty of small brewers under no obligation to desist from supplying unlicensed houses; indeed they even came to depend for their survival on the unlicensed trade.

By the 1820s there was widespread recognition that excessive regulation had polarised the alehouses between licensed, well-appointed public houses on the one side and illicit, smaller and poorer houses on the other. These latter had no incentive to become more respectable in case they were suppressed. Where they found supplies of beer hard to come by they turned to spirits, and by the 1820s the number of houses retailing spirits was again on the increase.

The early decades of the nineteenth century saw a population boom. Evidence of this can be seen today in the relative sizes of public houses built in expanding parts of London at this time – the north, the west and the East End. The increased investment in the pub by the larger brewers engendered in the public an expectation of perpetually improving standards. The parlour replaced the kitchen and the taproom, beer engines were increasingly widespread and as the century progressed the saloon and public bar emerged. In the meantime, the relative increase in pub size failed to compensate for the decline in the ratio of public houses to people. This further encouraged the growth of dram shops.

In 1818 the agitation for reform of the drink trade, occasioned by the petition against adulteration submitted in the same year, was eventually defeated by a combination of brewers, magistrates and their Tory allies. The debate was loud and wide ranging. Parliament was deluged by opinion from all sides on the issue of licensing reform. Many publicans also supported the brewers since they feared any major increase in competition, especially those whose overheads were artificially inflated by the actions of the magistrates. The Friendly Society of Licensed Victuallers had been formed in 1794, producing its own paper – the *Morning Advertiser*. It soon became a vocal lobby and one that was not, as a rule, sympathetic to brewers, but on this issue it was.

The brewers may have won a respite, but the gradual increase in gin consumption meant that the pressure for reform would not go away. Various Tory measures were enacted during the 1820s as half-hearted attempts to defuse the situation without radically altering the status quo. In 1822 a reform bill failed at its third reading. The 1823 Intermediate Beer Act was an attempt to encourage more brewers to set up to counteract charges of monopoly practices. The act was ineffectual. In 1824 the Retail Brewers Act permitted small brewers to sell up to sixteen bushels per annum over their doors for a licence of £5 5s. Its impact on consumption patterns was negligible, although it did have the effect, along with the 1830 act, of giving the ancient craft of domestic brewing a shot in the arm before it disappeared into history once and for all.

Year	Retail Brewers
1830	1,269
1839	18,017
1880	6,157
1914	880

Source: *A History of the English Public House*, H.A. Monckton.

The 1820s were a decade of much visible activity and change in the high streets, the effects of which were such that these piecemeal measures were not going to satisfy the pressure for reform. The 1820s were also a period of declining beer consumption and rising gin consumption, as well as the period of emergent gin palaces. In 1823 Scottish and Irish spirit duties had been hugely reduced, and in 1825 they also fell in England, from 11s 8½d per gallon to 7s (2s 3¾d in Ireland and Scotland). In the same year spirit licences were slashed from 5 guineas to 2 guineas. These measures had received unusual cross-party support, for they were primarily proposed as an anti-smuggling measure. The Whigs favoured them for their Free Trade overtones, while the Tories looked forward to an anticipated agricultural bonus. Neither side thought to look to the lessons of the previous century, and as a result they failed to see the obvious consequences. Gin drinking increased overnight. The duty-paid volume doubled within a year. By 1828 the need for reform was now incontrovertible. The licensing system was denounced as, 'one of the most enormous and scandalous Tyrannies every exercised upon any people', and it was declared that, 'we must have a small massacre of magistrates, nothing else will do.'[2]

It is important to be wary of the chronology of events during the 1820s and 1830s, for popular history and actual fact are not always the easiest of bedfellows, and the reality of what happened does not always square with people's retrospective interpretations. The popular misconception is to associate the rise in gin drinking with the emergence of the gin palaces and to see the 1830 Beer Act as a means of combating them. This is incorrect. There would appear to have been a 32 per cent increase in the legal amount of gin drunk in the 1830s over the 1820s, yet there were, by all accounts, no gin palaces until late 1829.

The 1820s saw changes which were necessary to enable gin palaces to evolve. As we shall see below, the principal impetus for gin palace growth was none other than the Beer Act. As described, there were changes in the appearance of many town public houses. Beer engines made pot boys redundant and radically changed the character of houses. Furnishings were becoming less Spartan, following the Victorian taste for clutter. The taste for fittings was no doubt in part determined by the diffusion of gas lighting and the atmosphere given off by reflected light.

Prints, clocks, glass cases, copper and plants were starting to make their way into houses, in such a way as would have made the plusher Georgian taverns look bare.

The inglenook was giving way to the stove and chimney piece, and the number of rooms were multiplying and acquiring different functions and class connotations. Upstairs rooms were made over to clubs, small side rooms may have been set aside for spirits, and bottle and jug departments were starting to appear.

Outside in the street there were changes that affected the pub. The late eighteenth century saw the establishment of a permanent retail presence on the high street. Shops and signs were becoming established features, and the combination of gas lighting with plate glass in the 1820s provided the opportunity for attractive and eye-catching 'shop windows'. As the street became a more colourful place, the external appearance of the pub had to brighten up lest it appear shabby by comparison.

As most pubs were still essentially domestic properties with internal alterations, they spruced up their appearance by means of gas illumination outside and a greater use of signs. Traditionally, the sign of the house had changed with the landlord; now it became fixed. As a result of increased literacy it was more likely that the brewery would write the name of the pub on the signs which also advertised their 'Entire', 'Porter' and 'Ales'. In 1809 Meux started to regard these signs as assets of the brewery. Within five or six years such signs were being considered part of the brewers' obligation to the landlord, and the era of advertising and brand names was silently ushered in.

At this time the coaching era was still at its height. The railways had not yet taken trade from the inns, so the retail liquor outlet was still sharing an intermediate status between a house that was open to the public and the modern pub. The 'bar' was making steady inroads into more and more houses, but it was the serving hatch type of bar typical of the taverns of the previous century. Today we would call it an office, since it often had glass panels so that good visibility could be maintained. The bar 'counter' was an innovation of the gin palaces and only became a universal feature of the public house when the railways finally killed off the inns, so that grooms, ostlers, waiters and chambermaids went the same way as pot boys, and the pubs started to ape the gin palaces rather than their traditional role models because of the adverse competition brought on by the Beer Act of 1830.

The magistrates had had their final warning two years before. The Licensing Act of 1828 was a poor attempt to reverse their policies. It provided for special sessions to grant one year licences, prohibited adulteration and the running of disorderly houses, and indeed it forbade opening during divine service, but failed to provide adequate sanctions. However, it did not tackle the problem at a procedural level and so failed, and bad drafting made it a dead letter. The message, however, was clear: at a time of falling beer consumption, magisterial oppression was unwarranted.

The year 1828 saw the gin drinking revival enter the public consciousness. In 1825 there were 8,500 more spirit licences than there had been twenty-five years earlier. At this stage, temperance agitation was largely anti-spirit agitation. The notion of abstemiousness still meant moderation rather than teetotalism, and it was not regarded as incompatible to rail against spirits while still believing beer to be a wholesome and nutritional beverage.

The conditions were right for drastic measures to be taken, and the concern at gin drinking and the unpopularity of the brewers, who were against any reform, stiffened the resolve of the reformers. In 1830 the Duke of Wellington, a Tory, rode roughshod over many powerful Tory interests and pushed through the Beer Act, which abolished all duty on beer and established the right of any householder to sell beer upon purchase of a two guinea licence from the Excise, subject to a £20 penalty for selling wines and spirits. The effects of the act were immediate, predictable and not entirely successful, as far as they were intended. All the illicit alehouses came out of the woodwork and traded legally, every craftsman's shop obtained a licence, and every blacksmith bought the right to sell ale as a refreshment for waiting customers. Brewers, who had feared the worst, benefited immensely from the increase in the beer being drunk. The production of Bass rose six-fold within ten years and the price of beer was halved overnight. Within the first year of the operation of the act 24,000 new licences were taken out. Liverpool witnessed fifty new beer shops opened every day for weeks after the introduction of the act. By December the 24,000 licences had risen to 31,000, by 1832 to 36,000 and by 1836 there were 46,000 beer shops in a country where there were only 56,000 fully licensed pubs and where the population was only 15 million. In 1850 in Manchester alone, excluding Salford, there were 475 public houses and 1,142 beer shops – one for every eighty men aged twenty or older.

Ironically, the areas where the justices had been the most severe saw the greatest rise in the numbers of retailing premises. The new premises were universally named Tom and Jerry shops after the rough characters in Pierce Egan's 1821 *Life in London*. There was also a cinnamon-spiced drink of the same name. Brewers' agents went door to door canvassing trade and offering to pay the two guinea licence if home owners would sell their beer. Competition was so intense that agents would even sell their beer on credit.

On 24 October 1830 Sydney Smith observed that 'the new beer bill has begun its operations. Everybody is drunk. Those who are not singing are sprawling. The sovereign people are in a beastly state.' Lord Palmerston more aptly summed up the position in 1853: 'The words "licensed to be drunk on the premises" are by the people interpreted as applicable to the customers as well as the liquor.'[3]

The 1830 act deserved to fare better than it did, for it was one of the very few drink measures prompted by concern for the well-being of the working classes that was not merely patronising. There were, of course, considerations of expediency. It was hoped that the act would stimulate agricultural revival and reduce gin drinking, but Parliament recognised that, for many, beer was 'the second necessity of life . . . which was in a great degree calculated to sustain their strength while at work.' There were also other motives behind the act. In an article in *The Times* on 3 May 1830, the Chancellor of the Exchequer, Viscount Althorp, expressed the opinion that 'the system . . . for licensing houses for the sale of beer had necessarily given rise to a greater or lesser degree of monopoly . . . that the existing system had led to a deterioration of the article, and operated, therefore, as a severe tax upon the poor man.' The Chancellor's belief was widely shared. Members of Parliament considered that 'if all persons were suffered to sell beer in their shops (and) there be no increase in the consumption of the article: it would only be a transfer of the trade from one class of the community to another.'

The members of the classes concerned, however, were well aware of the effects of the act. A publican writing to *The Times* in

May 1830, before the act received its Royal Assent, accurately forecast some of the turmoil that it would engender.

> Two years ago I purchased the lease of a public house, which cost me £2,500: £1,000 of this was my own bona fide property which I had slaved 12 years in the same business to accumulate. The brewer lent me the rest, and took my lease and a power of attorney as security. My house under this new measure will probably be reduced in value to the £1,500 the brewer has on it. The deficiency which my trade will experience will prevent me paying off so enormous a loan, and I must resign my house to the brewer, or he will legally take possession of it. Thus the brewer will get all his money in a house which from its construction will, under the 'frees system' secure him good interest, but I must be compelled to resign the hard years of earnings and be driven into a world penniless. Well may the brewers be content. The bill is a positive good to them, by the spoilation of the publican.

Such arguments did not win much sympathy. It is interesting to note the degree to which it resembles the publicans' complaint (to be discussed in the next chapter) made in 1834, after the bill had come into effect.

While the number of beer shops soared astronomically, life became harder for the full on-licence publican and helped drive him further into the arms of the brewer. Large numbers of petitions against the bill were presented to both houses of Parliament by licensed victuallers, but the popular feeling was very much in favour of the measure. When the Duke of Richmond failed in his attempt to scupper it, by preventing liquor being drunk on the premises where it was purchased, *The Times*, on 9 July 1830, commented that, 'We really have no wish to say anything offensive to the Peers who opposed this bill, but if we were to judge by their speeches alone, we would say they had not read it; most certainly they do not understand its object or effect.'

In many respects the act was bound to favour the brewer, come what may. The following table illustrates the varying economies of scale attainable between different types of brewer, and is calculated from the 1830 returns for the amounts brewed from a quarter of malt.

	barrels	firkins	gallons	quarts
Common Brewers	2	2	3	3 strong
		1	5	1 table
Retailing Brewers	1	3	8	3 strong
		1	1	1 table
Victualling Brewers	2	0	1	3 strong
		1	4	3 table

Source: Peter Haydon

The intention was that, by encouraging the smaller producers who used comparatively more malt, the demand for malt could be stimulated. This takes no consideration of the market, which does not differentiate between the types of producer, as far as malt prices are concerned, unless the larger common brewers could negotiate discount prices – in which case they derived even larger benefits. The encouragement of increased selling by small houses would therefore result in a transfer of sales away from the high overhead outlets – the public houses – to the cheaper beer shops and cakeshops, and from the retailing brewers to the lower input common brewers. This is exactly what happened, and the large brewers, originally very anti-act benefited enormously.

Naturally, the impact of the act went far wider than just increasing the number of beer shops and providing protection for illicit houses. It destabilised the whole trade. The magistrates saw their good efforts at ridding the streets of disorderly houses undone at a stroke. There was only one remedy available. Since they could no longer refuse licences to beer shops, the granting of full licences was the only course open to them by which they could exercise some control. The magistrates then pursued a policy of granting full licences to those beer shops that applied for them, in the hope that they could then induce them to become more respectable. The number of public houses rose by 15 per cent between 1830 and 1840, and by 1876 the total number of full licences stood at 69,000. The result of this policy was to further increase the availability and consumption of gin. Gin drinking had actually fallen in the immediate aftermath of the act, but then gradually increased again, peaking in 1836.

The brewers were worried that deregulation would effectively abolish the cartel they operated, meaning that the large amounts of money laid out to keep others out of the market place would be lost. As ever, they need not have worried. The boom in beer consumption more than offset any collapse in the values of their estates, which in turn was offset by the increase in the numbers of premises that fell to them, and the 1840s were, once again, a period of expanding brewery capacity. New brewery companies were established, Davenports in 1846 and Ansells in 1858, for example. Both, interestingly, were Midlands brewers brewing the northern Burton beer. The act helped accelerate the decline of porter. The free-for-all gave the 'bitter' brewers access to the London market. Often these firms had very tight controls on their own local estates, and being more dispersed, were less vulnerable to outside incursions, while they were advantageously placed to poach from the London market. The abolition of the tax on glass in 1847 gave them a further fillip, since the clear bitter looked better in glass than the darker porter.

The real loser was the existing publican. He had gone to some expense to jump through the hoops held up before him by the bench. He had had to become indebted to take on the business, and his continued solvency was dependent upon the beer retailing for 4d a quart. Overnight the price of beer fell by much more than was justified by the mere removal of taxes. Publicans like Mr Ivory, of the Anchor at St Mary-at-Hill, who had already been deceived by the brewer's agent into believing the turnover of the house to be greater than was the case when he bought it, now found themselves in debt, trading insolvently and with a depreciating asset on their hands. Mr Ivory, having paid £3,000 for the house and taken on a loan of £1,500 from Whitbread in 1829, was forced to sell the premises for £800 in July 1832 to an agent of Whitbread. Interestingly, this same house that Mr Ivory was assured turned over 144 butts per annum, but that could only manage 117 in 1829, was turning over 300 in 1824.

Clearly not all landlords went to the wall like Mr Ivory. Many managed to run profitable houses. Many others decided that if their profit margins on beers were to be cut, they should provide another commodity – gin. It was the irony of the 1830 act that the sudden opening up of a market heavily distorted by the actions of dominant monopolists should have the exact opposite effect than that which was hoped. Intended as a means to popularise beer at the expense of gin, it forced publicans and magistrates to further popularise gin. The result was there for all to see, and was recognised as such – the gin palace.

The beer houses very much interfered with the business of the regular publicans . . . and this is the cause of a great number of what are called in the newspapers, Gin Palaces. The old public houses where a man could have his steak dressed and sit down and take his ale are extinct; they are obliged to convert themselves into splendid houses, and sell gin at the bar.[4]

The first gin palaces predated the 1830 act, though not by much. Commonly acknowledged as the first was Thompson and Fearon's on Holborn Hill, in London, though closely behind came Weller's on Old Street. The appearance of these new establishments caused great comment and much antipathy. By our standards they were very modest concerns. Thompson and Fearon's was designed by the architect Papworth, who specialised in the newly fashionable styles of shop front and who also left his mark on much of Cheltenham.

Thompson and Fearon's did not style itself as a gin palace, but rather described itself as 'wholesale and retail spirit and wine stores'. What was revolutionary was the layout of the premises. Its inspiration was the shop and not the public house. The relationship between proprietor and patron was not one of host and local resident or traveller; it was a purely commercial relationship between retailer and customer. The decor was influenced by the new ideas of the shop front. It was meant to be eye-catching, to draw one in, but once in there was no inducement to linger for longer than was necessary to conduct one's business. There were no seats, no partitioned areas, no food on offer; merely a long counter, behind which were the serving girls, dressed, according to one report of 1833, like the 'belles limonadiers' of the Paris coffee houses.

Dickens was among those to comment upon the sudden speed of the appearance of gin palaces, which he described as a 'revolution' which 'burst forth with tenfold violence among the publicans and keepers of wine vaults. Onward it rushed to every part of town, knocking down all the old public houses, and depositing splendid mansions stone balustrades, rosewood fittings, immense lamps and illuminated clocks at the corner of every street.'[5] However, what was new were the premises and not the drinking.

> Honestly to speak it was a dismal spectacle. In every broad thoroughfare, and in every close alley, there was drunkenness abroad; not shamefaced drunkenness creeping in maudlin helplessness to its home by the side of the scolding wife, but rampant, insolvent, outrageous drunkenness. No decent woman even in broad daylight could at the holiday seasons dare to walk alone in the Strand or Pall Mall.[6]

This description of urban debauchery sounds as if it comes from the 1750s. If the reaction to the appearance of the gin palaces is to be believed, we might assume that it came from the 1830s. In fact it came from 1824, during the period of the most rapid increase in gin consumption.

Few descriptions of the gin palaces were as impartial as Dickens's.

> At one place I saw a revolving light with many burners playing most beautifully over the door of the painted charnel house; at another 50 or 60 jets in one lantern were throwing out their capricious and fitful but brilliant gleams, as if from the branches of a shrub. And over the doors of a third house were no less than three enormous lamps with corresponding lights, illuminating the whole streets to a considerable distance. They were in full glare on this Sunday evening; and through the doors of these infernal dens of drunkenness and mischief, crowds of miserable wretches were pouring in that they might drink and die.[7]

What is interesting is that once the style of the gin palace was established, courtesy of Weller's, and Thompson and Fearon's, it varied relatively little, even despite the injunction of the London magistrates in 1834 that licence renewal would be dependent upon the provision of a parlour or tap room.

> Everyone remarks the increase of gin shops. In all those parts of Leeds and Manchester, and of London too, where the poorest people live, there you find in almost every dirty street, not one,

but several fine houses, handsomely stuccoed, curiously painted, ornamented with plate glass and polished brass . . . inside, great barrels of spirits gaily painted and disposed for show, carved mahogany and more polished brass, with men and women, smartly dressed, smiling welcome to all who enter.[8]

It is easy to see in the gin palace the forerunner of the modern town pub. The great barrels may have been the hallmark of the gin palace but the essential characteristics were these, the bright polished surfaces, the deep warm colours of the wood and above all the glass and lights. In the days before street lighting the appearance of the gin palace would have been like a beacon in the darkness for the miserable poor who thronged their doors.

This was all very predictable. In the teeth of falling beer and rising gin consumption, the Middlesex Quarter Sessions were able to warn, before the 1830 act, that,

The attention of the Middlesex Magistrates had been called to demoralising consequences likely to ensue in the middling and lower classes from the alarming increase of gin shops in every direction, in and around the metropolis, by the conversion of quiet respectable public houses where the labouring population could find the accommodation of a tap room or parlour in which to take meals or refreshment as they require, into flaming dram shops, having no accommodation for persons to sit down, and where the only allurement held out was the promise of 'cheap gin'. This court do most earnestly recommend to the Justices . . . not to license any publicans who shall be found to have obtained a beer licence, as a mere convert or pretext for obtaining a spirit licence.[9]

The final injunction is full of irony, for within a year the first of 46,000 beer shops were created, all of which were allowed to apply for a spirit licence.

The divorce of eating and drinking was felt to be particularly harmful, though to what extent the gin swillers would have victualled while drinking gin is a moot point. Pubs certainly found that savings could be made by abandoning victualling, while many alternative food outlets were springing up to cater for the nation's food needs apart from the pub. The connection between the pub and provision of food was one that was not re-established until the turn of the century, and it is only within the last twenty years or so that it has become unusual to find a pub that does not do food.

It is one of the mysteries of the drink trade that, win or lose, the brewer always wins. If a course of action is beneficial to the brewer and a second course is detrimental, it is a general rule that, by adopting the first, the second, if subsequently embarked upon, has mysteriously become transformed so that it too now works to the brewer's advantage.

It might be thought that by flooding the market with thousands of new retail premises the brewers' tie would be massively weakened. This was not the case. The number of oligopolistic brewers may have increased and the cost of entering the market and acquiring an estate may have fallen, but with the shift towards the gin palace style this required investment. The investment could be funded by the fact that the cake had suddenly become larger, irrespective of the relative share of the cake, but the investment needed to be protected, and the tie was the best means of protecting investment. The process was easy to see in action.

The 1834 Select Committee on Drunkenness heard the following illuminating evidence on the transition of a public house to a gin palace in premises in Tothill Street, Westminster.

A public house, nearly opposite to my residence, where the consumption of spirits was very trifling, was taken for a gin palace. It was converted into the very opposite of what it had been, a low dirty public house, with only one doorway, into a splendid edifice, the front ornated with pilasters, supporting a handsome cornice and entablature and ballustrades, and the whole elevation remarkably striking and handsome; the doorways were increased in number from one, and that only 3' or 4' wide; to three and each of those three 8-10' wide. The floor was sunk so as to be as level with the street, and the doors and windows glazed with very large squares of plate glass, and the gas fittings of the most costly description. When this edifice was completed notice was given by placards taken round the parish by a number of men, that it would be opened on Saturday evening at six o'clock; a band of music was stationed in front of the house; the street became almost impassable from the number of people collected and when the doors were opened the rush was tremendous; it was instantly filled with customers and continued so till midnight.[10]

Two interesting points are clear from this passage. First, the conversion of a property is an expensive business. Frequently it was not the case that the pub landlord refurbished the premises as a gin palace; more often he sold out to a different type of proprietor. Neither should it be implied that the big brewers were necessarily keen to include gin palaces in their estates, for although they certainly sold beer as well as spirits, their fundamental *raison d'être* was the sale of gin. From the point of view of the brewer and publican, they spelt competition. Some landlords threw in the towel, others decided to join the ranks of the gin sellers, and others realised that the public house would have to adopt the trappings of the gin palace in order to hold their own. In 1833 three public houses in Lamb's Conduit Street were refurbished with the expenditure on the bar area alone in excess of £2,000 in each instance. Here was the opportunity for the brewers to continue to extend their influence, but this shall be examined later.

The other thing to be gleaned from the evidence of the grocer of Tothill Street is the completely changed nature of the premises. For example, the growth in numbers and width of doors was to maximise access and exit from the premises in order that people coming and going would not hinder each other. The expenditure on advertising and the impressive opening night celebrations occurred because the building was now a piece of working capital, the returns on which must be maximised from the very outset and before nearby competition could get in on the act.

The Times of 14 December 1829 reported people entering Thompson and Fearon's at the rate of a six a minute. These people could not all have been spending the same amount of time within the premises as they would if it had been a pub; the building would have been filled to capacity within half an hour. Clearly, the customers were not staying for very long, since they were buying liquor to take home (the frequent presence of a low counter for children sent on errands supports this) and much of the trade was passing. Thompson and Fearon themselves reckoned that one-third of the trade was for off-sales and considerably more than one-third of the takings. Volume of turnover was the key to success of the gin palaces. In the eighteenth century the brewers had concentrated on maximising the benefits associated with production; in the nineteenth century the next stage was to maximise the benefits derived from consumption. The distillers and the new breed of proprietors, the gin palace owners, briefly took the initiative from the brewers in the 1830s and extended the principles of industrial manufacturing and applied them to the gin palace. The architectural biographer of the Victorian public house, Mark Girouard, neatly encapsulates the whole process.

> The 1830s saw the first beginning of one of the major nineteenth century marketing discoveries, that if the turnover is big enough there is money to be made out of the poor and they can be given something approaching the amenities of the rich. The rich found this very upsetting.[11]

This was the crime of the gin palaces. They were incongruous surroundings for poor people to get drunk in. What offended middle-class sensibilities was not that the poor were getting drunk (they had always been getting drunk), but that they were getting drunk in opulent surroundings that were lavish out of all proportion to the status of the customers. The increased profile of the gin palaces meant that the people were getting drunk more publicly. The gin palaces relied on passing trade and were not to be found in the slums, where children might return from fetching their parents' tipple unseen, but were on the principal highroads where, thanks to the terms of the 1828 act, the middle classes would be incommoded as

> The Church bells chime out
> And out stagger the queer'uns
> From Wellers in Old St,
> And Thompson and Fearon's.

Chapter 14

PUB BUILDING

I have been in love and in debt and in drink
This many and many a year;
And those three plagues enough one would think,
For one poor mortal to bear.

Twas drink made me fall in love,
And love made me run into debt;
And though I have struggled and struggled and strove
I cannot get out of them yet.

'The Mad Lover', Alexander Brome (c. 1650)

A small man with his scanty capital is induced, by the great
man, to build a house; if his money happens not to be quite
sufficient, the great man is willing to advance the deficiency
and to take a mortgage on the premises. By the interests of the
great man, a licence is duly obtained, and stock is supplied
either on credit or on a future mortgage. Now it must be
evident to everyone that a lucrative and steady custom is not
to be obtained for a house in the space of a few months. The
losses at first, in a new house are considerable, since to secure
what may be deemed a good customer, credit is too frequently
given and when the indulgence stops the good customer is
seen no more. What follows? The great man intimates that no
further credit be given and the great man's lawyer steps in and
forecloses the mortgagor. Thus [is] the unsuspecting individual
ejected by the kind friend who helped him to buy his house,
who obtained him his licence and who supplied him with his
stock – penniless and unpitied; and the house adds another to

the list for the display of the 'Co.'s Entire'. Nor is this all . . . a
sum is demanded for the goodwill from the next comer, who
becomes a still more dependent vendor of his commodity.[1]

The parallel between the state of affairs by which the brewer's
estate is expanded and the case of the unfortunate Mr Ivory is
clear from this complaint of 1834. In Mr Ivory's instance he was
'induced by the great man' to buy his house; here he is induced to
'build', and it is in the important area of new public house
construction that the battle for the tied estates is fought during the
middle decades of the nineteenth century. The new suburban areas
provided rich ground away from the sordidness of rude beer
shops and gin palaces of the city centre. Here customers were
wealthier and more respectable and the premium was gained by
getting in on the ground floor, when a new area was being built.

On the pastures lately set out for building you may see a double
line of trenches with excavation either side and a tavern of
imposing elevation standing quite complete, waiting the
approaching row of houses. The propinquity of these places to
each other in Camden and Kentish Town is quite ridiculous. At a
distance of 200 paces in every direction they glitter in sham
splendour. In some instances one speculative builder, reserving
all the angle plots, run up a dozen public houses; he obtains
licences for all that he can, and lets or sells at such incredible
prices or enormous rentals; others he sells to adventuring
publicans who try for the privilege, or, in case of failure, open as
beer shops at war with the bench.[2]

Public houses became, literally, the corner stones of urban
development. The developer built the public house first, since it
would prove the largest drain on his capital. He knew he could sell
it rather than any house that stood in an unfinished development,
and the revenue from the public houses would finance the
completion of the remainder of the terrace. If, as was often
the case, he was a publican who became a builder, he would be
aware of the value of getting the building workers to part with
some of their wages in the pub they had just completed.
The builder was secure in the knowledge that a pub
development would sell. In the last resort, the competition among

brewers for new outlets meant that they effectively acted as underwriters for the project, and the practice just described gave London many of its characteristic Victorian terraces and corner pubs. If the builder could not secure the corner location the head of a 'T' junction would do as second best, with the frontage of the pub dominating the approach from the adjoining road.

The new public houses took much from the gin palaces. The brewers were not slow to catch on to the economies of scale that the gin palaces were enjoying through their low value/high volume turnover and sought to achieve the same gains for themselves. The *Building News* of 15 May 1857 acknowledged the changing style of public house furnishing, and did not approve.

> Settled or backed benches, with a plank to each, sufficed in primitive times for the enjoyment of a cup of brown nappy, with a pipe and a joke; the light of a coal fire, or the glimmer of a tallow fat, illumed satisfactorily the boozy meeting of our ancestral artisans and swashbucklers, tonight it is otherwise – the corner public is radiant of gas, redolent of mahogany, and glittering in mirrors, there are no settles, no stools nor an easy smoking with hard drinking. . . . At the bar the dropper in to drink must stand their drink and move on when tired.[3]

Such changes in the character of the pub may have made commercial sense, but socially and politically they were unwise. Socially, by the end of the century, there were conscious efforts to correct the errors of the gin 'palacifying' of public houses, to encourage the provision of food, to provide more in the way of leisure facilities and generally displace drinking from its central role, to which, in the mid-Victorian decades, all other traditional activities had been subordinated. Politically, it hastened the inevitable transfer from the gin palaces to the public house as the national scourge and sickness, and the shift from the calls for moderation to complete abstinence by the temperance movement. Nothing upset the temperance campaigners more than the gradual decline in provision by the public house.

To suggest that the design changes undertaken during the 1830s and 1840s produced public houses whose features and functions were commensurate with the gin palaces would, however, be incorrect. The single room with a traverse bar

designed to maximise the serving area and standing area were the
basic characteristics of the gin palace; only the rudest beer shop,
however, was a one room affair. Public houses were based around
several rooms of varying functions. Gin palaces were strictly on
one floor only; the public houses may very well have been on two
or even more. The public bar was the principal area with the
taproom becoming a smaller and withering adjunct, surviving
along with the 'vault' as a northern idiom. The 'parlour' or 'bar
parlour' was to develop into the saloon; the bar parlour may have
been a kind of inner sanctum of the landlord where favoured
cronies drank. It would have been a remnant of the old hatch-style
bar, which had been a form of office where the landlord had done
his paperwork and kept his receipts. The bar, in the modern sense,
had opened out and left his original sanctum more exposed. The
bar *per se* had not acquired the straight nature of the gin palace
variety, nor yet embarked upon its gradual evolution and
elongation, but the bar *was* undergoing change.

> Its [the bar's] situation ought to be central in the interior of
> large buildings, commanding views of the front entrance hall
> and back entrance; and as far as practicable, of the foot of the
> staircase and along the principal passages. These objects can
> only be obtained by having the room of some size, almost
> insulated by broad passages and with windows on all sides, or
> having the sides formed by glazed partitions. Considerable
> assistance might be afforded to the barwoman to enable her to
> see in every direction by looking glasses judiciously disposed
> without, and within the bar, as these would reflect places and
> persons which could not otherwise be seen. The situation of the
> bar in a narrow building may be at the end of the entrance hall
> with one side looking towards the yard. In size, the bar need
> never be too large, because, though in small public houses and
> inns, it is used as a shop or storeroom, as well as an office, yet in
> general it is used in the latter capacity only. Here the books of
> the inn are kept or orders given to the cook, the keeper of the
> cellar, the ostler or the stable yard keeper.[4]

This account from 1833 is already a trifle naive, but it is important
to note that the principal function of the bar was supervision
rather than service, and the idea that the two could be made

identical by extending the bar area into all rooms so that all drinks would be handed directly over the counter was still a year or two away.

The development of the bar provides an illustration of how evolution will come up with the optimal solution. In 1840 Brunel was faced with a problem at Swindon railway station. Trains in those days had no buffet cars, heating or toilets, which meant that there was a great demand for the facilities provided by the station during the time the train stopped. At Swindon trains stopped for little more than ten minutes, which raised the problem that, although there were plenty of staff, people would still be trying to get served in the station bar when it was time to reboard the train. As an engineer, Brunel's scientific mind saw that the stopping time of the train was a fixed element in the equation, but the area of the bar was a variable. He concluded that a perfect circle was the most efficient means of dispensing drinks to the most people with the fewest staff, travelling the shortest distance. The nineteenth century saw the gradual elongation of the bar. As the vogue for partitioned pubs increased, the bar became longer still. Finally, in the 1890s, the public-house bar conformed to Brunel's specifications, as the island or stillion bar, examples of which can still be seen in many pubs.

The 1830 act, like virtually all drink legislation passed since AD 975, was a failure. The 1854 Select Committee on Public Houses noted, 'The distinction between beer shop and public houses gave rise to unhealthy competition under which both parties are down to extreme expedients for the attraction of custom.'[5]

The act had the perverse effect of encouraging gin consumption and boosting beer consumption, which had been suffering from the competition from tea as much as gin. No one perhaps had more experience of the vagaries of successive pieces of legislation than the hard-pressed alehouse keepers and publicans, so the Licensed Victuallers Association were perhaps best placed to summarise 1,000 years of drink legislation: 'in all the acts created to restrain the amusements, or, if it pleases to amend the minds of the people, where stupidity is absent, arbitrary rule presides.'[6]

The act also failed in another main purpose – weakening the tie. The brewers were not interested in making beer shops part of their estates; the quantities sold were too insignificant, though increased sales through beer shops provided extra revenue which could be spent on acquiring full licensed premises. Where new pubs arose, or magistrates licensed beer shops as pubs to keep the poorer houses down, there were new opportunities to expand tied estates. Despite the huge increase in retailing premises, the expansion in public house numbers during the 1840s failed to meet demographic changes, and the nineteenth century was consistently a period of a falling pubs-to-people ratio. Per capita beer consumption rose from the middle of the century onwards – perhaps as a result of less adulteration – but the number of public houses did not increase, and post-1877 the absolute number of pubs started to decline, a trend that has persisted to this day.

If all these factors combined to strengthen the hand of the monopolist then the act also failed in its signal aim of breaking the collusive understanding between brewer and bench. The creation of so many beer shops overnight had pulled the rug from underneath the magistrates as far as their efforts at repressive regulation went. Therefore, they were very receptive to any measures that would restore their influence. Barely three years after the act the publicans were again crying 'foul play'.

A popular brewer's ploy was, where a free publican commenced construction of a public house, to use their superior capital to build a rival establishment nearby, complete it first if possible, and so deny an opportunity for free trade. This policy could not have succeeded without the collusion of the magistrates. It had only been a matter of twenty years since magistrates had resolved to favour free houses instead of tied ones. The situation was now turned on its head.

The licensed victuallers will remember that this subject was brought under their notice some time ago, it was a dispute at issue between Mr Curtis, late landlord of the Gun Public House, situated in Union St . . . and the firm of Messrs Truman, Hanbury, Buxton and Co., which resolved itself into an application, on the part of Mr Curtis, to the magistrates to have the licence, which he held as lessee of the Gun Tavern, transferred to premises adjoining, or near those he now occupies. The bench decided in favour of the great brewers and their new tenant obtained a licence, and Mr Curtis was informed that he might renew his application on next licensing day. Mr Curtis, it appears has been virtually ejected by the firm, because he would not sign an agreement to quit, if required at three months' notice, and as his counsel justly observed their propositions 'tended to make him their complete slave'.[7]

There was one significant event in 1830 which was to have a profound effect on the developments in the rest of the century – the death of George IV. England had always been a country where national sobriety was partly influenced by the individual proclivity of the monarch. George IV had been exceedingly intemperate, and was also exceedingly unpopular, but, with the exception of Edward VII, was the last of the rake kings. William IV and Victoria were both temperate and this had two effects. First, it helped accelerate the divorce of the public house and the respectable classes. Second, it meant that future measures were rather better considered and less hastily imposed. The act of 1830 is the last drink-related statute of which it can be said that 'the act was a failure'. Select Committees and Royal Commissions considered various aspects of the drink trade in 1830, 1833, 1834 and 1854, producing recommendations, some of which became law. The next major piece of legislation was not until 1869, but there were additional acts in 1834, 1839, 1840, 1848, 1850 and 1856, which were more level-headed attempts to correct the absurdities and imbalances produced by the 1830 act.

Without going into too much detail, the 1834 act sought to improve the character of the beer shops, raising the licence to three guineas and demanding certificates of character outside London. In 1840 this act was strengthened when the signatories of the certificate, who had to be owners of properties of at least £15 rateable value in London, now had to be £11 owners in other towns and £8 owners in the country. In 1839 the Metropolitan Police Act caused an immediate reduction in drunkenness following vigorous campaigning on the issue of drinking on Sunday. A Select Committee on Drunkenness reported

it appears that trading prevails to a great extent in various districts on Sunday morning, and that such a commencement of the Sabbath tends very much to its general desecration throughout the rest of the day. The state of some of these places is described as 'more like a fair than a market'. So that the neighbourhood is quiet upon any other day of the week compared with Sunday. The people who frequent these shops and market are chiefly the improvident who generally speaking might have made their marketing to greater advantage on Saturday evening . . . a higher price is paid for commodities paid on a Sunday, and that they are also generally of inferior quality.[8]

Sunday, while for some a day of rest, worship and divine contemplation, was for the masses a day of divine debauchery, which had acquired traditional status in the minds of the people. The London markets were the principal locations of Sunday drunkenness. Earlier attempts in the 1830s to suppress the drink trade on Sunday in Lambeth had met with outright defiance. Drink shops and stalls placarded themselves with signs declaring 'This shop will be open on Sunday as usual', 'No Jesuits', or 'No Religious Persecution'.

The anomaly was that the law only forbade people from drinking during divine service. People on their way to church were frequently incommoded and abused by the recently ejected gin-shop revellers. A Mr C. Wilson gave evidence to the 1833 Commons Select Committee.

It would be impossible for myself and my family to attend Church in the Broadway. I have attempted to take my family there; I have six children, and it is not safe for their persons to approach the church, for at eleven in the morning the public houses are disgorged of their contents, and the great proportion of the people who come out of them are in a state of beastly intoxication; mechanics, labourers, prostitutes and the rest, who are quarrelling and sometimes fighting and talking in a most obscene manner, and it is impossible to pass on the foot pavement for the obstruction caused by their numbers, in addition to the obscene language . . . I have seen public houses discharge men and women on a Sunday morning when, being unable to walk they have been brought out and laid on the road.[9]

The 1839 act closed the public houses in London between midnight Saturday and noon Sunday, as well as prohibiting the sale of spirits to the under sixteens in all licensed premises within a

fifteen mile radius of Charing Cross. The act was immediately
successful in reducing public drunkenness. Though often ignored it
was ignored prudently, and was extended to the rest of the country
in 1848.

Sunday closing was extended in 1854 between 2.30 p.m. and
6 p.m. with 10 p.m. final closing, with the traditional waiver for
bona fide travellers, while the following year the act was relaxed to
the more realistic 3–5 p.m. afternoon closing with 11 p.m. final
closing. This act, too, was successful and led to an almost
immediate reduction in gin consumption of approximately four
million gallons per annum. The 1830 act had far-reaching effects.
It prompted new areas of pub development, and new heights of
hostility towards public houses. It also radically changed the
physical appearance of public houses. All three trends were to
dominate the middle decades of the century.

An Old Norfolk Gentleman

Chapter 15

THE MID-VICTORIAN ERA

That flows from the empoison'd still,
Thither the fiend loves to repair,
And Death, oft too, attends him there
Who, in his never ceasing rounds,
The still-man aids as he compounds
Each mixture that's in daily strife
With Health, with Honour and with life.
The Dram shop is the spot that yields
More various ills than all the fields,
Where grow the vices that disgrace
Th' existence of the human race.
The town with beggars it supplies,
And almost fills th'Infirmeries,
Gives half their inmates to the jails,
And multiplies the hangman's vails,
Question the sturdy Labr'er, why
He wears the rags of poverty?
Wherefore his well paid, daily task
Denies the Bread his Children ask?
It is the Dram's alluring cup
That swallows all his earnings up.
Behold the squallid Mother's breast
By the faint, sickly infant prest,
That ne'er the milk of Nature gives:
Instead, the suckling's lip receives
The sad infusion, which at length,
Destroys its puny, struggling strength;

Till life its very aid denies
And the poor, shrivelled pigmy dies.
'The English Dance of Death', William Combe (1816)

The mid-Victorian era was one of a rapid divergence and expansion in recreational opportunities, the vast majority of which were for the comfortably well to do. The public house was being gradually denuded of its traditional social and recreational functions, and where they detracted from the serious business of liquor consumption the brewers were not sorry to see them go. Naturally the fewer traditional functions there were associated with the public house, the more odious it became in the eyes of the prohibitionists, and it was not until the end of the century that the brewers realised that they must reverse the process and relocate the public house in the mainstream of responsible community life or lose to the temperance lobby.

In other respects the public house was powerless to defend itself against change. Whereas coaching had sustained the inns, the railways sustained little. Very early stations had pub names, since it was not foreseen that railway travel would be radically different from coaching travel. Before 1845 Forest Hill station, south London, was the Dartmouth Arms, and Norwood Junction was the Jolly Sailor. Any large town boasted a Railway Hotel and this was indeed a hotel rather than an inn and the premises which grew up in the wake of the railways were clearly hotels rather than 'inns'. The nature of rail travel and the new class distinction meant that there was very little interaction between the railway hotels and nearby premises, unlike the old coaching inns, which had often clustered together to form a kind of sprawling terminus. If the railway hotel proved to be the starting point for a tram or omnibus, this also was of no benefit to public houses.

As mentioned, part of the strength of the gin palace trade was its 'passing' nature. In the days before public transport everyone likely to go into licensed premises was a pedestrian. Those public houses that happened to be the omnibus terminus did very well. The Yorkshire Stingo was the departure point for the very first omnibus route in 1829 from the Marylebone Road. Famous termini included the Royal Oak, the Monster at Pimlico and the Adelaide at Chalk Farm. The Plough at Clapham is still in existence (though now a Goose and Granite), as is the Bricklayers' Arms at Bermondsey.

The Elephant and Castle, the Angel, Nag's Head and Swiss Cottage all gave their names to areas of London, while elsewhere the same thing happened at Nelson, Lancashire which – previously being called Marsden – took its name from the Lord Nelson pub.

If the termini pubs did well, those along the route did not. One Select Committee heard that, 'we have known the establishment of a coach or omnibus in some road abolish public houses along its line.' There was a decline in riverside pubs in the nineteenth century as Thames traffic declined in volume above the Pool of London, and the distribution of London public houses took on a distinct bias towards the north/south and east/west axes with the relative densities of pubs in different areas showing that they were primarily catering for a mobile working-class population engaged in an increasing amount of commuting rather than a static wealthy population.

This hypothesis is supported by contrasting wealthy areas where the rich lived and areas where the rich lived but large numbers of poor came to work. In 1896 St James had one public house for every 116 head of population. In Edmonton the ratio was 1:727. Outside London William Hoyle deduced in 1877 that the greater density of pubs in Manchester than in Bolton was a result of the greater number of people working outside in the streets in Manchester. Pubs were very much a facet of the life of the street, hence the number of entrances found in pubs and the preference for corner locations. The advance of urban public transport materially affected the activities going on in streets and reduced the numbers of hawkers, porters, costermongers, stallholders and tinkers just as it reduced the numbers of pedestrians.

In London and other cities, pub location was determined by other factors than mere class and transport. In areas like Bloomsbury and Pimlico – aristocratic estates – there were conscious efforts to exclude pubs. The borders of the temperance-supporting Duke of Bedford's Bloomsbury estate can still be determined today by anyone walking around the streets to the east of the Tottenham Court Road, marking the surviving pubs on a map. The domestic servants on the estate provided an excellent market to support a number of pubs on the perimeter of the estate in the same way that the requirements of the cellars of the houses on the estate meant that there was a healthy band of wine shops rubbing shoulders with the pubs on the periphery.

Domestic servants were a traditionally large and identifiable sector of public-house custom throughout the eighteenth and nineteenth centuries. Engaged in an occupation where saving was fairly easy, many domestic servants made the transition to publican, especially during the early decades of the nineteenth century. In other estates, such as the Grosvenor estate in Belgravia, the architect Thomas Cubitt (who also worked for the Duke of Bedford) ensured that the pubs needed to serve the domestic staff were discreetly tucked away in mews locations such as the Star and the Grenadier, both just behind Belgravia Square. In other parts of Belgravia, as well as parts of Mayfair, Camden and Notting Hill, the intention was to make the pubs blend in with the surrounding terraces and so endow them with a particular character. In these circumstances the positive decisions of the estate owner or architect had a definite impact on the incidence of public houses, and elsewhere small developers may only have built one side of a street of terraced houses or even one half of one side of a street. This building pattern ensures the characteristic pub every 200 yards described in the last chapter. As the century progressed, therefore, the factors determining public house incidence and density were becoming more complex and were gradually shifting as the social mores of the day shifted. Superimposed upon this pattern were the policies, often fairly arbitrary, of the magistrates.

The next major institution to come out of the public house was the music hall. A gradual innovation of the 1830s was a 'saloon'. The pub had always been the venue for a singsong, conjuring tricks, dancing, juggling and all forms of popular entertainment. With the gradual process of specialisation of various rooms in the public house for different purposes, it was only natural that 'entertainment' should also evolve its own area. Just as pubs had billiard rooms and club rooms, so they developed new rooms – saloons – where entertainments were laid on. With the demarcation of a space for a specific purpose it became possible to charge admission to the area or charge a different rate for drinks and food served there.

What often started up as a back room soon became sufficiently popular to warrant additions and extensions, with the result that an increasing number of purpose-built rooms meant that greater variety was possible. This helped to make the entertainments ever more popular, and various houses specialised in different forms of entertainment. Some did plays and small operatic revues, others concentrated on variety, others on music. Thus the music hall was born. Yet other premises decided to move slightly more upmarket and styled themselves 'song and supper rooms' where patrons could eat as well as drink while watching the entertainment.

The most famous of these saloons was the 'Grecian Saloon' of the Eagle in the City Road of 'Pop Goes the Weasel' fame. The Eagle's rooms were very grand indeed and catered for a middle-class clientele. More in tune with working-class entertainment would have been premises such as the 'Bower Street Tavern' attached to the Duke's Arms in Staggate Street, Lambeth, which managed to survive until 1877. Lambeth had more than its fair share of music halls, and the Kennington Road was the fashionable address of famous music hall stars. Charlie Chaplin recalled watching performers alight from their coaches and enter the Horns, the White Hart, and the Hercules public houses after their performances for after-hours relaxation.

The music hall was no sooner born out of the saloons than it was rudely separated from them. The government decided that drinking and the passive enjoyment of organised entertainment were incompatible, and the Licensing Act of 1843 ruled that saloons had to register as theatres if they wished to provide spectacles – in which case they were prohibited from providing drink in the auditorium. The majority of the saloons went solo and set up as theatres and music halls, and no doubt the public house now adjoining did very well on pre- and post-performance trade. By 1866 there were some twenty-three major music halls in central London. By 1890 there were thirty-five principal halls with many smaller venues, and outside London music halls numbered several hundred. Their names were more redolent of theatres and coffee houses than pubs.

The evolution from saloon to music hall entailed a degree of upmarket movement and many of the working-class saloon patrons would have soon found themselves priced out of some, though not all, of these establishments. Some theatres, like the Royal Victoria (now the Old Vic), had exclusively working-class audiences.

The Industrial Revolution had managed to sustain itself by providing little more than subsistence for the millions of workers

who were as so much grist to its mill. Their spiritual well-being
was not a matter of great concern to the administrations of the
time. They were more concerned lest they became unruly. The
alehouse and public house were the means by which the labouring
classes – agricultural and urban – joined among themselves to find
sociability, assistance and entertainment. The alternatives that
existed when provided by municipalities or philanthropists such as
Tate and Carnegie – the public libraries and the Mechanics'
Institutes – had the condescending rider of education and self-
improvement. They were, of course, extremely popular. Many
thousands used them as a means of escaping from the slums, but
they were not institutions for relaxation and leisure.

Nor was it a case that any powerful or vocal lobby was arguing
that things should be otherwise. Indeed, the opposite was the case.
Bodies such as the Society for the Prevention of Mendicity were
only too happy to bring proceedings against publicans for running
a disorderly house. In London at the time, a disorderly house was
defined as any place within twenty miles of Charing Cross
permitting singing, dancing or the unlicensed performance of
music.

It was no small wonder that 'the sovereign people were in a
beastly state'; they were subject to the harsh double standards at
which the Victorians excelled. As the middle classes followed the
upper classes away from the public house, they took with them
that which they liked and denied those same pleasures to those
who remained. As the wealthy decamped elsewhere, specialist
institutions catered for their needs. Casinos became fashionable,
but it took a court case and judicial ruling in 1854 before it was
decided that the playing of dominoes in a pub was not a criminal
offence. Even in the 1830s magistrates were still condemning
outdoor pursuits, especially football.

With the casinos and hotels came the restaurants and cafés. The
Café Royal opened in 1863, Kettner's in 1867 and Pagani's in
1871. These were the grandest, but many others followed of more
modest proportions. They tended to eclipse the traditional chop
shops and ordinaries and changed the nature of eating out, which
became more recreational. When, however, the question of
licensing the ordinaries arose, there was much outcry and a lot of
effort was expended to ensure that they would not be properly
licensed.

In the field of politics one expects to find double standards, and so naturally they are not confined to the Victorians. Paranoia that the alehouses and public houses were potential cauldrons of political ferment was nothing new' and – given the history of the eighteenth century and fears of Jacobites, French revolutionary ideas, Mughouses, October Clubs and Gordon Riots – not entirely unjustified. This unease continued into the nineteenth century. The combination laws had been repealed in 1824, and now with working men free to meet more or less openly it must have appeared that unions were crawling out of the very woodwork of the public houses. Occasionally this paranoia reached ludicrous heights. Just as the rebellion of Jack Cade in 1450 was blamed upon the evil effects of the hop, certain Tories tried to blame the agricultural incendiarism of the Swing Riots on the Beer Act. There was a certain irony in this, for it was the introduction of threshing machines that further threatened the depressed nature of the agricultural labourers, and barley mows were frequent targets of the incendiarists.

> The neighbours thought all was not right
> Scarcely one with him ventured to parley,
> And Captain Swing came out in the night,
> And Burnt all his beans and his barley.

The political threat from the public houses was not from the countryside, however, but the town, and in the decades of the first half of the century it was Chartism. The public houses had been crucial for the survival of the Whig opposition during the long Tory ascendancy of 1807–30, yet it was a Whig government that threatened publicans with suppression in 1839 should they let their rooms for meetings of Chartists. The old practice of magistrates refusing licences to landlords of known radical or awkward sympathies still continued and was regarded as an effective and important means of facilitating canvassing. With the passage of the 1832 Reform Act, the role of the public houses took on extra significance with the enfranchisement of the forty shilling householder. This posed a problem, as the pubs were now the preserve of the disenfranchised and poorer electorate. In deserting the alehouse the ruling classes had no idea of what was being discussed in them, and during the age that saw the birth of socialism this was vitally important. George Eliot's *Felix Holt* (1866) describes how the Reform Act changed the relationship between public house and hustings. '"Ay, that's sin the Reform," said a big, red-whiskered man, called Dredge. "That's brought the 'lections and the drink into these parts; for afore that, it was all kep up the Lord knows wheer."'

Anthony Trollope in *Phineas Redeux* (1874) draws attention to the widespread nature of this form of corruption. 'Members of the House, as individuals, knew very well what had taken place at their own elections, and were aware of the cheques which they had drawn. Public houses had been kept open as a matter of course.' What made the public houses suspect was the localised nature of productive labour. Trades were still highly concentrated in definite areas of towns or in villages, so pubs were often frequented by people of common occupations. This was a bonus for the fledgling unions, and as a result some trades became notorious for their political activities. The early Chartists had come from the skilled, articulate working and artisan classes, as did the early socialists. Printers were known for their political literacy, while at least one other group in London, the costers, had their headquarters at the Roebuck, Holborn, which was popularly known as the House of Lords since the costers were known to be republicans, socialists and 'Chartists to a man'. The politically aware Street Mechanics, Labourers and Hawkers Association met at the Lamb, Holborn; the National Union of the Working Class met at the Argyll Arms, Oxford Street, while the London Working Men's Association first met in February 1837 at the Crown and Anchor in the Strand.

The proximate relationship between pubs and trades had other side effects apart from political organisation. Among skilled labour certain pubs became known as places to find work and, depending upon your trade, a certain pub in the town would act as a hiring fair in the same way as drovers and merchants knew the inn in a town where they could carry out their trade. The pub as labour exchange would appear to have been restricted to fairly skilled occupations, to people who in days gone by would have been called 'journeymen'. For the unskilled worker the association between pub and pay was not always so advantageous.

Your great master manufacturer is too great a man to attend to the morals and comfort of the lower orders in his employ; all he

wants from them is their labour; and having made his bargain
with them as to the price of that labour, he deputes a foreman
to see they do their stipulated labour, and do pay them their
wages. The foreman being a shrewd and clever tradesman, like
his master, sees no reason why he also should not turn the lower
orders to some account; and as the master leaves him no chance
of getting anything out of their labour, he contrives to screw
something out of their relaxation, and this is the way he goes
about it: he contracts with a neighbouring publican to supply
them daily, and every day with beer, gin, tobacco etc. He
undertaking to pay the score upon condition of receiving a
percentage thereon. By this contrivance the men can 'drink and
drive care away' all week; and by doing so oblige the foreman –
which is much; and the foreman, when Saturday night comes,
in order that they oblige him more, keeps the account open, and
the spigot running until the first or second hour of Sunday
morning. And this admirable contrivance for the accumulation
of capital is called the pay table.[1]

The pay table was without doubt a pernicious practice in no way
justifiable on grounds of convenience or custom. Paying of wages
in a pub on a Friday or Saturday night was merely a device for
clawing back as much of the money as possible, and only the
publican and the foreman benefited. Saturday night was also
the night when most women were to be found in public houses.
Most of them wanted to get their hands on their menfolk's wages
before they managed to drink it all – a not uncommon practice.
Others wanted to assist in this method of its disposal, while yet
others came to join their husbands before adjourning to the Sunday
markets. The pay table was then in part responsible for the riotous
nature of Sundays, and also for some of the domestic violence
which was endemic in Victorian society when drunk and penniless
husbands confronted hungry and reproachful wives. Domestic
murder flowing from drink was common, as shall be seen.

Although the Sunday markets were much reformed by the 1854
act that introduced Sunday closing, a degree of indignation was
felt among those enlightened temperance reformers who realised
the repression of the poor was an insufficient remedy against
drunkenness in itself without the gainful occupation of the poor.
The public houses of the poor were precluded from opening

on Sunday, but the clubs, lounges and gaming rooms of the rich were more popular on Sunday than at other times of the week, as the upper classes sought to escape the stultifying boredom of a Victorian Sunday. Measures like the Lord's Day Observance Bill of 1833 was a case in point, resented for its attempts to curb the pleasures of all except the rich.

Indignation was very much the stock-in-trade of the temperance movement. The poor were not unduly perturbed by the proscription of their traditional Sunday recreations. They had two very successful remedies to the problem of Sunday closing. In the first case they ignored it. In the second instance they would head out of London and enjoy themselves at some of the more notorious country pubs.

That which made this part of Battersea Fields so notorious was the gaming, sporting and pleasure grounds at the Red House and Balloon public houses and Sunday Fairs, held throughout the Summer months. These have been the resort of hundreds and thousands, from royalty and nobility down to the poorest pauper and the meanest beggar. And surely if there was a place out of hell that surpassed Sodom and Gomorrah in ungodliness and abomination this was it. Here the worst men and vilest of the human race seemed to try to outvie each other in wicked deeds. I have gone to this sad spot on the afternoon and evening of the Lord's Day when there have been from 60 to 120 horses and donkeys racing, foot racing, walking matches, flying boats, flying horses, roundabouts, theatres, comic actors, shameless dancers, conjurors, fortune tellers, gamblers of every description, drinking booths, stills, hawkers and vendors of all kinds of articles.[2]

If the middle classes and petty bourgeoisie spurned such evils as donkey racing, the rich did not. In the words of Lord Randolph Churchill; 'The aristocracy and the working class are united in the indissoluble bonds of a common immorality.'[3]

This was, however, becoming ever less true, and the cockpit or the ringside of the bare knuckle fights were not as classless as they had once been. The gradual abandonment of the pub, starting in the late eighteenth century, by the upper and then middle classes has been repeatedly stressed. Like all things associated with the pub, such a statement requires qualification. The picture painted during the last two chapters is of a fairly dissolute scene, and while it is true that the grandest gin palaces were in the less well-off areas and would have had an overwhelmingly working-class clientele, that is not to say that there were not grand premises elsewhere and that they did not retain a genteel or even aristocratic clientele.

The gradual influence of the restaurants inspired many public houses to go upmarket. The remnants of taverns that survived enjoyed a brief renaissance, becoming 'smart rendezvous with counters, glasses and pretty girls coquettishly dressed'. By the 1850s taverns were virtually high-class chop-houses. The largest were the London in Bishopsgate; the Tory Crown and Anchor in the Strand and the Thatched House in St James Street. Dr Johnson's Tavern in Bolt Court and the Mitre in Fleet Street were specifically chop-houses trading on the excellence of a particular dish. In such an establishment a meal of mockturtle soup, roast or boiled beef, pork or mutton pudding, cheese and a pint of porter would cost around 2s. Another effect of the restaurants and cafés was to open up opportunities for women once more by providing a greater variety of premises where it was considered respectable for them to appear. Previously they had been confined to the private rooms in taverns. Middle-class women were very deprived in this respect. Poorer women were frequent visitors to the gin palaces, if not so much the pubs, and even by the turn of the twentieth century (when female drinking was frowned on in all classes) it was common for pubs to have discreet side doors into the parlour or snug where women could enter and leave without attracting attention.

For better-off women there were few opportunities to indulge in the relaxations of their menfolk. There were, however, luncheon bars.

The West End luncheon bars have, I think, made a considerable improvement of late years. They cannot indeed cook a mutton chop or a beefsteak. That interesting branch of the fine arts has never flourished west of Temple Bar. But they can do most other things very well. You can take ladies with you to Verrey's in Regent St and they will take their carriages and do their own very satisfactory luncheons in Oxford St elsewhere. I think Spiers and Pond deserve well of the community for the good luncheon purposes to which they have applied their Australian expertise. . . . At the Corner of Burlington St the Messrs Blanchard have one of the best possible luncheon bars, you stand . . . but the system is excellent and the viands are good and you may make any number of observations, if you are so inclined, on life and character.[4]

Contemporary illustrations of the luncheon bars demonstrate that luncheon was not necessarily the primary objective of those crowding their portals. There appear frequently to have been more customers than could be seated to eat, and many were seemingly happy drinking at the bar.

There were, however, some proper public houses where one would have been expected to eat – indeed to eat would have been the principal reason for going, aside from the desire to see which celebrities happened to be there also. If it is said that these public houses were not convenient for the centre of London, one might deduce, then, that people went there to eat something in particular. If one was told that something in particular was whitebait, one might also guess that what was being referred to were the famous Greenwich riverside pubs. The Trafalgar is still there but, sadly, its slightly more famous cousin – the Ship – is not, having closed in 1908, while the third of the Greenwich taverns, the Crown and Sceptre, closed in 1900. Indeed, the Trafalgar itself was closed from 1915 to 1965.

The Ship was opened in 1857 when Greenwich diners were already fashionable, an earlier inn of the same name having been pulled down in 1846. Its rooms were thronged with the great men of the day. Once a year on or near Trinity Sunday, the senior members of Parliament would board rival barges and sail down the Thames from Westminster to dine at these famous weatherboard-fronted taverns with their sweeping balconies where one might digest one's meal and contemplate the serenity and splendour of the traffic on the Thames. In these times the Tories dined at the Ship and the Liberals at the Trafalgar, and the sheer volume of traffic from the four corners of the globe passing to and from the docklands must have filled these powerful men with a sense of their own importance. The following description is taken from 1863. Although the pub is called the Vessel, contemporary readers would have had no trouble in identifying the Ship.

> From the First of April to the 30th September. Pleasure's business is in full swing here, and never allows the smallest relaxation. With a view to such business, and nothing else the vessel was built, on the heading of its bills it calls itself an Hotel, but . . . you will never find rows of boots . . . standing outside its chamber doors, nor regiments of bed candlesticks on its hall table; no boots lurking up its stairs at the chilly hours of the morning to call anyone who is going by the first train, nor, too, has such a thing as a 'breakfast order' ever been heard within its capacious walls. From its cellar to its attic the Vessel means dinner, and nothing but dinner. On its ground floor are its hall, a lavatory, and the coffee room with its numbered tables and its cheery lookout on the river. On the first floor are the large rooms used for city companies' testimonial dinners, and such like, at which between 200 and 300 guests often sit down simultaneously; above are the smaller rooms used for private parties.[5]

It has been the intention in this chapter to cover a wide range of subjects to show the state of affairs during the middle decades of the century. However, the diversity present at the time makes description of the characteristics of the public house problematic. It was true that the middle classes patronised public houses less, but in 1865 the Reform League was still meeting in pubs, as was Birmingham's Sunday Evening Debating Society in 1870 and the Ancient Order of Cogers.

It is true that in the 1870s Ruskin could complain that, 'There is scarcely a public house near the Crystal Palace but sells its gin and bitters under pseudo-Victorian capitals copied from the Church of the Madonna of Health.'[6] But for every one of these there was a rude beer shop tucked down a dark alley where the ornamentation was almost as rude as its alehouse parent of a hundred years previously. It is true that credit continued to be the publicans' plague, and that many pubs and beer shops doubled up as pawnbrokers, but there were also houses of splendid proportions and laudable pretensions. The East London Etymological Society convened at the Bell in the Mile End Road, not a nice part of London at that time, while on the same road the Mackerel was spacious enough to house 20,000 stuffed animals displayed in cases. Today's pubs pale into insignificance by comparison. The cases of beautiful butterflies and fearsomely large beetles at the World's End in Camden could not even hold a candle to the Mackerel, while the Prince of Wales on Clapham Pavement, with its floor to ceiling bric-a-brac and memorabilia, has nothing to rival the collection at the Edinburgh Castle, Mornington Crescent, which – when audited on the landlord's death in 1908 included a two-bodied pig, a Benin bronze, a marble head of the Emperor Justinian, the alleged spear with which General Gordon was killed at Khartoum, the bugle which allegedly sounded the Charge of the Light Brigade, two pictures by Ruskin, three great auk eggs and 80,000 butterflies and moths, among other things.

The famous maps of Charles Booth show how in Victorian England the rich and poor lived almost on top of each other. The street hawker would walk past the off licence – a product of the 1834 act – where the well-to-do purchased their wine, on his way to the beer shops, while the professional man might pass a gin palace on the end of an alley where stood a beer shop, as he strode off to the wine merchants. Indeed, there is a stronger correlation between the density of wine shops and wealth and beer shops and poverty than there is between the density of pubs and the density of street traffic. This should not be surprising. With the exception of areas of Bloomsbury, pubs were ubiquitous and were of infinite variety, from the relatively rare Gothic style to the Italian Renaissance fashion, from small to big, from disreputable to respectable. Finally, we are approaching a period where the modern pub is almost in sight. However it was, too, almost the time when the temperance movement was at its height and when the pub grew in stature and appearance. Then, at the end of the century, after a gleaming and golden age in the 1880s and 1890s, the pub suddenly collapsed as an institution. It was clear that it would never be the same again.

Chapter 16

TEMPERANCE, INTOLERANCE AND ABSURDITY

Britannia this upas tree bought of Mynheer
Renamed it through Holland and planted it here.
'Tis now stock plant of the genus wolf's bane,
And one of them blossoms in Marylebone lane.

The House that surrounds it stands in the first row,
Two doors at right angles swing open below,
And the Children of misery daily steal in,
And the poison they draw they denominate – GIN.

There enter the prude and the reprobate boy,
The mother of grief and the daughter of joy,
The serving-maid slim, and the serving man stout,
They quickly steal in and they slowly reel out.

'The Upas of Marylebone', James Smith

Let me set downe this for my general proposition. That all
Droonkards are Beastes. (1576)

Consider also how much this beastly sin of drunkenness doth
debauch, defile, deform the body of man which should be the
Temple of the Holy Ghost. (1677)

Now, intemperance in itself is nothing less than the voluntary,
and entire subjection of the rational and moral part of man to
his animal nature. (1838)

Anti-drinking campaigners had been around for hundreds of years,
and while they became most vocal and influential during the

nineteenth century, in truth all they had to say had already been said to death even before the start of the seventeenth century. Drunkenness was a 'beastly', animal state, an abnegation of reason and rationality. Such was the common argument of the temperance agitator. 'O, the folly and madness of sin! It is a continual acting against reason, a treasuring up of wrath with the God of all power, a providing for the society of Devils and damned fools, who will be cursing their maker and one another to all eternity.' (1633)

The argument was always consistent; drunkenness was beastly, it resulted in abandonment of reason, would lead to a destruction of reputation, credit and estate – usually in that order – which would result in moral depravity and, most importantly, the damnation of the eternal soul.

> What sin is so odious that a drunkard in his cups will refuse to do, when the drink is in and the wit is out, and when he is heated in his Drink, he is pot-valiant, and will prove the Devil's champion, and undertake any enterprise; we have known, *or hear it at least* when in drink some have killed their Fathers and Mothers, ravished their Sisters, murdered their best friend and nearest relation. (1677)

Characteristically, the temperance tract contained innumerable Biblical references, examples and justifications, exclusively from the Old Testament, which may have looked impressive on paper, but counted for nothing by way of argument, given the religious indifference of those to whom the tracts were seemingly addressed. More to the point is the question, to whom were the tracts actually addressed? A brief perusal of many of them makes it apparent that a large proportion of temperance literature was for consumption by the converted. This led to the unhappy discovery that preaching to the converted requires a little more ingenuity than simply repeating the same homilies to the unconverted and unimpressed. In order to keep the good word interesting, wholesome and uplifting, some absurd *non-sequiturs* and contortions of logic were resorted to.

> Men who are good singers are very apt to become drunkards, and, in truth, most of them are so, more or less, especially if they have naturally much joviality or worth of temperament. (1829)

By the last grant of Providence to man his life is 120 years, and that, where disease arising from other causes does not shorten it, the reason why do few attain to that age is to be found in the excessive stimulation to which the mass of the community are continually subject. (1838)

The foundation of the argument, which was actually submitted as evidence to the 1834 Select Committee on Drunkenness by a doctor, no less, was that Abraham lived to 175 years of age, Isaac and Ishmael to 180 and 137 respectively, Jacob to 147 and Joseph a mere 110.

One of the most popular temperance *non-sequiturs* went as follows.

Six penny worth of barley is the utmost quantity which is used in the brewing of a gallon of beer, which costs the consumer two shillings; out of this small quantity at least three-quarters must necessarily be lost in the various processes of making, of brewing and separating the sugar from the grain, of fermenting etc. So that from two shillings not more nutritious matter can be obtained than is worth three halfpence. (1838)

To most people who drank beer daily as a matter of course and whose ancestors had done likewise for almost 1,000 years, such 'facts' were not worth repeating. To take them as justification for repudiating alcohol and embracing abstinence was cause for open-mouthed astonishment. It is not surprising, therefore, to learn that, in the early days of organised temperance campaigning, the arrival of a temperance advocate or preacher in a town was sufficient cause for the populace to turn out and gawp in amazement at such a peculiar and unnatural creature.

The original author of the Malt Liquor Lecture, as the above homily was known once it had entered the temperance canon, was Joseph Livesey, a cheese seller from Preston and the founder of English Temperance. 'Two shillings worth of barley gives you two shillings worth of food, but two shillings worth of ale gives you one pennyworth of food. Ale is simply the juice of the pump, coloured, flavoured and fired.'[1] Livesey's favourite trick was, at this point in his sermonising, to ignite the spirit distilled from a quart of ale for the edification of his audiences.

Organised temperance societies were an American idea; societies springing up in Saratoga, New York, in 1808 and Massachusetts in 1813. By 1818 they had crossed the Atlantic as far as Skibbereen, Ireland, making their first appearance in England in Liverpool where ships' captains from the US used to distribute temperance tracts. By 1830 temperance societies in Ulster, Lancashire and Yorkshire could boast 23,000 paying members, their own newspaper – the *Temperance Societies Record* – and 60,000 registered abstainers. The following year saw the foundation of the British and Foreign Temperance Society with the Bishop of London and Archbishop Sumner as respective president and vice-president, and of which Queen Victoria became patron, upon her accession.

However, things were not always easy in the early days. Enthused by the Americans example, one John Finch established libraries and schools for the dockers of Liverpool, who responded in typical fashion. They took the benches out of the schools and swapped them for beer in the pubs. As is so often the case in history, it required the talents of one man to really galvanise the whole movement. The temperance movement over the years had several powerful and dedicated missionaries, some of whom became national celebrities. The most famous of these was Father Theobald Mathew, from Cork, whose missionary zeal was such that in 1841 the numbers of abstainers was said to be 4,647,000. The Irish population today is only 5,090,000. The Apostle of Temperance, as Father Mathew was known, worked mostly in Ireland and the US. Under Father Mathew's guidance 20,000 took the pledge in one day at Nenagh, and in Galway 100,000 took the pledge over a two-day meeting. When Father Mathew came to London a crowd of some 20,000 people met him at Blackheath. His death in 1856 was an occasion of national mourning and 60,000 people attended his funeral.

In England Father Mathew's mantle was worn by Joseph Livesey. Impressed by the efforts of Finch, Livesey founded the Preston Temperance Society in March 1833. Within six months Livesey had instituted the idea of 'the pledge' and a former drunkard reformed by Livesey, one Dicky Turner, himself a famous missionary, coined the term 'teetotal', almost as a spoonerism due to the stammer he had. The term caught on overnight as it identified those campaigners – initially drawn from the ranks of the radically minded (Chartists, socialists and the educated

working class) – who refused to draw any distinction between beer
and gin. They detested alcohol in whatever form, and argued that
moderation was no substitute for abstinence.

Among the London 'moderates', Livesey and his firebrands were
regarded as 'Lancashire fanatics', but the advocates of moderation
lacked the zeal of the nonconformist northerners, and many
'moderates' gave up the temperance movement altogether. There
were internecine splits and feuds, and although the vanquishing of
the moderate tendency took many years to accomplish, it is
enough to say that the 'moderates' left the field of combat and
retired to take no further major part in the campaign.

The history of the temperance movement is a chequered one.
It certainly managed to make drink a political issue in a way it
had never been before, but the lasting effect of that was not so
much a long term reduction in alcohol consumption as long
term damage to the Liberal Party. Temperance campaigners had
their successes: the 1839 Metropolitan Police Act, the 1848
Sunday opening laws, the prohibition of alcohol from the 1851
Great Exhibition. However, campaigners also suffered from
insensitivity to others and the class nature of English society. In
1855, when the bill to ban all Sunday trading was being debated,
crowds booed pro-bill MPs and bishops as they drove out on
Sundays. Large numbers gathered weekly in Hyde Park to see
how the aristocracy spent their Sundays. The passage of the bill
caused rioting, and people out driving were liable to be pelted
with earth and stones by the angry mobs.

The temperance movement also tended to wash their laundry in
public, much to the amusement of their enemies. The UK Alliance
for the Suppression of the Traffic in All Intoxicating Liquors came
in for criticism by stricter temperance bodies, in 1853, when it
advocated domestic production and consumption but not retail.
Their critics stung them with the palpable charge that they would
'close down the beer shops but not their own cellars'.

Temperance supporters tended to be tactless, as is the way of
people blinded by the certainty of their convictions. In the west
country the grubbing up of cider-apples trees caused much
resentment, and when in Cirencester a wealthy local convert to
teetotalism bought up the Hole-in-the-Wall public house and razed
it to the ground in order to build a temperance hall in its place, the
floor of which was made from smashed beer vats, that smacked too

much of rubbing people's noses in the dirt. Acts of seeming callousness were highly provoking to people for whom drink was either an important part of life or a ready means to escape the misery of their situation, and physical attacks on teetotallers were not unknown as a result.

Several of their number suffered from astounding naiveté, and so attracted ridicule. In 1834, when the report of the Select Committee on Drunkenness was published, its chairman, Buckingham, included several ludicrous proposals, not least of which was the complete abolition of gin palaces. The report was literally laughed out of the House and the newspapers had a field day, many printing the recommendations as a matter of universal hilarity, with the earnest entreaty that they should be repeated at regular intervals in order to keep the nation happy.

Perhaps their greatest weakness was that with their religious overtones and their strait-laced, po-faced manner they failed to bridge the gulf between themselves and those they were trying to save. This is not to say they were without success. The temperance societies were able to boast memberships of tens and hundreds of thousands, and their youth movement, the Jesuitical 'Band of Hope' founded in 1847, was a self-sustaining organisation with its own newspaper. As a movement, however, it could never decide on a social policy to underpin its stated aim of the complete prohibition of all alcoholic beverages.

At different times several of its members showed a willingness to provide an alternative to the public house. In 1836 the first temperance hotel was founded, by 1865 there were some 200. However, the movement seemed unable to make a success of them. There was no shortage of willpower, but experience seemed to be lacking. The only people they could get to run such places were either failed innkeepers, who could not be trusted not to sell drink on the premises illicitly, or reformed drunkards, eager to show their devotion to the cause, but not necessarily able to show much business aptitude. On the whole, the temperance hotels were of poor standard and reflected badly on the movement, confirming in many minds the popular prejudice that 'teetotalism' was a scheme got up by the masters to see how little working men could live on. One American visitor to a London temperance hotel refused to eat a steak served there, on the grounds that 'it was an infringement of Goodyear's patent for India rubber'.

Those who argued, in 1829, that, 'it would be well if the liquor vended to the poor possessed the qualities furnished by the contraband dealer, but instead of this, it is usually a vile compound of everything spurious and pestilent,' ran up against those, who since their aim was absolute prohibition, were indifferent to the state of that which was served up in the meantime. Yet others opposed reform of public houses in case they became less objectionable. This would, of course, make it harder for them to produce such statements as, 'the return of the UK Temperance and General Provident Institution shows the lives of abstainers to be 26½ per cent better than those of moderate drinkers.'[2]

Other temperance voices recognised the world for what it was.

If a man is resolved to continue a drunkard it may be proper to mention in what manner he can do so with least risk to himself. . . . One of the principal rules to be observed, not only by him – is never to take in inebriating spirit upon an empty stomach. . . . In addition drunkards should shun raw spirits, which more rapidly bring a disease of the stomach. (1829)

Such sound advice ran the risk of bringing down the wrath of those who would rather have a drunkard than a moderate drinker, or those who sought to impress by means of statistical nonsense.

If the 30,000,000 barrels of beer were emptied, they would fill a river 300 miles long, 21 feet wide and 5 feet deep, and if this river were pumped dry, it would take a pump throwing 100 gallons per minute, running day and night 20 years to empty, and yet this beer was all swallowed by the people of Great Britain last year.[3]

Some temperance tactics were plain silly. One painstaking and learned treatise demonstrating that alcohol was a disgusting poison by virtue of the poor condition of cabbages raised on alcohol produced a public reply from a newspaper reader, to the effect that he was grateful to the authors for the lucid exposition of their thesis and that as a result of reading their paper he would, in future, be as careful to avoid feeding alcohol to his cabbages as he was in planting his feet in the soil.

If the deadly serious nature with which the temperance campaigners took themselves, compounded with a bit of natural

Victorian pomposity, makes much temperance literature look slightly absurd to today's eyes, we must not lose sight of the fact that temperance was deadly serious. The *Liverpool Daily Post* of 25 April 1878 reported

On Tuesday afternoon the attention of a constable was drawn to the not very unusual phenomenon of a drunken man and woman in Johnston St. The woman had a child in her arms. It was taken from her and found to be in a shockingly diseased and neglected state. The constable afterwards visited the home of the inebriates. The sole piece of furniture was an old table. In the top room the woman's father was lying on the bare boards without a vestige of clothing upon him, and covered only by an old rug. In another part of the house was an aunt who was much the worse for drink, around her were three young children. There was not a particle of food in the whole place, and when the children were given some buns to eat they devoured them savagely. Drunken parents reeling in the street with an unhealthy and neglected baby; a house in a court with only an old table in it, an old man lying on the bare boards, with simply a rug for clothes or coverings, a tipsy aunt and three hungry, dirty children around her, make up a picture which would be considered unusually terrible if the scene were laid in the hut of a savage, and which is certainly a bitter satire on nineteenth century civilisation. The father and mother were brought to the police court yesterday; and the court ordered that the children should he removed forthwith to the workhouse.[4]

In this instance there is no doubt that a poor family had drunk their way to destitution, and only the intervention of the constable prevented them from continuing to the grave. Drink-related deaths were running at some 60,000 a year, and drink-related crime was at record levels – the 1870s was the age of the mugger.

The temperance movement, having chosen their path, saw in prohibition a cure for society's ills and the means of salvation of the souls of so many sinners. This made them very reluctant to confront the chicken and egg question head on. Were the poor poor because they drank, or did they drink because they were poor? Temperance logic said, simply, stop drinking and you will no longer be poor, and while it is a truism that not spending a sum on alcohol meant that the sum is free to be spent on other items, that is a long way from saying that this results in liberation from the privations from which refuge was sought in the first place. This shortcoming was undoubtedly a major failure of the movement. Even the licensed victuallers, not usually on firm ground when tackling the teetotallers, were able to sneer. 'They would muzzle the mouth of the ox that treadeth out the corn and make his yoke and harness as hard to bear as possible in the interests of pure virtue from their point of view.'[5]

There was no shortage of Victorian social reformers able to see through this flaw in temperance logic. Dickens, for one, felt obliged to point out to the teetotallers that

> Drunkenness, as a national horror, is the effect of many causes. Foul smells, disgusting habitations, bad workshops, and workshop customs, want of light, air and water, the absence of all easy means and decency and health, are commonest among its common everyday physical causes, mental weariness and languor so induced, the want of wholesome relaxation, the craving for some stimulus and excitement, which is as much a part of such lives as the sun is, and last and inclusive of all the rest, ignorance, and the need there is among English people of reasonable, rational training, in lieu of mere parrot-education, or none at all, are its most obvious moral causes.[6]

Ironically, the author of the tract that prompted this reply from Dickens was George Cruikshank, the satirical cartoonist, prominent teetotaller and occasional illustrator of Dickens's works. As a celebrity in his own right, Cruikshank was a high profile campaigner, and perhaps this prompted the reply, for he was one teetotaller to whom such remarks would not normally need to be addressed. Cruikshank showed a holistic approach to the temperance issue, notably lacking in many other quarters. His concern was not so much with the spiritual salvation of drunkards but their physical salvation and, indeed, protection. When, in October 1869, a Miss Rye proposed to take a party of girls aged five to ten years, abandoned by or the orphans of drunkards, to emigrate to the US and Canada, Cruikshank denounced the scheme as no better than white slavery. The fate of women and domestic violence at the hands of drunken husbands were of particular concern to him.

In 1853 he reported the case of a man named Mubbs, an otherwise good, honest and kind husband, who under the influence of drink murdered his wife and was subsequently hanged. The brewers, distillers and Excise, Cruikshank argued, were no more than accessories to the murder, since without them Mubbs would not have been induced to partake of the alcohol that caused him to murder his wife. What Cruikshank found ironic was that the crowd who turned up to see Mubbs swing on the gallows were also drunk.

Cruikshank was the most eloquent of the temperance campaigners who operated in print. There were many fine orators who toured the country after the fashion of hedgerow priests, but Cruikshank's use of illustrated verse provided a medium of formidable impact. His series *The Bottle* and its sequel *The Drunkard's Children*, which prompted Dickens's reply, were reprinted countless times, and he could cut his cloth to suit his audience.

> This is the woman, with woebegone face,
> The wife of the drunkard, in rags and disgrace,
> Who is served by the lady, all jewels and lace,
> The wife of the landlord, who coins his bright gold,
> Out of the ruin of youthful and old,
> Who drinks the strong liquors he sells night and day,
> At the bar of the gin shop, so glittering and gay.

One point of Dickens's explanation for drunkenness requires closer examination. 'Bad workshops and workshop customs' certainly assisted the perpetuation of an alcohol-centred workplace culture. Drinking practices were remarkably consistent across most nineteenth century industries.

> Scarcely has the stripling commenced his apprenticeship, in some towns, to the business of the joiner or cabinetmaker, than he is informed that the custom of the shop is, to pay a sum, as an *entry* to be disposed of in drink by the workmen . . . the first wages of a journeymen also are consecrated to the same unhallowed purpose, being in many cases the commencement of a course of inebriation, that ends only with poverty and death.

If one leaves the shop his station at a particular bench is
'rouped' [sold by auction] by the men who remain and the price
spent in drink: sometimes six shillings are thus obtained.

Similar *entry* practices were obtained in literally hundreds of
occupations. In any workplace, especially those with apprentices,
complicated systems of fines provided for a constant and
permanently accruing supply of money to be spent on drink.

He [the apprentice] receives charge of the fire in the premises,
and at every failure of kindling, mending, or extinguishing at
night, he is fined a small sum, to be expended in whisky; failure
in putting out candles at the proper time, or in watching the
works at meal-hours and a number of other petty offences, are
met by small amercements, for the same purpose.

These practices were incredibly entrenched. 'A respectable man
with a family, going lately to work at a smith's shop, refused to pay
entry; he was maltreated, and finally knocked down and bled; on
the aggressors being summoned, they actually pleaded, in bar of
judgement, before a magistrate, the *custom* of the shop having
been infringed.[8]

The impact of temperance was understandable, for it certainly
had great effect in shaping public opinion – one could not be
impartial on the drink question – and it stiffened the resolve of
government to tackle the question as well as emboldened
their supports in the legislature to introduce measures that would
have been unthinkable previously. Not all the measures they
introduced succeeded. In fact very few did. Yet a number of
measures were discussed and mooted during the Victorian period,
and necessarily so, for there was much truth in the lament that:

We drink the very strongest liquors that can be brewed or
distilled; the classes among us who are not decent are in the
habit of getting mad drunk, and of fighting after the manner of
wild beasts when they have a chance of using their fists, their
feet or teeth on each other and on the Guardians of the law. Our
places of licensed victualling are merely ugly dens, where the
largest number of sots can get tipsy in the shortest space of
time; and Sunday in London with all public houses, all the

music halls thrown unrestrictedly open from morning till night, would exhibit the most horrible terrestrial inferno that eye ever beheld, that the ear ever hears, or the heart ever sickened at. We are so very strong and stalwart, and earnest, and English, in a word, that we need in our diversions a number of restrictive checks and kicking straps, which the feebler and the less pugnacious of the Continent do not require.[7]

Chapter 17

BILLS AND ACTS
AND ARGUMENTS

> Our wish is to place the article within reach, not only of the
> class which now use it, but within reach of the whole middle
> classes – of the lowest orders of the middle classes and even
> the better portion of the working classes – I do not say as an
> article of ordinary consumption but one which they may use
> on those occasions when they provide themselves with
> something better than their daily food.[1]

The article was wine and the speaker was Gladstone, addressing
the Commons during the second reading of the Refreshment
Houses and Wine Licences Bill in 1860.

Once passed into law, it was important in that it was the last act
that liberalised the supply of drink, and that was, in part,
prompted by financial and diplomatic concerns unconnected with
drink. It was the first act in a number, from 1860 to the Defence of
the Realm Act in 1914, that effectively ended the drink question,
concerned with the management of the drink trade. The opposition
to the bill marked a watershed in pressure-group politics in Britain.
Finally, the act was the first – but not the last – which saw both
the licensed trade and the temperance movement united in
opposition to it.

The bill sprang out of Gladstone's Free Trading budget speech,
which indicated that it was fiscal rather than a social measure.
Richard Cobden had recently concluded a commercial treaty with
France, and while colonial wines were permitted to maintain a
favourable customs rate, the duties on brandy and wine were
almost halved. Gladstone, however, was not a man likely to
promote alcohol consumption to satisfy the Treasury, or in blind

obedience to the principles of Free Trade. It was his intention that the act should have a beneficial effect upon people's habits. He hoped, like legislators before him in the 1750s and 1830s with beer, to induce people to substitute less harmful wine for the damaging and foully-concocted gin. He wanted to more closely associate eating and drinking in the national consciousness, to try to stem the separation of the two activities by the publicans and gin palace owners. The act proposed the granting of licences to pastry cooks and eating houses, and permitted grocers' shops to be off-licences for the sale of wine.

Public reaction was instant. If the man in the street was pleased, or even indifferent, the teetotallers were not. They were not interested in the substitution of wine for gin. They wanted the suppression of wine *and* gin. To them the encouragement of any form of indulgence was reprehensible.

The publicans' position was built on rather less solid foundations. They feared a loss of business and were highly embarrassed by the charge that they were 'victuallers who provided no victuals'. The charges made by the publicans were patently ludicrous: the national character would be seriously damaged if people were to be allowed to drink at pastry cooks. The measures would lead to an epidemic of female inebriation, they warned. 'Not only shall we have the working classes degraded by these temptations to intemperance, but our females and domestic servants, and even the children will be tempted to these places for their pennyworth of wine.' Ironically, the publicans had never been known to complain of children being sent into pubs on errands for their parents' pennyworth of gin. 'These houses will become the resort of all the dissolute men and women in London, and the facilities which will be given to indulgence will make these places the high road to ruin.' The licensed victuallers were thus arguing that food was bad for the dissolute classes, since the only attraction these 'houses' had over pubs and gin palaces was the provision of food. Eating was the high road to ruin.

Mr Gladstone . . . will be an immense favourite with a certain sort of ladies. They have taste for stimulants which it would be awkward to gratify; they cannot go into a public house – that would be too conspicuous. A pastry cook's shop of Mr Gladstone's stamp is a very thing they wanted. . . . A man perhaps, might not infrequently alight in one of Mr Gladstone's beer shops on his wife dead drunk at the back parlour, or his daughter debauched upstairs.[2]

Was this passage taken from an irate temperance tract? It certainly reads with the usual smug assurance and superior piety often to be found in temperance literature. No, it was from the pen of an anonymous correspondent writing in the *Morning Advertiser*, which throughout the campaign was nicknamed the 'Gin and Gospel Gazette'. The ludicrous aspect of the unholy alliance between prohibitionist and publican served to explode their arguments, and the act was passed amid a popular mood that if both these groups were against it, it must be a good thing.

The act led to huge increases in the amounts of wine drunk, but consumption was largely confined to the middle classes, who took advantage of increased purchasing power. There is very little evidence of a wine-induced increase in working-class drunkenness. The amounts imported, however, were staggering. In 1859 France exported 695,911 gallons of wine to Great Britain, while Spain and Portugal exported 4,893,916 gallons legitimately. In 1876 France exported 6,745,710 gallons and Portugal 10,186,322 gallons, and this was during the height of the phyloxera plague. The scale of the increase must indicate that a side effect of the act was to make the illicit running of wine less profitable. How much is accounted for by a reduction in amounts smuggled must remain a mystery.

The take up of licences by pastry cooks and grocers was less than anticipated and was certainly insufficient to panic the licensed victuallers into a rush to recommence victualling themselves. Part of the lack of impact was due to the fact that, for technical reasons, the Excise permitted, in 1861, the retail of spirits in single bottles. This measure was brought about in order to legitimise a reality, so allowing the Excise some benefit. Wholesale spirit dealers could, for a £3 fee, retail single bottles which had previously only been available from public houses. Naturally, the result was an increase in the availability of gin, though it probably also meant an increase in the quality of gin provided. As a measure it did tend to rather sabotage the intentions of the 1860 act.

Neither was 1862 a good year for teetotallers. The Free Traders abolished the hop duty, while further Free Traders in Liverpool opted for a policy of licensing laxity, granting licences to 427 new premises between 1862 and 1865. The experiment was a failure – drunkenness was endemic – so it was abandoned, but not before it gave weight to the teetotallers' argument that repression was the only solution to the drink question. This was unfortunate, since it blinded them to the realisation that repression brought with it its own attendant dangers.

There were new attempts at Sunday closing legislation in 1863. The last, in 1855, had been assisted in its passage by public revulsion at the state of affairs in the Crimea. Military humiliation combined with reports of drunkenness among the troops had stiffened resolve that 'something must be done'. In 1863 there was no such resolve and the measure failed. The 1855 act had shortened opening hours on Sunday, and the 1863 bill argued for all day closing on Sunday. Such provision for Scotland was passed in 1853, and similar acts for Ireland and Wales in 1878 and 1881, but no such law ever made it to the statute book in England. The 1863 bill aimed to prohibit the sale of liquor from 11 p.m. Saturday to 6 a.m. Monday, but was felt to be too harsh. A further bill in 1868 failed because it permitted off sales for supper and dinner parties, and was so class biased that it was rejected lest it produce the kind of rioting that had accompanied the passage of the 1855 act. A subsequent bill accompanying that passed for Wales failed to make it to the statute book, and in 1883 there were no fewer than eight such bills – three national and five local.

The local bills were an extension of the policy of prohibition which had first been attempted in 1864. In 1851 the US state of Maine had voted for prohibition, and its example strengthened the resolve of teetotallers and forced some to the conclusion that the policy of abstention was only a partial solution since vast numbers of people were either incurable recidivists or impervious to the manifest logic of the Malt Liquor lecture. Thus teetotallers, Cruikshank among them, became converted to the view that prohibition was the correct solution to the drink problem.

In 1864 Sir Wilfred Lawson of the United Kingdom Alliance Party introduced the first local option bill. Known as the Permissive Bill, it made provision for parishes to vote on whether or not to impose total prohibition, a two-thirds majority being required for prohibition to be introduced. The problem was that the electorate consisted only of ratepayers, who were unlikely to be a majority in many parishes. A decision taken by two-thirds of a minority was to bind the majority. Not surprisingly, there was uproar. Even moderate temperance campaigners balked at this measure, both in 1864, and at the subsequent and frequent attempts to introduce local option. Canon Ellison of the Church of England Temperance Society expressed the view of many in a letter to *The Times* of 28 September 1878.

> As I have been understood to be aiming at prohibition only by a more circuitous route, I may as well say once and for all that so long as there is a minority able to show that houses for the sale of beer etc. are necessary for the supply of (as they hold it to be) a national want, or necessity, the imposition of the arbitrary will of the majority in prohibiting such houses would be, in my opinion, a tyrannical use of abstract right, to which the majority would never have recourse.[3]

Public outrage ensured the downfall of the bill and subsequent local option bills. It did, however, exhume the old spectre that had effectively been laid to rest in 1830: this was the suppression of houses regardless of their character, record or behaviour.

Indeed the principle was implicit in the 1869 Wine and Beerhouse Act, the first in a long series of acts and measures designed to restrict the drink trade and reduce the numbers of pubs. The act was introduced as a Private Member's Bill by a Tory and had cross-party support. It sought to bring the vast numbers of beerhouses under the purview of the magistrates and away from the Excise. The intention of the act was clearly to enable a clean-up operation to proceed against the beer shops. They had always been rough and ready, but with gradual improvement in public houses in the intervening forty years the beerhouses had failed to keep pace and were becoming less acceptable in the climate of the time. Beer shops that had existed before 1869 were given a modicum of protection under the act, but in future new licences were granted only when demographic pressure made it absolutely necessary. From 1869 the merits of the application became secondary to the existing pattern on the ground. Naturally, over the years many temperance campaigners had insinuated themselves onto licensing benches, for whom the act was a God-sent opportunity to do what they had long wanted; reduce the absolute number as well as proportionate number of licensed premises.

This measure obviously meant properties now acquired a premium. The relative positions of the Liberal and Tory parties on the issue of the reduction of the number of premises, added to the effects of the 1869 act, saw the recurrence of large scale public house investment and the renewed acquisition of tied estates.

The 1869 act had been a Tory-sponsored measure passed under a Liberal government. The next attempt at legislation was to put an end to cross-party consensus. The Intoxicating Liquor (Licensing) Bill of 1871 ran to a weighty 177 clauses. Its proposals were radical and drastic, and once again forged an unholy alliance between pub and pulpit. The main proposals of the bill were the introduction of higher licence fees, the establishment of a corps of licensing inspectors, a reduction in opening hours, Sunday closing at the discretion of local JPs, a fixed scale of licences to population, licences to go the highest bidder and, finally, suppression of 'surplus' houses without compensation.

The 1860 act had contributed to a fall in beer consumption. In 1861, 1.3 million fewer barrels were brewed than in 1860. The 1860s, however, were a period of steadily rising consumption. In 1869, 25,108,000 barrels of beer were brewed, 4,622,000 more than in 1860. By 1871 consumption had risen by a further 1.3 million barrels. In perspective, the total increase between 1860 and 1871 was only a fraction less than between 1830 and 1860. Prosperity was the principal cause of this increase. Clearly, the measures set in train in 1869 would take time to work, but for some they were not working fast enough, hence the 1871 bill.

The bill was universally reviled. Popular agitation against it was widespread. Eight hundred thousand people petitioned against it. The licensed victuallers organised themselves to campaign on a scale as never before. The bill was depicted as an attack on property and an attack on the customary freedoms of the common man, backed up by a system of spying. Even some temperance figures thought it went too far in this respect, while others feared that, if successful, it would defeat the need for the absolute prohibition they wanted. In the face of such opposition and as a result of Liberal by-election losses, partly occasioned by hostility to the measure, the bill was never pursued and the following year a much watered down version was drafted. Opening hours were reduced, but by less than originally proposed (5 a.m. to 12 p.m.), fines for drinking offences were increased, inspectors were appointed (by local police and not central government), and the sugar on the pill was the prohibition of drinking by those under sixteen years of age, a measure to which no one could reasonably object.

This bill of 1872 was passed and became known as the Aberdare Act. Even though some Tories had supported it and some Liberals opposed it, it was commonly regarded as a Liberal measure. The polarisation of the parties on the drink question was a direct result of the Aberdare Act. Many publicans had previously been staunch Liberals, but now they increasingly tended to support the Tory party. As the Liberals recognised this trend they became more openly pro-temperance, and in 1891 adopted the policy of the UK Alliance – local option – as official policy. The 1893 attempt at reviving the initial 1864 local option measure was postponed due to the Home Rule crisis, and when reintroduced in 1895 it would have received Royal Assent had not the Government fallen. In the election of 1895 the drink trade lobbied vigorously for the Tories, who were returned with a crushing 152 majority. Likewise in 1874 the publicans and brewers had combined to lobby support for the Conservative party, though they need not have tried too hard. The unpopularity of the 1872 act was still fresh in people's minds, and Gladstone, in his own words, was 'borne down in a torrent of gin and beer'.

The Aberdare Act sought to put an end to gin palace-type premises. Section 45 stipulated that at least two rooms must be given over to the public for premises with spirit licences. Gin shops and gin palaces had traditionally had just one large room.

Other clauses were designed to make life difficult for the landlord. Twenty-two years after the passing of the act, the Licensed Victuallers Association were still giving guidance to their members to assist them in avoiding getting caught out, for they well knew that temperance radicals were au fait with all the nuances of the act's provisions, and were ready to pounce upon the slightest slip.

For the guidance of licensed victuallers, bad characters may be divided into thieves and prostitutes . . . Section 14 of the Act of 1872 enacts that if any licensed person knowingly permits his premises to be habitual resort of or place of meeting of reputed prostitutes, whether the object of their so resorting or meeting is or is not prostitution, he shall, if he allow them to remain thereon longer than is necessary for the purpose of obtaining reasonable refreshment, be liable to a penalty not exceeding £10 for the first and £20 for the second and any subsequent offence.[4]

Disraeli's second administration was not slow in paying its debts, and what became known as the 'Publicans' Parliament' extended opening hours by thirty minutes as a mark of gratitude.

This is not to imply, however, that the Tories were in the pay of the brewers or were lax on the drink issue, but no further legislation was passed by the administration that had any bearing on the trade. In 1879 the government passed the Habitual Drunkards Act, which established a number of sanatoria that people could voluntarily enter, though once in they had to pay and stay the distance. It was also a Conservative government that extended this measure in 1898 so that 'criminal inebriates' could be confined in sanatoria, and while these were not particularly pleasant places, it was at least a recognition that alcoholism was a disease rather than an inclination.

The Tories, too, were committed to reducing the number of retail outlets, but, unlike the Liberals, regarded suppression without compensation as unjust. The brewers were realists and were prepared to accept the Conservative position rather than play into the hands of the temperance radicals. As will be seen, the declining number of retail outlets combined with the increase in volumes consumed was to the brewers' advantage. Although throughout the 1880s consumption was fairly level at between 27 and 28 million barrels, the 1890s saw an immediate jump in sales, finished the decade 6.8 million barrels higher, and this despite falls in 1895 due to a Liberal increase in beer tax the previous year.

In 1880 a Liberal government was again returned to power and set about further reforms. Perhaps on the principle of once bitten twice shy they preferred to avoid legislation, but instead reformed the tax. To save the cost of collection of excise the Liberals abolished the taxes on malt and sugar – hop duty already having gone – and replaced them with a tax on wort, a system which survived until June 1993. So while in 1879 the duty on beer consisted of 2s 7d and 5 per cent per bushel of malt and £1 1s 6d per cwt of brewing sugar – sugar had been permitted as an adjunct in 1847 and taxed from 1850 – in 1880 the duty became 6s 3d per standard barrel, or a farthing a pint, at a gravity of 1057°.

The obvious effect of the tax was to reduce the strength of the beer. Original gravity is a measure of the wort taken before any alcohol is present. It is, therefore, a measure of the potential alcoholic content of the beer. It is theoretically possible for a beer of a low original gravity to end up with an alcoholic strength in excess of a beer with a higher original gravity, but this is unlikely as it implies bad brewing. In the past the tax on the inputs rather than the strength meant changes of recipe or proportions of ingredients could be used to offset tax changes; now there was an immediate check on beer strength. If the government wanted beer strengths reduced it merely had to raise the tax or reduce the definition of the standard barrel, which it did in 1899 by downgrading it to 1055°, where it has stayed. The European Union harmonisation to 'factory gate' duty payment, as of 1 June 1993, had the same effect, and beer strengths fell as a result.

Just because the government was not proposing legislation it does not mean that others failed to do so. In the 1880s dozens and dozens of bills were put forward. Obviously, more bills' sponsors fancied chancing their arms under a Liberal administration, but even in Conservative 1890 there were twenty-five licensing bills proposed, fourteen on a single day.

A popular model for these bills was the Gothenberg System, which caused much excitement in temperance circles. In the 1870s there had been a number of coffee public houses. These, like the temperance hotels, were a recognition that some alternative had to be offered. What better alternative to a public house that sold alcohol than one that did not? These buildings looked and were supposed to feel like pubs, except that they provided food, coffee, tea and a variety of non-alcoholic beverages, and even early attempts at alcohol-free beers, such as Cox's Anti-Burton. There were not many aspects of the public house life that they did not try to imitate, even the best of them could not help but sanitise what it attempted to replicate, and the overall effect never really rose above a slightly sanctimonious pastiche.

The people who ran the underwriting organisation that founded these coffee public houses – the Coffee Tavern Co. (1870) and the

Coffee Public House Association (1877) – disliked the genuine pub too intensely to reproduce them without resorting to sermonising of one sort or another, even in the naming of the ersatz beer. As a result, they were not places where a man could feel at ease – and what else is a pub for? In addition, 'their tea, coffee and food were frequently disgusting and the surroundings they provided were gloomy and squalid enough to be compared to a workhouse dining hall.'[5]

Interestingly, the coffee public houses tended to be supported by the aristocracy, wealthy middle classes and the moderate arm of temperance. It was the money of the wealthy that sustained the coffee public houses, and when they despaired or tired of the project it collapsed. The coffee public houses barely lasted into the 1880s, though in the north a few struggled on to the 1890s. They all got stuck on the same nail. Something that looks like a pub, smells like a pub, sounds like a pub, opens and closes like a pub but does not serve alcohol is not a pub.

The demise of the coffee public houses and temperance hotels was a blow to the morale of moderate temperance supporters, who realised that an alternative to the pub was the key to the drink question. They could see that where alternatives existed, people used them. Chatsworth House and Kew Gardens were popular Sunday outing venues, especially among servants, always a group disposed towards using pubs. For a period Chatsworth ceased to open on Sundays, but parties still turned up to the locality and frequented the hostelries. When Chatsworth reopened the local pub trade declined. As a result, the 1854 Select Committee recommended that the Royal Zoological Society and the Crystal Palace open on Sunday too, as well as other gardens and museums. As other alternatives tried by these moderate reformers had failed they decided on another approach – the Gothenberg System.

The Swedish Licensing Law of 1855, while controlling the drink trade gave to urban municipalities the right to assign the entire local drink trade to a 'bolag' or controlling company, on condition that all profits went to public works. In 1865 the municipality of Gothenberg gave all on-licences to such a bolag. The Gothenberg bolag encouraged the sale of drink and had the power to determine arbitrarily the minimum drinking age and the strength of the liquors sold. Much of the profits derived were used for the establishment of eating houses for working men where liquor was available but not encouraged, and, with time, could only be purchased with a food order.

The Gothenberg system enjoyed a vogue in the temperance movement, and although attempts at legislation to introduce it into Britain were unsuccessful, several private companies were established on Gothenberg principles. This scheme was called Disinterested Management, the idea being that pubs were run by limited companies. Landlords were employees of the company rather than tenants and so were relieved of the incentive to push liquor.

The largest numbers of Gothenberg pubs, such as the Boar's Head at Hampton Lacy, were run by the Public House Refreshment Association (1876), and while the experiment was more successful than coffee public houses or hotels it still fell foul of the operators' temptation to 'improve' the public house, with the result that a sanctimonious air pervaded them too. In Gothenberg, of course, there were no alternatives establishments, but in England there were and the public voted with their feet.

Meanwhile, suppression was again the order of the day and the magistrates had a fairly free hand. There was at this time no compensation for the landlords of suppressed houses and this caused much resentment throughout the trade, and, through the lobbying that took place over the bar counter, in the community as a whole. The United Temperance Councils issued a guide entitled 'How to Shut up a Public House'. Temperance groups would use this as a blueprint for objecting to licences at sessions, and many a landlord lost his livelihood with no recourse to compensation. In 1904 the Conservative government brought in a system of compensation paid for by the trade itself. A levy on public houses went towards the compensation of the interests concerned when a pub was suppressed, for reasons other than for disorder. It goes almost without saying that the majority of the money paid out went to the brewers rather than the landlords.

The last piece of legislation to concern us at this stage was the bill of 1908. Just as the 1860 act ushered in the era of temperance, the 1908 bill ushered it out. There were two main considerations behind the 1908 bill. First, there was the new influx of Labour MPs many of whom, like George Lansbury, were committed teetotallers. They shared with many Liberals a distaste for the compensation scheme then operating, favouring the brewers as it did. Second, was the fact that the Liberals were itching for a fight with the Lords over a number of issues, friction that resulted in the budget crisis of 1910 and the constitutional crisis of 1911. The battlefield for the first skirmish of the campaign was the drink trade.

In essence, the 1908 bill was a local option bill with knobs on. It took its brief from the 1899 Peel Commission, which had resulted in majority and minority reports; the majority favoured generous compensation for suppression, but the minority and the bill did not. It proposed to get rid of one third of all licences, introduce a sliding scale of licences per capita ranging from 1:100 in densely populated areas to 1:400 in the country; a doubling of the prevalent ratio. After a phasing-out period for surplus licences, which was to take fourteen years, licence renewals could be treated as applications for new licences. A system of local option was to come into force, and if this was not enough, it also proposed stricter Sunday licensing laws, the refusal of a licence to a tied house, a ban on off-sales to children, the outlawing of the 'long pull' (serving over measure) and, to cap it all, a ban on the employment of women.

The temperance movement loved the bill and, equally, the trade detested it. There was to be no unholy alliance on this occasion. The uproar was sufficient to put the previous opposition to the Aberdare Act in the shade. Not only was the trade better organised to coordinate opposition, but they were unencumbered by any awkward logical contortions to hamper the fight for the hearts and minds of the population.

The Liberals were very confident. Asquith himself admitted that the central act of the bill was a massive reduction in the number of public houses, even though between 1904 and 1908 their numbers were falling by 1,200 a year. The government was looking to provoke its fight with the Lords, but although they got their fight it was not the one they had wanted, for the battle was lost on the streets before it ever got to the Upper House.

The impassioned pleas of the nation's barmaids to 'Save our Jobs' must count as one of the first and greatest victories of modern public relations, which triumphed in the face of widely-published evidence of the poor living conditions, health and life expectancy of female public house employees. The Barmaids'

Political Defence League was founded on 6 November 1908, declaring that, by its inception, 'the trade of 100,000 women has been protected from arbitrary government suppression.' (Although the 1901 England and Wales census put the number of barmaids at 27,207, both figures are unreliable.)

The brewers and licensed victuallers – never comfortable bedfellows – united to orchestrate mass popular opposition to the bill. The brewers played up their munificence by publicly suspending their philanthropic activities. Every public house was a soap box for the anti-bill interest, to the extent that shopkeepers were forced, if not already inclined, to advertise their dislike of the bill in the face of a general business boycott, the motto of which was 'I can only deal with an honest man!' The level of public debate was immense. In 1908 *The Times* contained no fewer than 1,660 references to the bill. In Parliament the bill attracted no fewer than 1,000 amendments.

In the Peckham by-election the Liberal seat went Conservative on the issue. The Liberal MP for Huntingdon – the brewer Samuel Whitbread – offered to stand down and fight his seat on an anti-bill ticket, but the clamour convinced him it was unnecessary. The Liberals lost eight other by-elections; Hyde Park was the scene of pro- and anti-demonstrations, with 800,000 turning up for one anti-bill meeting. These public demonstrations were in addition to those occurring in Kent and East London, which culminated in a mass rally, under the auspices of the London and Provincial Hop Growers and Pickers Defence League, in Trafalgar Square, which became known as Hop Saturday.

The whole country was involved in the 1908 Bill. Passions were inflamed and the 'politics of the public bar' took on a significance it had never done before or has since. The bill gave people the opportunity to express their indignation, not only at the measures contained in the bill, but also at the compensation scheme of the 1904 act, whereby the licensed trade funded its own suppression. A correspondent to *The Times* of 6 March 1908 described the bill and the extension of suppression thus: 'In a deserted country district a man was walking along quite temperately when a man came up to him and, pointing a loaded pistol at his head, said, "Your money or your life." The intended victim replied, "Sir, I think you are most reasonable, the last man I met of your fraternity wanted both."'

The debate was not without humorous incident. When the Bishop of London took a torchlight procession of pro-bill marchers through the East End, he was confronted by a mob of drunken Londoners. Beseeching them to join him in singing *Lead Kindly Light*, he and his entourage were drowned out by a chorus of *For He's a Jolly Good Fellow*. This does not mean to say that all reason was lost. The same year saw passage of the Children's Act, which forbade under fourteens from entering a bar. Intended to stop children from running errands, it actually had the effect of preventing women from entering public houses and, as a result, led to the popularisation of 'jug and bottle' departments.

In the midst of all this the bill passed through the Commons, as everyone knew it would. The Tory House of Lords was where the debate that counted was to take place, and the nation waited for their judgement. Edward VII pleaded with their leader, Lord Lansdowne, to amend the bill rather than reject it, but they too were in belligerent mood, not so much because they wanted to precipitate the coming battle with the Commons, but because they shared a common revulsion for the measures proposed. It must be remembered that the Lords had already passed Trade Union legislation affording immunity to Trade Union finances. If they were purely out to scupper Liberal measures this bill, too, would have fallen at their lordships' hands. On suppression, Lord Salisbury summed up the mood of the Lords when he said that 'though he had a great many bedrooms he did not find this led to his sleeping more.' He may not have been a noted pub goer, and his views on the relationship between premises and indulgence were simplistic, but he struck a chord. After three days' debate the bill was rejected, to the rejoicing of the non-temperance majority.

Temperance as an issue died with the bill. Other more weighty matters occupied the national forum – the budget of 1910, the Constitutional Crisis, the death of Edward VII, the spectre of European conflict and the First World War – which resolved the drink question once and for all.

By 1908, however, the Victorian pub was under threat. It had grown too fat too fast in the 1890s and the reduction in absolute numbers that had been the order of the day had whetted the appetite of the brewers into a frenzy of estate accumulation that was unsustainable.

Chapter 18

SNUGS, SALOONS &
SHORT-LIVED
BOOMS

Some few years ago almost every public house had its parlour and taproom, the former devoted to the social foregatherings of neighbouring tradesmen, the latter provided with fire and cooking utensils for the use of the labouring classes. The old fashioned public house was the scene of right pleasant social meetings, after the labours of the day. Neighbours and cronies gathered together to discuss the affairs of the parish or the politics of the nation over a pipe and a pint of ale. In most modern houses, however, the parlour and taproom are done away with altogether, or converted into bars where the customer must come like a bucket to a well and fill himself and go away again. There are only a very few places for friendly gathering and social converse left and those few that remain are made as uncomfortable as possible. All games, however, are forbidden, not by the law, but by the publican, because they interfere with drinking. The harmless bagatelle board has long been banished, cards and even dominoes are interdicted on any pretence whatever. (1864)

The landlord of the latter half of the nineteenth century was unlikely to be quite the portly, jovial Boniface of popular memory. Instead, he was a man weighed down with problems. His enemies consisted of the brewery, the temperance chapel, the bench and any rival publicans with a bit of cash to invest in refurbishment.

If lucky, with a profitable house and as an able businessman, the 1880s and 1890s gave some publicans the opportunity of becoming men of considerable wealth, owning small chains of sizeable houses. Speculative trade in public houses became popular.

The last phase in the development of the nineteenth-century pub really begins with the passage of the Aberdare Act and ends with the collapse of the market for public houses and the act of 1902. The chronology of the period is very important since the policies of magistrates and brewer changed frequently as a result of legislation. Between 1870 and 1879 no fewer than fourteen acts passed through Parliament which had a direct bearing on public houses. Between 1880 and 1889 no fewer than seventeen acts were passed.

In the initial post-Aberdare period there was little immediate impact on numbers of premises. The number of beer houses was already falling. Some had become full on-licences after 1869, while others were suppressed now that they came under the purview of the bench. At this time the magisterial attitude generally inclined to the view that an orderly house should be re-licensed, though they would not allow it to flourish in any way, and so would adamantly refuse to countenance any expansion or structural alteration.

In little over a decade the policy of the magistrates would undergo a *volte face*: licences could be taken away from law abiding publicans (by the 1890s forced surrenders were negotiated, between bench and brewer) while expansion of floor area was encouraged as tending to respectability. Increasing demographic pressure on a fairly constrained floor space necessarily demanded a rethinking of the best utilisation of that space and with it a re-examination of the materials used in it. The bar had already changed shape to maximise its circumference in relation to area. Now the evolutionary process vaulted over the counter and begun to work changes on the drinking area.

In pure modern marketing parlance the process underway in the 1870s might be termed 'market segment identification'. The snugs had originally been a private recess away from the bar area, a sort of hybrid offspring of the tavern booth, and had been popular with customers because they were intimate, cosy retreats out of the way of prying eyes. Snugs were unpopular with magistrates for the same reason, for they saw them as places where prostitutes could solicit trade with ease. There were reported cases of intercourse in the snug. The snug extended itself from the walls and came to meet the bar. The 1870s saw a rise in the number of multi-barred premises, much in the fashion of the Argyll Arms, Argyll Street, London, as it is today, though the booths of the pawnbrokers' shops, so familiar to the pub's customers, were equally as much an inspiration for this phenomenon. By partitioning off the bar area into small segments, more people of more varied classes could be accommodated within the same space, without being permanently condescended to by their superiors or disturbed by their inferiors.

Although the multi-barred pub was a short-lived fashion, many of its accoutrements still exist. Examples of snob screens still abound, though few are in their original condition. Movable frosted glass windows, mounted on the bar at head height, allowed people to drink in a bar and order drinks from the bar staff without compromising their anonymity.

Glass windows which disguise must be either distorting or opaque. Plate glass had long been available, but not immediately as frosted glass. The history of glass and the pub is an interesting study in cause and effect. The introduction of gas lighting led, in the 1830s to the increased use of plate glass. The development of the gin palace depended upon the attractive interaction of the two to produce a pleasant and warming image. The abolition of glass tax in 1847, as an incentive to glass manufacture, led to a rapid rise in the use of mirrors in pubs, which at first received magisterial blessing as mirrors improved the visibility and supervision of all areas of the pub. With the introduction of cut plate glass in the 1850s – though not widely popular until the 1880s – and the development of frosting by means of the application of hydrofluoric acid, visibility was again reduced. In the 1860s mirrors became less popular with the bench with the introduction of gold lettering and the subsequent use of mirrors to advertise brewers' products. Magistrates tried to restrict the amount of decoration applied to glass, in the name of maintaining good supervision, but by the 1870s glass was the material of the town pub and was engraved, etched, French-embossed, enamelled, lettered, illuminated and cut in the most magnificent styles, of which, thankfully, many fine examples still exist. By the 1890s sheet glass was becoming available, and this lighter and cheaper form meant that beautiful ornamental glass work was within the reach of even fairly modest public houses, while the introduction of incandescent gas mantles in 1895 meant a reduction in the numbers of gas lamps needed to produce the same effect. This increased the potential of what it was possible to do with glass, and defined the style of what has become known as the 'Victorian pub'.

In 1830 the aim of combining gas and glass was to draw people in off the street, to attract passing trade. By the 1890s passing trade was, for the majority of pubs, no longer their prime source of trade. Glass and gas were now combined to create a pleasant atmosphere in which the customer was induced to remain. A splendid, grand interior was now more important than the face shown to the outside world. Gas and glass could not achieve this sumptuousness alone, but, fortunately, Victorian inventiveness had provided a range of decorations to add to and soften the brightness of the mirror's shine.

In 1841 a firm by the name of Potters, from Darwen, produced a commercial wallpaper by successfully printing designs on calico. Wallpapers became very popular, so much so that artists like William Morris found in them a means of expression for a whole school of late Victorian thought.

Paper was not without its competitors. The first of the embossed wall coverings was known as Tynecastle. Developed in the early 1790s it was first made of leather, before the technique was perfected sufficiently for canvas to be used. In 1877 the firm of Frederic Walton patented Lincrusta, which onomatopoeic term was used to describe the squares of solidified linseed oil, built up into relief. This covering was light enough to be applied to ceilings and became very popular, having a virtual monopoly of the market until 1887 when a former Walton employee patented Analgypta. Made from paper pulp, this was lighter and more versatile. With the coming of Analgypta, Louis XIV ceilings became popular.

The addition of hydraulic presses to the production process allowed a very great degree of relief to be attained. The introduction of Analgypta had forced Walton's to pull an ace from its sleeve or face ruin. In 1888 it came up with Cameoid, a hollow-backed version of Lincrusta.

The pubs of the 1870s and 1880s had an expanding range of materials with which to work. Innovation occurred frequently enough for there always to be impetus for change. Beer consumption was rising throughout the 1870s, peaking in 1876 at 34.4 gallons per capita per annum. Since the number of pubs was not yet falling, but instead rising demographically, existing publicans saw profits rise, so more money was available for investment, which in turn resulted in an increase in drinking.

Many of these improvements were condemned for leading to an increase in drinking among women. The privacy afforded by the small bars was attractive to them, as were the new surroundings, the respectable ceilings and the rich Queen Anne styles adopted in the furniture of the pub especially the stillions. Occasionally these small bars were referred to as 'ladies' bars', presumably as an attempt to convince women that they are respectable places to enter.

That the temperance movement linked such changes in decor to increases in female drinking is unsurprising. However, the increase in cases of female drunkenness that occurred in the 1890s coincided with the reduction in the numbers of bars occasioned by the introduction of the 'saloon' bar. The increase in drinking among women, prior to the Children's Act, was probably a result of the policies pursued by the temperance movement, and indicative of the split within that movement. The prohibitionists had always resisted public-house improvement since it would make drinking respectable. If it were more respectable it would be harder to proscribe. The issue of female drinking, therefore, is a tribute to the effectiveness of the brewers and publicans in defeating the prohibitionist argument, via their quest for respectability, on the one hand, and the moderate temperance movement on the other, whose success during the period in restraining the number of licences forced the trade to adopt the approach it did.

Whatever the reason, the landlord of the 1870s and 1880s found himself able to adopt new measures to improve his public house, and this was before considering any of the clutter of which the Victorians were so fond. For on the newly hung flock wallpaper were to be found shelves full of books, clocks, jugs, bottles, kettles, stuffed birds, fishes and animals in cases. Watercolours and political cartoons appeared on walls, and mirrors sported adverts for whiskies and fine ales. Pot plants rested on art nouveau porcelain, or on top of the new upright piano. Walls were adorned with nautical artefacts in nautical pubs, swords, firearms, regimental badges, and bugles in military pubs, agricultural implements in rural pubs. Brass rails ran round the bar to complement the highly polished mahogany, which sported newfangled 'gasogenes' – early soda syphons – and whisky urns, which acted as polished supporters to the upright handles of the pub's centrepiece – the beer engine.

In many ways the Victorian public house, having been reviled for most of the century as the shame of the nation, the fountainhead from whence sprang a national curse and affliction, finished the century as a temple-cum-museum to the endeavours of the age. The pub opulence which reached its apogee in the 1890s was made possible through the application of the system of mass production to the wealth of empire. The craftsman's skills, replicated by ingenious machinery, were everywhere to be seen, from the Lincrusta imitations of the plasterer's craft to the taste for extravagant faience, glazed brickwork, terracotta and Doultonware. Everything in the pub was ornate, yet it was ordered from a catalogue and increasingly was done by the same architect who designed the exteriors. The public house, rather than the great lord's stately home, gave us the modern concept of 'interior design'.

The 1880s opened with a change of administration. Gladstone's second ministry was painfully aware that the drink question had kept it out of power for six years. It was not about to rush into a new fight with the drink trade, though many acts were passed. What did change were magisterial attitudes. The 1870s had seen the number of beer houses decline but not the number of public houses. In 1881 the total number of publicans' full on-licences was in the region of 71,800. By 31 March 1884 this number had fallen to 67,944. Not all of this fall was due to the actions of magistrates. A rate revision and a new beer duty in 1880, plus the election of an anti-beer government, all helped to raise prices. In 1881 beer consumption was some 3.4 million barrels lower than the previous year. This represents a per capita decline of 7.2 gallons per annum between the peak year of 1876 and 1881. Total volumes brewed did not match the 1880 amount until 1890, and not until 1896 was the 1876 total exceeded, but the rise in population of some 7 million people over twenty years meant per capita consumption was 33.26 gallons per annum – still 6.5 gallons per capita less than in 1876.

In the face of a sudden and dramatic fall in demand there was bound to be a reduction in the numbers of licences. Slum clearance accounted for much of this reduction. The effects of policy in one area frequently require reassessment of attitudes in another. The policy of the Board of Works in overseeing slum clearance operations, of permitting one new licence for every three public houses demolished – even higher in London – prompted magistrates to consider how many pubs were desirable in any area.

In 1887 the Kendal division of the Westmorland Licensing Board suppressed the public house of a Miss Sharp on the grounds of superfluity. Miss Sharp sued the chairman of the licensing board, Mr Wakefield, on the grounds that he was acting beyond his powers. The case rose through the courts to the House of Lords in 1891, where the long-suffering Miss Sharp lost her appeal. The effect of the ruling was immediate. The principle of suppression without compensation was enshrined in law and a new period of suppression was heralded, culminating with the celebrated Farnham case where local magistrates, in 1902, demanded the surrender of six licences as a result of *Sharp v. Wakefield*.

A brief examination of public house licences throughout the 1880s illustrates the effects *Sharp v. Wakefield* had on magisterial policy as well as the effect on the complexion of the government in power. On 31 March 1884 there were 67,944 full on-licences; a decade later, on 31 March 1893, there were 67,028. The overall decline of 4.17 per cent does not seem a lot, but this was a period of tremendous urban expansion. Villages and hamlets found themselves on the outskirts of towns, outskirts became suburbs and new licences were applied for in these new areas, so offsetting the thinning out of public houses in older, inner urban areas. In 1884 there was one public house, excluding beer shops and off-licences, for every 197 people; by 1893 the ratio was 1:1,444. To maintain the ratio would have required the granting of a further 7,922 licences by 1893. In fact, there were 916 fewer.

It is, of course, impossible to chart the progress of a non-event. It cannot be said that more licences were not granted in one year than were not granted in another, since the chance of success would affect the number of applications. The most that can be done is to examine the visible trend. The last full year of Gladstone's second ministry saw a reduction in licences of 122 in total. This figure was modified the following year to only ninety-seven as the Conservatives interrupted Liberal rule from 24 June 1885 to 6 February 1886. The Liberals were in power again for only five months in 1886, but the number of licences in the year to 31 March 1887 fell by 165. Gladstone was not to be Prime Minister again until 18 August 1892, and during the period of Conservative government prior to the *Sharp v. Wakefield* ruling the number of licences rose by twenty-two. The effect of *Sharp v. Wakefield* was dramatic and immediate: 368 licences were lost by 31 March 1892, and the following year of Liberal rule saw licence numbers fall by 186.

Sharp v. Wakefield actually produced a sharper reduction in publicans' licences than in beerhouse on-licences, which had been declining in real terms under the Tories as well as the Liberals. The number of beerhouse on-licences had only fallen by 346 to 31 March 1892, and there were only 131 fewer beerhouse off-licences.

The effect on the trade was profound. In 1893 there was, in real terms, a 32 per cent shortfall in pubs over 1884, although the amount of beer sold rose by 15.4 per cent. The majority of that rise took place after 1889, that is when the demographic trends were most pronounced. Publicans' profits rose. The situation of the 1880s, when it cost more money to sell less beer, was reversed. Now it cost more money to sell more beer, but the returns were greater. An expanding market with contracting outlets is an unstable environment when there are large numbers of players. The economic boom of the 1890s, *Sharp v. Wakefield*, and a Liberal government from August 1892 to July 1895 set the tone for the tied house wars of the 1890s.

Chapter 19

THE TIED HOUSE WAR

In 1892–1900 certain Young Bloods of the Brewing Companies started to loan money on public houses, and to take over hundreds of them, which were to all intents free to take their business elsewhere, if another brewer was willing to take over the loan. So came it that Watney's and half a dozen others saw outlet after outlet vanishing from their books till it looked as if the old fashioned London brewers were going to be brewers without the means of selling their beer. So they had to join in the race for tied houses, and get what pubs they could at what prices they could. A good many, however, had vanished into the maw of new combinations, and naturally, as the article – the public house – became scarcer, up went the price to the scarcity figures usual when the holder knows the needs of the buyer. This new tribe of brewery companies was not of the 'fine old English Gentleman type' who were content with a 'tie' for beer of a semi-moral kind. The new type tied his publican in newly forged fetters of steel, and having got most of the houses at prices short of the top ones of the 'boom' he stands to lose less by the valuations akin to which the older brewers are now bewailing. In short the new brooms sweep all the profit to be got out of a 'tie' into their coffers and in many cases associate with beer a 'tie' for almost everything.[1]

The Young Bloods were, for the most part, the same Burton Brewers who had been eroding the supremacy of the great London porter brewers throughout the nineteenth century by the gradual popularisation of their bitter, but this was not the first time that the big brewers had had to react to the predatory advances of their northern cousins. In 1834 Whitbread had started brewing a pale ale, in line with most of the London brewers, who had learnt to 'Burtonise', or replicate the qualities of the famous brewing town's water. In fact, today Burton Brewers themselves 'Burtonise' their water, as farming and modern life have made it too impure to use naturally. What caused the second assault by the raiders from the north on the traditional fiefdoms of the southern brewing dynasties was the peculiar nature of the London tie.

Outside London brewers tended to own their estate in order to guarantee continuity of outlets. In London the sheer multitude of premises and the fact that many pubs, unlike those elsewhere, were leasehold and not freehold, had made this unnecessary. The London cartel had, in their gentlemanly fashion, avoided the need for buying estates by operating what was known as the 'London System'.

The London System was a mechanism by which London beer outlets were loan-tied to breweries, who felt secure from the need to add extra expense to their operations by agreeing not to poach each others premises. This agreement worked well, until, as is the case with cartel agreements, it did not. All cartels rely on trust and a fair knowledge of what other cartel members are up to. This is easy as long as things are going well, as they had been until the economic downturn of the 1880s. The beauty of the London System was its self-regulating nature. Brewers all lent to landlords at a basic 5 per cent. Few others would lend at that rate since the risk of losing the licence was too great, so the brewers cornered the market of credit, though a small amount of public-house finance was advanced by distillers. Any landlord could change his supplier – should he so choose. There was no binding agreement with the brewer, though both parties understood that, if the publican did change, the brewer would call in the loan. While another brewer might advance another loan, the cash flow crisis the change in supplier would cause was sufficient to apply enough deterrence to enforce the working of the system.

In the 1880s, however, the publicans were feeling the pinch of higher prices for beer and lower sales. They resorted to watering the beer – the eighteenth century was very much repeating itself. The brewers announced that adulteration would result in loans being called in and supplies stopped. This would spell ruin for a landlord and provide the bench with an excuse to suppress another licence. The publicans sought alternative sources of capital, and found in the Burton brewers willing providers. This threatened the market dominance of the London brewers, who needed to defend themselves from the northern predators, but defence costs money and extra money was difficult to produce in an uncertain market, consumption not rallying until the early years of the 1890s. The London brewers had countenanced a gradual reduction in the numbers of houses as a result of magistrates' decisions, since it improved the overall respectability of their estates, and as the market was not expanding, closing marginal pubs improved the performance of the remainder. This was acceptable so long as all members of the cartel suffered proportionately and magistrates did not favour one brewer over another, as they had done in the 1830s. For all members of the cartel to lose out to the interlopers from Burton was not acceptable. Extra capital was needed, but where were they to get it?

Ironically, the answer was provided by the one brewer with no tied houses at all, and which to this day has no estate – Guinness. In 1886 Guinness announced their impending flotation on the stock exchange. The intention of Edward Cecil Guinness, later Baron Iveagh, was to provide capital for expansion of Guinness abroad, since it was already being widely exported.

The flotation raised some £6 million and was a huge success, being oversubscribed some fifty times. The Guinness flotation prompted a wave of brewery mergers and flotations. Brewery flotations became highly popular and they were ideal public company material. They were already household names and the bulk of their assets were property, and property values were rising.

Between 1890 and 1900 the number of actual breweries – not firms – declined from 11,322 to 6,460, though output rose by 20 per cent. Brewers were merging in order to become more attractive flotation prospects, or to enjoy the economies of scale necessary to inflate margins as a defence against price competition made necessary by aggressive public house purchases by rival breweries – though this was avoided as much as possible.

In the 1780s the London System had come into being as a result of the policies of the magistrates and as a defence against adulteration. Now in the 1890s the wheel had come full circle and the London System was no longer adequate in the face of renewed threats of adulteration, suppression and encroachment.

Between 1886 and 1899 brewery floatations raised a staggering £185 million. Obviously, some of this money went to finance expansion and investment in new equipment and new brewing and bottling techniques, but the bulk was spent on purchasing properties. In July 1898 the well-known and large London firms of Watney, Coombe and Reid combined to float a successful issue of £15 million, this being a full £6 million over the combined book values of the companies. The vast bulk of the flotation proceeds were used to purchase an estate.

The effect of a contraction in the number of premises available at a period of huge once-and-for-all capital injections into the trade was clearly inflationary. In 1886 there were 67,725 publican's licences and 36,067 beerhouse on-licenses in England and Wales. By 1906 that total had fallen to 98,742, but over the same period the population had risen by approximately 6.8 million.

The following table will illustrate how the policy of mergers and flotations produced a smaller, leaner brewing industry, but one with a larger capacity.

Number of Breweries (133)

Barrels Brewed p.a.	1870	1880	1890	1900	1910	1914
<1,000	26,506	16,770	9,986	4,759	3,141	2,536
<10,000	1,809	1,768	1,447	910	722	580
<20,000	210	272	274	262	214	191
<100,000	128	203	255	308	274	280
<50,000	23	23	34	42	41	46
<1,000,000	3	3	2	6	4	5
>1,000,000	0	1	2	3	2	3

Source: Alcohol and the Nation, B. Wilson

There were clearly two phases to this period of expansion. Breweries combined to create firms capable of outputs in excess of 20,000 barrels per annum, and these firms again combined in the 1890s, or combined with slightly smaller firms to create firms with even greater outputs, the mechanism being very similar to the incremental size differences of the porter brewers discussed in chapter ten. The whole industry took a considerable knock in the first decade of the twentieth century with the spate of public house bankruptcies combined with a slump in demand to produce a severe downturn in the industry.

Clearly, many smaller breweries could not find the capital necessary to provide an estate. The increasing price of public houses, plus the increasing investment in their refurbishment, tended towards consolidation of the industry. This fact is borne out by examining the fate of those public houses which still brewed on the premises. These houses had been in decline ever since the late sixteenth century, but although their numbers were dwindling they had received a boost in the nineteenth century both with the 1830 act and with the 1880 transfer of duty to the wort, which permitted anyone to brew on payment of a 6s licence. In 1880 there were 12,417 such premises. In 1914 there were 1,447, and these were confined to rural areas. The inflation in the liquor trade in the 1890s simply forced them out.

In the 1880s the number of bars in pubs had increased as the area inside the public house was put to best use. In the 1890s, faced with demographic pressures and falling absolute numbers of public houses, the policy of the brewers was to extend the size of the premises. The magistrates were, at this stage, happy to permit expansion to take place. The 'bigger but fewer' mentality of the improved public house movement was starting to become fashionable.

When the Liberals were in power the tendency was to refurbish public houses to attract custom in an increasingly competitive market and improve the house in order that magistrates would be more likely to suppress another. Under Conservative administrations licences were felt to be more secure, larger numbers of pubs would be bought by brewers and more public houses would be commissioned from architects and builders. The two-party system, therefore, was very effective at completely changing the appearance of public houses. Expansion under Conservatives would be followed by retrenchment under Liberals, which would lead to increased pressure to buy under Conservatives. The whole together created a highly inflationary spiral.

The Crown, in Cricklewood Broadway, was sold in 1873 for £2,000. It was sold again for £5,000 then £15,000, £32,000, £42,000 and in 1898 it sold for £86,000. It was bought then by the Cannon Brewery of Clerkenwell, a small aggressive brewery of the kind whose activities sparked the tied war. The upward spiral was a speculator's bonanza, and the entry of non-trade interests stoked the fires of inflation. The Cannon Brewery spent £1,363,010 on acquiring 125 pubs between 1893 and 1898, paying maximum amounts in each year of £23,000; £24,500; £28,200; £50,000; £55,000; and £84,000 in addition to £250,000 spent on rebuilding pubs once acquired.

Once acquired, pubs had to recoup the inflated prices that had been paid for them. In order to do this they had to attract more custom, and to attract more custom the pub had to be rebuilt or refurbished. Frequently pubs that had been redecorated in the late 1880s would be further redecorated or rebuilt in the 1890s. The net effect of all this was to ensure that very few surviving town pubs date back much earlier than the 1880s, for pubs of an earlier date would either have been suppressed or would have lost customers to more luxurious newcomers. While the amounts spent on acquiring properties were well known and a source of national fascination as they increasingly diverged from reality, the amounts paid for refurbishment and rebuilding were not so well publicised. Nor were the sources of such funds, though it was nearly always the brewers who extended further loans to landlords and speculative purchasers where they did not install a landlord themselves.

The upward spiral could be justified so long as alcohol consumption could be seen to be rising, but alcohol consumption was not going to rise indefinitely. Between 1889 and 1890 consumption of wine rose by 10 per cent, rum by 12 per cent, whisky and gin by 7 per cent and beer by 4 per cent, despite a rise in the duty on beer. These rates of increase could not be sustained for any great length of time, and, indeed, after peaking mid-decade, per capita alcohol consumption subsided – but public house prices kept rising. Naturally, a point was reached when the prices paid for public houses were greater than could possibly allow a positive return to be made on the business. In that eventuality bankruptcies became inevitable, and it only took a few insolvent pubs coming onto the market at cheap prices to prick the speculative bubble on the surface of which the tied war had been waged.

The bubble burst in 1899 and a string of bankruptcies followed, continuing throughout 1900 and well into 1901. The fact of the matter was that many pubs had been becoming increasingly unprofitable over a number of years as retail outlets, but money could be made by selling pubs, buying others and selling them again, for as long as the price carousel was going round. The trick was not to be on the ride when the music stopped. This was all right as far as the speculators were concerned, but the brewers were into the pub-buying business for long-term reasons. They must have realised that the situation was both unrealistic and unsustainable, and while most brewery money had been lent to landlords, the brewers had also bought estates. In 1881 Whitbread's own pubs were making a comfortable profit of 10 per cent. By 1888 this had fallen to 4 per cent, and as early as 1890 they had ceased to make a profit at all. Similarly of the money they lent, bad debt rarely reached 10 per cent pre-1900, but by 1903 it was 28.5 per cent, rising to 40 per cent in 1912.

When the money to constantly upgrade the pubs dried up so did the rise in alcohol consumption, and when the growth in alcohol consumption went into decline the number of bankruptcies began to increase. The publicans were the losers, and while the brewers were in an unpleasant position, foregoing dividends and writing off bad debts, they at least gained the freehold of many of the insolvent properties. By 1915 the brewers owned 95 per cent of all licences, but many of these pubs were still paying off the interest on which they had been purchased, never mind the principal sums.

The collapse in pub prices and bankruptcies among speculating landlords put a halt to pub construction. Ironically, the finest surviving houses of the Victorian era were those, like the Philharmonic in Liverpool, still under construction as the bubble burst. The collapse of new public house construction meant a greater decline in the number of licences, as no new premises were opened to offset those that were being closed. The 98,742 licensed premises, pubs and beer shops that existed in 1906 had fallen to 88,445 by 1914, and yet the population had risen by a further 4 million over the same period.

Not all was gloom and despondency, however. Although the average length of tenancy in a pub at the time was approximately five years, an average is a misleading figure. Many landlords were speculators, men who had built small empires on the basis of buying, building and rebuilding pubs with a view to selling. But others were people who wished to be publicans and wanted to stay put. Many, therefore, bought houses early in the boom and were content to see the value of the properties rise.

Since they had not rushed to sell, when the bubble burst their losses were merely on paper. Not only did these public houses survive, but many benefited from the collapse of the inflationary spiral. Deflationary fallout from the 1899 market implosion worked to their advantage. They could afford to have their houses refurbished too.

What happened in the 1890s was that as pubs became physically larger – and some were huge affairs with ballrooms capable of seating upward of two hundred or so – the 1880s vogue for a large number of small bars disappeared. Part of the process of investment into the bars of the 1890s was the introduction of the saloon. The class division of the pub came to be 'public' and 'saloon'. Various pubs, especially in the north, might have a third bar – either a tap of very basic appointment, or a parlour, especially for women, with rather more plush surroundings than even the saloon.

In many ways the pubs had priced themselves out of their own markets. The tied war was initiated by the fear of losing outlets to the caprices of magistrates. Vast sums were spent on improving pubs to meet what the brewers thought would please the magistrates, but in order to do so prices had to rise sharply. This was a dangerous policy since the working classes were the bread and butter of the brewers, as can be seen by examining the distribution of licences among the London licensing districts in 1894.

Bethnal Green	848	Islington	832
Bow	1,051	Kilburn	721
Camberwell	792	Lambeth	614
Chelsea	354	Marylebone	430
Finsbury	692	Paddington	333
Greenwich	832	St James	533
Hammersmith	952	Southwark	579
Hampstead	560	Wandsworth	977
Highgate	853	Whitechapel	742
Holborn	387	Whitehall	147
		Total	14,103

Source: Licensed Victuallers' Official Annual, 1894

The more desirable the borough the fewer pubs there were, the reasons for which have been discussed earlier. The brewers ran the risk of pricing themselves out of the traditional markets. In a way, it was fitting that the party ended when it did. Queen Victoria died in 1901, and very quickly the nation realised that the new century was going to be very different from the old. For the public house it was to be a century of decline, a century of increasing control by bureaucracy. Not just the bureaucracy of the Board of Control or the Ministry of Food, but also the bureaucracy of the accountant. The spontaneity and individuality of the pub was to be consciously eradicated during the twentieth century – at first by the public house 'improvers who wanted the pub to resemble anything except a pub, and today by the marketing men who create theme pubs to target the young affluent drinker. Just as inn signs virtually died out in the 1880s and 1890s to be replaced by painted lettering advertising the brewer rather than the pub, so the same fate befell the pub again in the 1950s and 1960s. Just as the publicans adulterated the beer in the 1790s and 1880s, so the brewers introduced keg bitter in the 1940s and lager in the 1960s.

There are still hundreds of Victorian pubs remaining, and we should not complain if they are refurbished occasionally today, for refurbishment is better than closure, even if refurbishment is sometimes merely a euphemism for vandalism. We must remember that those that survive show us only a brief glimpse of Victorian public life. Very few interiors give a picture of the public house of the 1860s or 1870s, while plenty of pubs today give fine examples of the huge diversity of styles embarked upon in the final two decades of the nineteenth century.

Chapter 20

TWENTIETH-CENTURY LICENSING PRACTICE

The Cross Keys Inn, near Caerleon, has failed to obtain a renewal of licence and will be closed. The bench appeared to consider that it should have more accommodation and that the proposed facilities would give 'increased facilities for drinking'. The licensee countered that the inn was at the corner of the roads and no extension of ground could now be obtained, that travellers did not wish to stay there, but that it was very convenient for motorists on their way to Caerleon or to South Wales and that no complaint of bad conduct had been made, but that the needs of the occasional crowd of persons desiring refreshment would only be met by extending the bar and throwing the old fashioned living rooms at the back into one big room. Several well-known teetotallers, not usually seen on the bench sat as magistrates on this occasion. It may be suggested that licensing administration is for the purpose of affording not refusing adequate arrangements for the consumption of alcoholic beverages.[1]

This 1920s correspondent of the *Southern Echo* has put his finger on the nub of the drink issue in the first decade or so of the twentieth century. The publicans and brewers, with the backing of the British people, won the battle over the 1908 bill, but they lost the war. The teetotallers on the bench abrogated to themselves more powers, and in the face of the market crash of 1899 the brewers were powerless to resist. In all truth the magistrates were operating in a fashion completely the reverse of the task they were there to perform, but to point this out was not to find favour.

The twentieth century is one of decline for the public house, and for all those intimately associated with it. The real loser of the twentieth century was the landlord. Up until the 1899 crash he was responsible for his pub. He may no longer have owned it, he may have been in debt, but he was still responsible for its appearance, decor and layout. This was true no longer. Design and construction of public houses was removed from its traditional domain and passed over to a planning system made up of people who, on the whole, disdained using public houses: magistrates, town hall officials and brewery-appointed architects. The result, in some respects right down to the present day, has been the emasculation of the public house. A pub could resemble anything so long as it did not resemble a pub.

The other loser was, of course, the drinker. Victorian particularity, combined with Chamberlain-style municipalism and a bigoted bureaucracy, produced a system whereby the wishes of the drinking man and woman counted least in the scheme of things. It could be argued that throughout the history of British civil administration, nowhere else has the British public been so consistently patronised, ignored and ill-served as in the area of public house management between 1897 and 1939.

The century got off to an awful start. Christmas 1900 was marred by an epidemic of mysterious illnesses centred on Salford. Seventy people died and 6,000 were affected. The cause of the outbreak was determined to be arsenic poisoning. After a period of intense public concern the source was eventually discovered to be a batch of contaminated sulphuric acid. Sulphuric acid was used in the inversions of sugars to produce glucose for addition to fermenting brews.

Once the origin of the arsenic was identified the outbreak ceased overnight, but the incident had a depressing effect on national morale, already subdued by the Boer War, rising beer prices and pub bankruptcies. Given the status beer enjoyed in the British national consciousness, it would have been hard to think of a more effective means of damaging the morale of the nation than by undermining the nation's trust in its beer. The death of Queen Victoria in January 1901 had a sobering effect, too. It was universally acknowledged that what was to follow would not be like what had gone before.

An idea of what was to come could be gained from the Birmingham Scheme. This was reputedly set in train in 1897 as a result of remarks made by Bishop Gore, who suggested, 'The public houses of that day, were all wrong, that they ought to be on the lines of a German beer garden, where there was no reflection on a man, or his wife and children, if they were seen going in or coming out.'[2]

Such a laudable intention may have been part of the scheme's aims, but what actually occurred was an attempt at urban eugenics. Essentially, the scheme was a mechanism for the transfer of licences from the city centre to the expanding suburbs.

> The scale generally accepted for the renewal of a publican's licence to a new site where there were no licensed premises before is three on-licences; for an entirely new beer off-licence, two on-licences; for a new beer, wine and spirit off-licence, two and a half on-licences. . . . For alterations involving considerable extension as many as two licences have been surrendered. Generally it is one on-licence or two off-licences for a considerable extension of existing licensed premises.[3]

It is uncertain how a system operating in this fashion was intended to fulfil Bishop Gore's ends. A brief analysis of the bishop's complaint raises a fundamental question. Are German beer gardens more respectable family environments because they are beer gardens rather than public houses, or because they are in Germany? The temperance campaigners liked to believe the former, whereas the latter was actually the case. As a result, the Birmingham Scheme's main achievement was to formalise and codify what had been going on already on an informal basis: the forced surrender of licences. The surrender of licences, and indeed the Birmingham Scheme, were completely outside the powers that magistrates either had or were intended to have. It was a great shame that no legal challenge was mounted to stop this abuse of power, but Sharp v. Wakefield loomed in the background as a salutary reminder of the complications of going to law and the inclinations of the judiciary.

The Birmingham Scheme, also known as the 'surrender scheme', clearly relied upon the collusion of the brewery companies, and for its successful operation, required the peripheralisation of the landlord as an actor on the licensing stage. The brewers combined to form a company which was entrusted with negotiating with the justices how licences were to be surrendered. The company then organised the distribution of compensation to its constituent brewery members paid out of levied subscriptions. The compensation went, however, to the brewer, *not* the licensee, whose livelihood was ruined not by his own actions or misconduct but by the collusion of the brewers and justices who were acting way in excess of their powers.

The brewers had no choice but to comply. The magistrates were intent on reducing the numbers of licences. Between 1904 and 1914 a thousand licences disappeared in Birmingham. By complying with the magistrates brewers at least were guaranteed the preservation of outlets in areas of guaranteed expanding trade. Unlike the early decades of the eighteenth and nineteenth centuries the twentieth century saw no popular backlash against the flagrant abuse of magisterial powers, indeed quite the reverse.

The 1910 Licensing (Consolidation) Act legitimised the activities of magistrates, giving them, *de jure*, powers they had taken *de facto*. Insistence upon the provision of food was the most common magisterial interference. The act required magistrates to determine what part of a public house's future profits was going to accrue as a result of a monopoly position that the house might enjoy. This gave to magistrates the sweeping power of deciding on the fate of a business, not as yet in existence, by reference to an estimated portion of its expected revenue, determinable only by assumptions of a highly arbitrary nature.

The act went even further. It gave to magistrates the power to insist upon or to veto proposed structural alterations. This clause was for the magistrates a charter for capriciousness. An act of 1904 had established the principle of compensation for landlords whose licences were suppressed or surrendered. Compensation being in place, however, the magistrates were able to salve their consciences with the knowledge that compensation existed (they had, in fact, opposed compensation). In this fashion the temperance lobby fought. Through the operation of an iniquitous system landlords could be denied a livelihood on the basis of what was unobjectively deemed to be the superfluity of their premises, by people who made no secret of their antipathy towards the drink trade.

The operation of the market place was held to be insufficient criteria for the determination of the current level of supply when drink was the issue. This was not, however, a good time for the market. The *laissez-faire* policies of the nineteenth century were now out. Joseph Chamberlain had launched his tariff reform campaign in 1903, and for the second time split a political party. Free Trade as an ideology was on the defensive, and the anti-drink lobby was not slow to exploit the fact. Temperance campaigners laboured to insinuate themselves onto licensing benches whereas representatives of the drink trade were forbidden. The poor publican was faced with having to pay for the suppression of his fellow licensed victuallers under a system heavily stacked against him. When his turn came to be suppressed he may be said to have subsidised his own redundancy.

The consistency with which the magistrates applied their powers under the 1910 act is understood only if one acknowledges that they were not trying to fulfil their duty as licensing magistrates, that is of ensuring a sufficient and orderly supply of liquors through the various types of licensed premises, but that they were trying to restrict demand by restricting supply. The function of the magistrates was to appraise the demand for alcohol and arrange for its supply in an orderly fashion, conducive to the maintenance of law and order and public safety. It was not their function to orchestrate deterioration in supply irrespective of demand or demographic changes. Nor was it their task to deny the existence of demand in the face of contrary evidence provided by brewers and landlords. This, however, was the key note of licensing policy between 1891 and 1939.

No clearer example of this policy need be offered than an examination of the attitudes of magistrates towards plans for building new public houses or for the alteration of the existing public houses. An apologist for the Birmingham System explained that,

> The system has worked excellently. . . . We have an extra-ordinarily good lot of houses. The new houses put up are splendid buildings, well equipped both for supplying food and drink. Plans are always submitted with the applications for removal, and the justices invariably make careful investigations to see that proper provision is going to be made for the supply of food and drink and that there will be recreation rooms.[4]

If, however, existing premises made application to incorporate the 'proper provisions' the justices 'invariably' wished to see, their attitude was rather different. In the aftermath of the 1910 act the South of England Brewery stated,

> The prejudicial attitude of our local bench of magistrates has been so well known to us for many years that we have refrained from making applications to improve our houses in any way which might be held to give increased facilities for drinking, as any real improvement must do. No such application stood any chance whatever of success, and we, therefore, held it useless to go to expense in preparing plans which we knew could never be carried.[5]

This policy was a direct throwback to the policy adopted after the 1869 Beerhouse Act when all applications for improvements by beerhouses were routinely refused. The hope was that by denying the opportunity to make changes the building would become unsafe and then the bench would be able to dispose of it by condemning the premises.

The North Cheshire Brewery, in Macclesfield, protested annually between 1904 and 1916 against the activities of the magistrates. In 1917 the brewery seems to have been broken and their mournful request was that they no longer raised an objection over the suppression of pubs, 'providing that they would leave just one of them alone'.

In 1906 no less than 2 per cent of all licensed premises were referred for compensation under the 1904 act. This represented 1,800 premises across England and Wales. The effect of this onslaught against the trade was to prompt an increase in prices as publicans sought to pass on the burden of the compensation levy to their customers. A side effect of the 1904 act and the strictures of suppression policy in years like 1906 was the success of the 'surrender schemes' that sprang up all over the country, as frightened brewers ate humble pie in an attempt to safeguard the outlets left them.

Besides the magistrates the trade had to contend with such bodies as the Public House Refreshment Association and the Trust Houses. These were institutions inspired by the Gothenberg System of disinterested management, which believed that the profit motive encouraged drunkenness. Founded in 1876, the PHRA started with the Sparkford Inn, Somerset, and by 1927 had 170 houses, while a further 260 non-profit houses were run by the Public House

Trust companies. Although the number of houses controlled by the PHRA and the Trust Houses was never large, they did set part of the standard in defining what an 'improved' public house was to be like. Their ideal was to recreate 'country inn' public houses.

The brewers took up their ideas, and in an effort to please, became even more pastiche than their opponents. The result of the improved public house programme in the 1920s and 1930s was to become known as 'Brewer's Tudor', as it manifested in the huge, characterless estate pubs promoted by the LCC and other metropolitan authorities. The architecture of the pub became all-important, and what would please the magistrate rather than any aesthetic consideration, became the overriding consideration of the architect's brief. This required cultural revisionism of Stalinist proportions. There was to be no concessions to the possibility that the gin palaces of the 1830s and 1840s, or the extravagant high Victorian styles of the 1880s and 1890s, were architecturally legitimate. These were merely vulgar aberrations, which had briefly erred from the family-centred, neighbourly, Merrie England reality of what inns had been. That they had never been like this was not considered, though the proclivity for prefixing everything with 'Ye Olde Worlde' should have been enough to put the lie to such grand scale delusion.

In their desperation, brewers held competitions to come up with appropriate designs. Allsop's held one in 1920, stressing that what they required was, 'a modern building, but one more on the lines of an eighteenth-century inn than of a nineteenth-century public house. Plate glass windows, bay windows and features generally are not desired.'[6] It was inevitable that sooner or later it would be possible to read manuals on how to design pubs with the conciliation of magistrates as the central theme. The satisfaction of the customer, unfortunately, was of secondary importance.

Any bar or compartment in the licensed area having a floor area no greater than $120'^2$ in front of the counter must not be further subdivided, the justices not favouring snugs and corners. . . . The planning of the house should facilitate the complete circulation of the house by the police, when making a visit of inspection, which can be made by entering the house at one door and going out through another, without leaving the cover of the house.[7]

The same author, an architect, informs us of the best plan likely to satisfy Liverpool magistrates. Traditional regional characteristics, therefore, were to be secondary determinants of appearance, after regional variations in magisterial preference. In Liverpool the bench were keen on the complete circumlocution of the premises by the police. The 1930s especially were a period of cloying self-congratulation by architects and designers for their efforts on some truly awful excuses for public houses.

After the collapse in prices in 1899, there was also a slump in the construction of public houses. Perhaps the last to be built in the classic style of the 1890s was the extravagantly opulent Vines in Liverpool, built in 1907, with its completely over-the-top Art Nouveau interior, which competes with its slightly older neighbour the Philharmonic (1898–1900), also with a splendidly rich interior. The Vines was the last of its kind. In 1909 the True Temperance Association was founded. This was a society established by members of the drink trade to steal much of the thunder from the temperance movement. Key among their strategies to forestall and dilute measures opposed to their interests was their firm, wholehearted embrace of the concept of the 'improved' public house.

This is not to say the TTA was merely a front for the organised trade. It clearly attracted a lot of sincere support from other walks of life, and frequently urged the brewers to invest more capital in 'improvement', at times when capital was short. Of course, they were free to 'urge' as much as they liked, but the creation of the TTA was an inspired move, for it successfully wrong-footed the teetotal opposition, who clearly had problems with the idea of improvement. By appearing to be more Catholic than the Pope, the TTA deprived the temperance movement of a key plank in its argument and left them open to the charge of being prohibitionist wolves in reformist clothing, which would likely alienate a lot of temperance support, for there is no doubt that a large body of temperance opinion found the fanaticism of the prohibitionist both exaggerated and distasteful.

What exactly was an improved public house? Under the terms of the 1924 Public House Improvement Bill it was:

> Where licensed premises are not merely places for the consumption
> of intoxicating liquors, but contain adequate provision, in view of
> the character of the house, and the wants of the neighbourhood,

for the supply of other refreshments, and are airy, commodious and comfortable and have proper seating and sanitary accommodation and contain provision of suitable recreation.[8]

The garden city pubs fitted this model – where they existed, for they are few and far between – as did the pubs turned out by the Birmingham Scheme that had gradually incorporated improvement as well as maintaining surrender. Improvement was by no means a short-lived policy. The remarkable thing to remember about the temperance movement was its preparedness to countenance the long-term. They were fantastically patient, and patience has its own rewards.

It was, therefore, still possible in the 1940s postwar era to speak about the desirability of improved public houses, and offer the following description of a typical Birmingham Scheme pub.

Plenty of drawing up space for cars, a good garden, including usually a bowling green; a pleasant kind of elevation recalling, on a larger scale, the old inn of domestic character; oak doors, clear glass in entrance doors, floor behind counter five inches higher than that in front; lavatories for bars outside; two smoking rooms, men and women; plenty of ventilation, and crosslighting wherever possible; assembly room lofty; garden service and no stupid inhibitions about alcohol served there; the bar to 'oversee' all entrances . . . refrigerator, provision for supply of meals and teas, separate garden for children to play in.[9]

Unfortunately we will never know what the natural style of the public house would have been if there had never been any campaign of improvement, if the magistrates had never abrogated to themselves powers they were never intend to have, or if popular sentiment had slapped down the magistrates as it had in the early eighteenth and nineteenth centuries. Probably new houses would have been bland, since they were built with the same materials and techniques that were creating acres of exceptionally bland suburbia in a similar mock-Tudor vein. However, public houses were not left to themselves, for as the magistrates were learning to make full use of their powers the First World War broke out, and for the next twenty years, the drink trade became fascinated by the town of Carlisle.

Chapter 21

THE CARLISLE SCHEME

The ale which could be had for fourpence a pot
Now must be had for one & four the jolly lot;
Let workingman combine to keep down the price,
The Brewers and publicans will climb down in a trice.

So at this price let Mr Bung keep his beer,
If it's good it makes you well, but too much makes you queer,
It's too much to pay for such dear doubtful stuff;
So I'm trying to do without it; my name is John Hadenough.
'Mr Bung's Beer – It's Prohibitive Price', 1917

On 4 August 1914 Britain and Belgium declared war on Germany. Nothing would ever be the same again, least of all the public house. Within four days of the war commencing, the government passed the first of the Defence of the Realm Acts. Initially, there were measures designed to give the executive very wide-ranging powers, but they were of an anticipatory nature, since hostilities had not commenced and the scope of the threat was unknown. Many of the measures passed under what became known as DORA were subsequently relaxed. Drink, however, was one area where regulations were not relaxed and indeed became constantly stricter until well after the Armistice.

Initial regulations came thick and fast. On 8 August 1914 it became an offence to treat a soldier or sailor 'with intent to make him drunk'. Closing times in the vicinity of a harbour were determined by the government. On 31 August the Intoxicating Liquor (Temporary Restrictions) Act gave magistrates the power to restrict opening hours of particular houses, and even to suppress certain houses. The Temporary Restriction Act was widely unpopular and regarded as an unwarranted infringement of liberty, even under the circumstances.

Naturally, for the magistrates the act was the kind of boon they had long wanted. Between September and 19 October, 259 out of 1,000 licensing districts had restricted hours in some way. Opening was permitted between 6 a.m. to 8 or 9 a.m., and then again from 12.30 p.m. to 11 p.m. The effect of such measures were reported to be fairly dramatic. The Brewers Gazette of 24 September 1914 reported that

> A transformation of the night scenes of London has followed the closure of the public house at eleven. Great traffic centres like the Elephant and Castle, at which immense crowds usually lounge about till one o'clock in the morning have suddenly become peaceful and respectable. The police instead of having to move on numbers of people who have been dislodged from the bars at 12.30 at night found very little intoxication to deal with, the last hour and a half being responsible for much of the excesses of which complaint is made. Many of the public houses were half empty sometimes before closing time.[1]

On 19 October 10 p.m. closing was universally imposed, to further public disgust. By the end of January 1915 the number of authorities instituting reductions in permitted hours had risen to 427, in which case many of these magistrates must have decided that the official 10 p.m. closing time was still too lenient. Further measures were enacted. On 18 November 1914 the beer duty per standard barrel rose from 7s 9d to 23s. In April 1916 it rose to 24s, and rose a further shilling the following years. In 1918 it rose to 50s while spirit duty rose from 14s 9d to 30s a gallon.

The beer duty was never to come down to its pre-war levels again. In 1920 it stood at 70s a standard barrel, 100s in 1922 and only fell in 1924, being 100s per standard barrel, minus 20s per bulk barrel, an anomaly which was a recognition of the degree to which standard barrels were no longer a realistic measure of strength, due to the progressive weakening of beer that had occurred throughout the war.

Strangely enough, convictions for drunkenness in October 1914 were actually 7 per cent higher than for the previous month at

15,362 for England and Wales although the convictions in Wales actually fell in October by three). The number of convictions for November, though lower than for October, was still higher than for January 1914, and the number for December not much lower than January's. It can be said then that the reductions in opening hours, much heralded at the time as responsible for an immediate improvement in law and order, were less significant in their impact than the increase in duty.

On 29 March 1915 Lloyd-George, then Chancellor of the Exchequer, declared, 'Drink is doing more damage in the war than all the German submarines put together. . . . We are fighting Germany, Austria and Drink, and the greatest of all these deadly foes is drink.'[2] The problem was not drink *per se* – the artillery scandal that embroiled Lloyd-George demonstrated that much traditional British unpreparedness was not drink related at all. The problem was the lack of discipline among the working class.

The problem faced by the munitions industry in 1915 was the remoteness of the newly constructed factories and the general lack of facilities. They required large numbers of workers to be brought in from outside. In early 1915 the population of Carlisle increased by between 20,000 –22,000 people, many of whom were Irish immigrants.

The early years of the 1910s had seen dramatic increases in alcohol consumption, the war being the only factor that stopped this trend. In 1911 and 1912 consumption of beer rose by 4.45 per cent to 1.55 million barrels. The heaviest drinking had always occurred in the north of England as a result of the thirst created by heavy industry, and most war production was in the north. In 1914, 51 per cent of all convictions for drunkenness were in the north of England, out of the total for England and Wales.

The problem for the government was that the production of munitions depended upon people who were earning more than they ever had, with traditionally little incentive to work, little interest in the war (at that stage at least), traditionally prone to drinking large amounts and with nothing else to do except drink anyway. Arrests for drunkenness in the Carlisle area rose from approximately five a week during the summer of 1915 to thirty-three a week a year later. Drunkenness convictions over the north of England as a whole – including Carlisle – declined by

42 per cent over the same period. Comparison is difficult, however, as arrests do not equal convictions.

On 19 May 1915 the Defence of the Realm Act No. 3 was passed. The act established the Central Control Board (Liquor Traffic) under Lord D'Abernon. Its brief was to improve national efficiency by a reduction of 'drunkenness, alcoholism and excess'. In contrast with earlier resentment caused by the measures of 1914 and 1915, DORA No. 3 was relatively well received by all except the temperance movement. They wished to see the acts used as an excuse for prohibition. In fact their opposition was counterproductive, because if the alternative was prohibition, then most people were happy to swallow the act.

There were several other factors assisting the act. Its passage was sweetened with the understanding that it would render unnecessary alternative drink control measures. The munitions scandal made people realise that domestic inefficiency cost lives at the front, and there was acceptance that compulsory restriction was part of the general patriotic response required from the population at large. Between the passage of the Temporary Restrictions Act and DORA No. 3 there had been the German capture of Amiens, the Battle of Aisne, the Battle of the Marne, the Battle of the Yser, the First Battle of Ypres, the Battle of Soissons, the Battle of Neuve Chapelle, the Battle of St Michel and the first use of poison gas.

The Central Control Board had very extensive powers. It could close any licensed premises or club – with compensation. It could restrict the sale of certain types of liquor and impose conditions upon the sale of liquor. It could dictate the level of supply and control the transport of liquor. It could establish the supervision of premises and inspect premises. It could create a monopoly of supply in an area, it could compulsorily purchase premises and acquire them as businesses, including stock-in-trade, and it could then carry on in business without reference to the licensing laws. It could prohibit the buying of rounds, it could provide entertainment, or suppress it at its discretion, it could grant excise licences. It could order the dilution of spirits without reference to the Sale of Food and Drugs Act. Lastly, it could provide postal and banking facilities.

However, if the prohibitionists thought the board was going to do their task for them, they were sadly mistaken. It began its operations in a very modest and discreet fashion. The first areas to come under its jurisdiction were ports, at the insistence of the Admiralty, but it should be noted that the board was not responsible for deciding which areas were to fall within its purview. First under its control was Newhaven on 26 July 1915. In August Southampton, Barrow, Dartford, Bristol and Avonmouth were added, along with the north-east coastline, Liverpool and the Mersey area, Newport, Cardiff, Barry and those areas of Scotland around the Clyde and the Forth. On 22 November the Midlands, the West Riding, Portsmouth, Plymouth, Falmouth, Pembroke and the West Borders also came under the Central Control Board's jurisdiction. A year later 38 out of 41 million people were under board control.

The board was not overly heavy handed. Under Lord D'Abernon it understood that cooperation would make its task much easier than coercion, and that resentment of the board would lead to abuses and attempted evasion of its regulations, with the result that resources would have to be expended in surveillance and enforcement. The board's regulations were not uniform. It examined what was necessary and appropriate for each area, frequently consulted beforehand and published its findings before enacting restrictions.

A fairly general regulation concerned afternoon opening hours. It restricted the afternoon sessions to 12.00 to 12.30 opening, usually 12.30 in the north of England where shift workers were in the habit of stopping off for a couple of a nips of spirits on the way to work. It was also intended to reduce alcohol consumption by women, whose traditional drinking time was midmorning when they could enter public houses unseen by their men folk, who were all at work, and when they had a little leisure time on their hands. The number of convictions for drunkenness among women had actually risen in 1914, and despite the measures enacted, only fell by 4,100 to 33,211 in 1915, or by 10.5 per cent, whereas among men the fall was almost 44,000 or 30 per cent. In 1916 the figure for women fell by 30 per cent once the board's policies began to bite.

The Central Control Board also frequently restricted off-sales, so that they ended before on-sales, though this must have been very hard to enforce. It did, however, ban weekend off-sales of spirits, to reduce the traditional Monday absenteeism. During the rest of the week spirits could only be sold between midday and 2 p.m. and in sealed bottles of a quart minimum capacity, so that it was not easily portable and could not be carried in small bottles in jacket pockets. Spirits were also banished from the railways as a further measure to protect the sobriety of troops.

The board also enacted other general measures. It prohibited the extending of credit, though how effectively is uncertain, and encouraged the provision of food. Where this was not feasible it established its own canteens, being equally anxious to ensure that the workforce was receiving proper nourishment as well as trying to moderate drinking by combining it with eating. As general public health measures the board's restrictions were fairly effective. There were immediate and pronounced falls in deaths certified as resulting from alcoholism and cirrhosis, a fall in suicides and a fall in infant mortality. In 1918 the total number of convictions for drunkenness was only 15.8 per cent of the 1914 figure.

While all this seemed to be highly satisfactory, it was noticed that there were one or two rough spots where these measures just did not appear to be sufficient. The worst of these was Carlisle. Within this area there were 5 breweries and 368 licensed premises. In Carlisle itself there were 119 public houses and 7 clubs. The board bought up all bar 47 of the pubs and all of the breweries. Two of the breweries were closed, a third was converted into a beer store. That left one brewery to supply Carlisle and another, at Maryport, to supply the Gretna region.

A total of 123 public houses were suppressed, 53 in the Carlisle region, while 3 new premises were opened. The first, and most famous, was the Gretna Tavern, which was to do the work of 6 former public houses. It was, in fact, a converted post office, and it looked like it. It was designed by Harry Redfern, who between 1916 and 1931 was to design many of the 'improved' pubs in the region. Redfern was a supporter of the Birmingham-inspired 'fewer and better' school. The pubs were intended to be unassuming and unglamorous, and if the creation of unglamorous premises was Redfern's brief, he was amply capable of discharging it.

The decor of the Gretna was grey. Not surprisingly, it was detested by the drinking public who felt that they were drinking in a post office, which they were. It is also not surprising that thousands of column inches of enthusiastic tributes to tile Gretna Tavern were produced after its opening. Improvement fanatics were still holding it up as a model twenty years later. The fact that its customers only patronised it because there was no alternative was not a consideration.

A decade later, Carlisle-Scheme apologists were seemingly contradicting themselves. 'Of the 119 licensed houses originally purchased in the city only 65 remain. These provide ample accommodation for the needs of the city, except on particular Saturdays such as Hiring Fairs and when there are important football matches. On ordinary Saturday nights there is still some overcrowding in particular houses.'[3]

This faulty logic – there being 'ample accommodation' for people's needs, except when there was not – was a direct result of the criteria used by the board to determine which houses should be suppressed. Volume of trade and location were secondary considerations behind the perceived suitability of premises and their economy. Pubs were not located where there was a demand for them but where they were thought to be suitable. Suitability was determined by people who did not patronise the pubs or understand the needs of the working drinker.

In 1921 the ratio of pubs to people in Carlisle was 1:810 – the national ratio was 1:375. This was a ratio guaranteed to cause overcrowding, or require exceptionally large houses. During the war, when the population of Carlisle was even greater, this overcrowding was made worse by the fact that all grocers' licences were suppressed and off-licences reduced by 80 per cent. This meant that the basic policy of the board in the Carlisle region was one of restriction of supply, irrespective of demand, which of course was what the magistrates had been doing prior to the war.

The board in its refurbishment of public houses and construction of new public houses tried to influence the behaviour of its customers. It disapproved of what the 'improvers' liked to refer to as 'perpendicular drinking', or what is more usually known as 'standing up'. To discourage this the bar area, in contrast to the evolutionary process of the previous century, was made as small as practically possible, and customers were confronted with waitress service. The bar staff were all dressed in uniform, which must have reinforced the impression of drinking in a post office. If the bar was small the rooms were large, in order to accommodate tables and chairs rather than people. The calculated effect was to slow down people's drinking. Drinkers would have to catch a waitress's eye, and wait for her to fetch the order and weave between countless other tables and chairs before their drinks would arrive. Short of immediately retaining the same waitress and promptly despatching her to the bar once more, it would be impossible to maintain Saturday night's drinking pace.

The next new house opened under the scheme was the London Tavern at Longtown, where there was, and is, a large ammunition depot. Opened four months after the Gretna Tavern, it was described in *The Times* thus:

> The model tavern at Longtown, which is the most recently completed seems thrown away in this bleak old border town. It is built of fine reddish stone, very solid and handsome round two sides of a court, holding a bowling green, with a raised flagged walk all round and an Italian pergola down one side. The rooms are plain and strictly adapted to their purpose, but they are large and lofty, and have an austere picturesqueness and refined dignity worthy of anyone. If architecture can lift the public house out of debasing associates it is done here.[4]

It is not surprising to find that people who learned to drink in the mellow warmth of Victorian public houses were less than impressed with 'austere, large, lofty and dignified', even if they did have a pergola to contemplate as they waited for their waitress. The main emphasis of the London Tavern was as a café-restaurant, the bar being presented as very much the intended secondary function of the premises, though this was not actually the case. Attempts at pushing food with drinks were, on the whole, unsuccessful. The temperance movement had discovered this already in 1903 when a campaign to identify drinking with eating had been a failure. There was just not the demand. Those pubs that sold hot take-away food, however, did quite well, though the board and improvers failed to notice the fact, for take-away food was never a deliberate feature of improved houses. The middle-class concept of sitting down to a meal brought to your table by a servant or waitress was held to be the desirable norm.

The praise heaped upon the London Tavern, again, frequently by people who had never been within a hundred miles of it, on top of the reception afforded to the Gretna Tavern, raised a popular clamour among the temperance movement for the nationwide extension of the Carlisle Scheme. This time it was the government rather than the brewers, publicans and punters who squashed the idea. In the first instance, it had a war to fight, which took up quite enough of its time, without having to extend a scheme covering a few hundred thousand people to one covering 41 million. In the second place, the government was well aware from the public demonstration over the 1908 bill and 1910 act that drink was a highly charged political issue. One of the reasons why the board's operations in the nationalised areas were successful was because of the remoteness of these areas. It was one thing to convert an old post office into a rather unattractive pub in Gretna, but to do the same thing in Liverpool docks, the Potteries, Leeds or London would have invited national civil disobedience and electoral ruin for the party concerned. Lloyd-George was a Liberal. He knew well what drink had done to the Liberal party. He also knew that it was wise not to fight the war on too many fronts.

The German submarine campaign was having serious effects on the domestic war effort. Barley, like anything else, became a precious commodity. It had proved necessary in April 1916 to pass the Output of Beer (Restriction) Act, which reduced output, in March 1917, to 26 million standard barrels, a cut of 4 million barrels and a reduction on 1914 of 10 million barrels.

In 1917 it was decided that original gravities of beers (OG) should be reduced. In 1917 the average OG was 1040°, although under the 1916 act the Food Controller decreed that one half of beer production was to be of a strength of 1036° or below. In 1918 the target was that the average OG of all beer production should not exceed 1030°–1045° in Ireland – and, shrewdly, no beer was to be brewed below 1010°. This was to protect public confidence and to prevent brewers from brewing some ludicrously weak beers in order that they might brew some strong beers and still maintain the required average. Between 1917 and 1930 the actual average fell from 1040° to 1030°. Beer restrictions did not end with the Armistice and restrictions were gradually eased through 1919. Average OG was permitted to rise by 2° and output was increased. In July 1919 volumes were unrestricted and the permitted average OG was raised to 1044° for the UK and 1051° in Ireland, and in July 1921 OG restrictions were abolished. In the event beer strengths never approached their pre-war levels and in 1923 the average strength was 1042.7°, from which level it fell for most of the century only starting to rise to this level again at the end of the 1990s.

Not only was the beer a full 16° lower in OG by the end of the war than it was at the turn of the century, it was also four times as expensive and popularly reckoned to be pretty poor at that. Still, consumption rose by 50 per cent between 1918 and 1919; there was a victory to be celebrated after all. What frequently happened, however, was the establishment of co-operative breweries to produce alternative superior beer to that which was otherwise on offer, since brewers, in the face of increasing sales, did not have to improve the quality of the beer, or its strength.

Normality was resumed with the 1921 Licensing Act. This abolished the Central Control Board and restored the supervision of the licensed trade to the magistrates. Houses were permitted to open for eight hours a day, nine in London, but with compulsory closing in the afternoon (a system that survived until 1 August 1988). The act also abolished the concept of *bona fide* travellers who were entitled to be served on a Sunday, who were by then precious few compared with those who claimed to be.

With the end of the Central Control Board came the end of nationalisation in Enfield Lock and Cromarty. Nationalisation remained the order of the day in Carlisle, with authority transferred to the Home Office, which enabled pub improvement enthusiasts – like Lady Astor – to continue to enthuse about Carlisle and make reverential pilgrimages to its grey public houses until the onset of the Second World War.

Improvement continued to be the buzzword throughout the 1920s and 1930s, but it masked the fact that once the effect of the war ended the temperance issue ended too. The war had, of necessity, achieved many of the aims of moderate temperance advocates, who had always run up against the problem that the fulfilment of their aims, under normal circumstances, required an intolerable restriction of the traditional liberties of the populace. For the less moderate temperance campaigners, the war had stolen their thunder. You could not seriously tell returned soldiers that they must not drink while the worst excesses of drink abuse had been eliminated. The health of the nation was now not related to drink but to the fact that the fittest sons of the nation, an entire generation of sturdy drinkers, had been cut down. In the US the Volstead Act of 1919 ushered in a period of prohibition. Mafia and moonshine in the US effectively destroyed the credibility of prohibition on this side of the Atlantic.

For those that returned from the war the 'land fit for heroes' failed to materialise. Unemployment was rising, and government in those days of 'classical economics' would do nothing to alleviate it. Beer duty and prices fell in the 1920s as a concession to public opinion, though even through the deflationary period of the 1920s and 1930s beer prices failed to fall in line with the retail price index.

Another nail in the temperance coffin came with the implementation of the Scottish Local Option Act. The outbreak of war had superseded the operation of the act, but in 1920 the local option question was put to the vote. Of the 584 licensing areas which voted, 511 voted for no change, 37 voted to restrict licences and a mere 36 voted to go dry. If Presbyterian Scotland was not interested in local option, soft Anglican England was never going to be. There were further attempts to raise the question, but it was dead, Wales already being divided into 'wet' and 'dry'. Temperance ceased to be an issue, because in large part it had secured what it set out to achieve. Drunkenness was not the national disgrace it had been and there was improvement across the spectrum of drink-related interests.

Two interesting points are worthy of note as a result of the war and 'improvement'. First, the two combined to improve the lot of women. In Victorian times female drinking was taboo, regarded as a furtive activity. The war was accused of encouraging female drinking, and it would be surprising that with newly won liberties in so many fields, women now would be drinking less. Although there was no great overall increase in female consumption, those women who did drink did so in more concentrated numbers and so achieved a higher profile. Having complained that women were drinking more, those who raised the complaint were left with little further to complain about. The logic of the improvement policy was that the improved public house should be respectable enough for women to enter without embarrassment. If, once in, they should then choose to order a drink, the improvers were hardly in a position to complain that this was unseemly or improper. Traditionally, women's drinking places were frequently inferior; women had less disposable income and often were encumbered with children, neither of which tended to endear them to landlords or male customers. It was right and overdue that much of the stigma should be removed from women using public houses, though it is amusing to see some of the limp attempts of the improvers to face up to consequences of their own logic.

Nothing is worse than furtive drinking among women. It is prevalent everywhere. In many houses one discovers a small, usually quite unsatisfactory 'snug' or corner, screened from view where women are allowed to congregate. It may be that some women prefer segregation, not because of a desire for secret drinking, but because they don't like entering mixed bars. If separate rooms are needed for the accommodation of those women who require them, they should at least be as commodious and well appointed as the rest of the house.[5]

The other important point to note is that the Carlisle Scheme failed. Despite the best efforts of the Control Board it was not possible to look back on the period and argue that Carlisle was any less prone to drunkenness than any other area. It had started off as more prone to drunkenness, due to extraordinary circumstances that were not unique to Carlisle but, where replicated, produced the same problem. Special measures were successful in ameliorating these circumstances, but there is no evidence to suggest that they induced Carlisle to become a naturally more sober place. In the words of one chronicler of the scheme, 'the conditions of the trade involved in such changes are not those that influence sobriety and public order.'

This conclusion is supported by subsequent history. In 1931 the True Temperance Movement was complaining that Carlisle was exceptionally drunk still. Cases of drunkenness were running at 9.58 per 10,000 population in 1930, compared with 4.2 in Liverpool, 4.1 in Newcastle, 2.4 in Birmingham, 2.4 in Salford, 1.3 in Leeds and a genteel 0.8 in Bristol.

Despite this evidence, the nationalisation debate raged on into the 1930s, way after the Gretna Tavern was no longer à la mode. However, to understand the argument it is necessary to understand what people were doing in pubs in the early part of the century.

Chapter 22

THE INTERWAR
YEARS

In this tavern you may find
Everything to suit your mind –
Good wine, good fish, and flesh in courses,
Coaches, chaises, harness, horses.

In the 1930s Gracie Fields and George Formby were the two
largest box office draws at the British cinema. The two of them,
with thirty-five film credits between them, were never shown for
what they were, working-class people from working-class
environments. They were fish out of water, working-class people
transplanted into middle-class situations. Films were made by
middle-class people, who had no idea how to put Formby and
Fields into working-class situations. Contemporary attempts to
portray the working class were universally awful. This was
because at this time there were, sadly, two Britains, completely
ignorant of each other on a scale unparalleled in our history.
With the rise of suburbia, the decline in domestic service, the
specific location of industry and countless other social factors that
had their seeds in Victorian England, the lives of the majority of
the population were a mystery to the educated minority, and so
was the public house.

Polite society in the 1930s was almost wholly unaware of what
working people did in public houses. A few people freely admitted
the fact and tried to do something about it. George Orwell gave
us the brilliant and incisive *Road to Wigan Pier*, while Tom Harrison
organised Mass Observation and launched a new sociological
approach – the Vox Pop. He set up Mass Observation since, as an
anthropologist, he knew more about the cannibals of the New

Hebrides than of the working populations of Lancashire and East Anglia.

It is with a sense of bathos that one discovers that much of the most detailed information about the habits, manners and attitudes of the English drinkers of the 1930s is a result of the methodology designed to make the lives of cannibals and stone-age tribesmen intelligible to members of the Royal Society.

Less voyeuristic are the accounts of those who were there. Shortly after her retirement in 1978, Bessie Beed, who was then, at 100, Britain's oldest licensee, wrote memoirs of her seventy years 'behind bars', first at the Red Lion, Blean, Kent, and then at the Old White Lion, Bradninch, Devon. The pub clubroom was used as a changing room for local football games; a prohibition on ball games in pubs meant that until the Second World War, bagatelle, billiards and 'devil among the tailors' had to be covered up on Sundays, Christmas and Good Fridays. On a Sunday morning her customers were all fishermen from Whitstable, posing as travellers to get a drink, and had trudged the statutory three miles from their own parish in order to qualify. During the Depression, the pub was a local means of self-help, where a box club was run and where, on share-out night, a big dinner was laid on and was eagerly looked forward to. Every day the spittoons were cleaned out and had fresh sawdust placed in them. In the years of the Great War the stock consisted solely of beer, porter, whisky, gin, rum and port, while, 'during the '20s and '30s beer was generally sold at about 5d or 6d with bitter 7d a pint, gin and rum were usually about 6d a drop and whisky was always a penny dearer, with Martell's brandy a costly 9d a drop.'[1]

In the south of England porter was clinging on, while in the north the universal drink was mild, with bitter being an occasional luxury. At 7d, a pint of bitter had doubled in price from the start of the war, and although there were calls for a fall in price during 1919, these did not bear fruit.

The Times of 22 January 1919 reported, 'The fact that beer of low gravity and poor quality costs more today than the more palatable and stronger beers of four years ago is resented, and it is stated that some of the dock labourers in Liverpool and other ports of the country are talking of extreme measures unless the situation improves.'

Some clearly hoped that the fear of popular revolt would lead to an increase in the quality and strength of the beer, since fear of bolshevism was rife, and England, under the banner of the White Army, was still fighting Trotsky's Red Army. A *Times* correspondent, signing himself John Barleycorn, warns, darkly, 'the fact remains that the contrivance of the excessive restrictions on the sale of alcoholic refreshment is causing so much discontent among the workers, that they are simply becoming ripe for revolution . . . what the Englishman wants and what he will take good care he gets is more, and better and cheaper beer.'

As a matter of fact, the Englishman did not get more, better and cheaper beer. He only got more and slightly better beer. After the initial euphoria of postwar victory celebration died down, it was quickly apparent that the country was a very changed place. There was no sustained campaign for a swift restoration of pre-war strengths of beer, nor was there a return to pre-war levels of drunkenness. In part this was due to the fact that a generation of drinking men were now dead, but also because there was a genuine sea change in public attitudes. In short, now that supply was no longer a problem and gravity was no longer restricted, it was found that the public were happy to accept weaker beer than previously.

In January 1920 the Versailles Treaty fixed the postwar settlement and the League of Nations came into being. Global events could not help but influence the national mood that in turn influenced every High Street saloon and every back street tap. President Wilson could not carry the United States with him into this 'new world order', but his vision of self-determination and his famous '14 Points' were topics of conversation and matters of inspiration in the rest of Europe as much as the German plebiscites that they provoked.

Other factors influenced society, which in turn, manifested themselves in the public house. The postwar epidemic of Spanish Flu claimed more lives than the war had, and this time the deaths were on the home front; while the rise of communism, the domestic growth of the Labour Party, the struggle for the emancipation of women and the methods used in their struggle for the vote – all had profound impacts on public attitudes and, therefore, the public house.

These social changes led to popular ideals of greater sobriety and moderation. The propagation of the wireless led to a growth in demand for bottled beer, while the inter-war years were ones of a gradual decline in the strength of drink, though the amounts drunk fluctuated widely according to the state of the economy. This naturally meant a reduction in the number of pubs. In 1905 there were approximately 99,000 licensed premises; by 1935 there were roughly 77,500. In the period between 1911 and 1939 and 5 million new domestic properties were built. Suburbanisation was itself a force for social change, most notably in the general health of the population, but it also provided for a continuance of the policies of 'surrender' and 'improvement'.

Inner city licences were surrendered in order that pubs might be built on the periphery of expanding towns. There was nothing new in this, except that, as simple geometry shows us, the faster towns expanded the greater the circumference of the perimeter of the towns, with the result that unless the rate of the public house construction increased – which it did not – then the density of public house location must fall. This, in turn, meant that the atmosphere of the suburban pub was affected by different competitive influences. The suburban pub was meant to have a distinctly suburban air. The houses of Mitchell and Butler in the West Midlands demonstrate this trend, mock-Tudor being very much their fashion, and while they were careful to employ a variety of architects – unlike Watney, who over the same period produced a number of houses of remarkably unimaginative drabness that could be almost described as a house style – half-timbering is, even today, very much an M&B hallmark. In 1934 Watney's architectural division had a staff of forty who were then engaged on no fewer than twenty public houses.

Mock Tudor was the first of the brewers' fads; unfortunately, it was not the worst. 'Tudor did at least have some visual appeal, whereas the neo-Georgian pub could easily have been mistaken for a bank or a post office, so far removed was it from the glitter and sparkle of the gin palaces.'[2]

If the period from 1900 to 1919 was one of improvement, 1919 onwards was one of improvement with a vengeance. The brewery trade quickly appreciated the changed national mood, and decided that by pursuing improvement further the changed national mood need not be disadvantageous. 'In the minds of the more thoughtful section of the industry there is no fundamental conflict between the financial interests of the licensed trade and the social environment of the people, and this social improvement can be carried out without antagonising the consumer. What we may call the backbone of this policy is the improved public house.'[3]

Improvement was a risky strategy, since it was a long term strategy. The brewers had learned from the excesses of the late 1890s that the more lavish the improvement the greater the security of the premises, but the smaller the chance of making a reasonable return. There was a tightrope to be walked. Improvement had the twin benefits of securing premises, since magistrates, who were entitled to make stipulations, could hardly suppress premises they had previously approved, and the act of investment by the brewers would, by the fact of the amounts of money involved, make state intervention less attractive from the point of view of all parties. The government would not wish to spend the money itself if nationalisation was an option, and indeed, in Carlisle, it did not. It must be remembered that at this time, although no further nationalisation was ever embarked upon, this was by no means a certainty, and there were plenty of vocal advocates actively campaigning for the extension of the Carlisle Scheme.

Between 1922 and 1930 approximately 27 per cent of the total number of public houses in England and Wales were improved in some way or another. In some parts of the country there was a chronic undersupply of public houses. Council estates of the period were ludicrously underpubbed. The Downham Tavern, in south London, was the only pub on an estate of 30,000 people. It had the longest bar in the country, but despite this 'perpendicular drinking' was forbidden, while no fewer than thirty-five people were employed to ensure that drinkers remained seated and served. The direct parallels between these new estate pubs and the early experiments of the Carlisle Scheme cannot be ignored. Pubs like the Goat Inn, at Enfield, and the Fellowship Inn, in Bellingham, south London, with its roof garden, were built on similar lines, and today remain, as they ever were, places noted more for their architectural interest than for conviviality and community spirit.

Naturally, the impetus for change was led by middle-class sentiment, which, as we have seen, was completely unaware of the needs and desires of the majority of the population. Orwell summed up the destructive side of the 'better and fewer' policy that was the reverse of the 'improvement' coin.

As for pubs, they are banished from the housing estates almost completely, and the few that remain are dismal sham Tudor places fitted out by the big brewery companies and very expensive. For a middle-class population this would be a nuisance – it might mean walking a mile to get a glass of beer. But for a working-class population, which uses the pub as a kind of club, it was a serious blow at communal life.[4]

Neither did one have to be as perceptive as Orwell to dislike the results of municipal paternalism.

> We haven't got a cinema
> We haven't got a pub
> We've got a hundred tennis courts
> And a splendid cricket club,
> And lovely rambling, rosy walks,
> And many gay parterres,
> And solid civic seats behind
> The houses built in pairs.
> We don't hold with such fallacies
> As pubs and picture palaces.

The philosophy behind these policies was incredibly entrenched, and as shall be seen, survived beyond the end of the Second World War, with the result that there are similarities between the construction of the large municipal estates of the 1930s and the development of the Garden Cities in the wake of the 1945 New Towns Act.

David Swaffler, a temperance agitator of the period, wrote of the Downham Tavern that 'more than any German beer house I have seen, than any French café I know, a centre of communal life . . . it had no bars. All drinks are served at small tables in large saloons . . . if all houses were like the Downham Tavern drunkenness would continue to die out even more rapidly.'[5] His comparison with French and German premises is instructive. Why should he compare public houses to German beer houses and French cafés? Most public house customers at the time never went further afield than Blackpool, Skegness or Margate. Swaffler is clearly talking to another constituency, one, as has been said before, that would never set foot in the Downham Tavern, but who felt entitled to dictate to those that would.

The aims of improvement would perhaps have been better achieved had not its most vocal supporters been so insufferably pompous and sanctimonious.

It is all to the good that some of England's public houses should be reformed, reconditioned, or improved, and made fit and decent places for refreshment and recreation of the people. The process is already taking place with all the celerity and enterprise that circumstances allow, and in countless places squalid and uncomfortable bars are being turned into pleasant and genial resorts to which Mr Citizen may, without local scandal, take his wife in the evening to listen to a fair little orchestra and, in the words of Bishop Brougham, 'see Truth dawn . . . over the glass's edge'.[6]

Tom Harrison did not see fit to direct his observers to ascertain what the drinking population of Bolton thought of Bishop Brougham, but he did ask them why people drank.

Why I drink beer, because it is food, drink and medicine to me, my bowels work regular as clockwork and I think that is the key to health, also lightening effects me a lot, I get such a thirst from lightening, and full of pins and needles, if I drink water from the tap it's worse, beer makes me better, the more I drink the better I feel, neither does it make me drunk, when a Boy a horn of Beer before Breakfast was the foundation for the day.[7]

The Bolton worker drinks because he likes it. He likes beer, he likes to drink, he has always done it, even if the surroundings he does it in are Spartan.

The pub isn't much different from the other houses in the block, except for the sign with its name and that of the brewery firm that owns it, but its lower windows are larger than those of the others, and enclosed with stucco fake columns that go down to the ground, and the door, on the corner, is set at an angle; it is old-looking, worn, brown; in the top half is a frosted window with VAULT engaged on it in handwriting flourishes; at the edges of the main pane are smaller ones or red and blue glass.

Behind the bar are shelves; reflecting themselves against the mirrors at the back of their shelves are rows of glasses and bottles, also stacked matches and Woodbine packets. Beer advertising cards and a notice against betting are fixed to the smoke darkened yellowish wallpaper; and on the wall besides the door, is a square of black glass, framed in walnut, that has painted on it in gilt, a clock face with Roman numerals, and the letters NO TICK.[8]

That was a Bolton pub one weekday evening in 1937. The following is a description of a rural pub from 1935, which the author is using as a template to which the improved urban pub should match. We may very quickly conclude that this pub was not in the vicinity of Bolton.

It is almost sacrilegious to break the silence, but here on one side of the passage is the bar, and here is the parlour with a wood fire, and here is the host, courteous, genial and quietly philosophical, draining our honest beer to two tankards. On either side of the bar in the 'tap' is the pleasant hum of rural dialect, and with quiet flick-flick of the darts into the board. The 12-year-old black spaniel, fat with years, rises from her place before the fire and gives her paw for a biscuit. Sibyl, the daughter of the house, comes in flushed from hockey and bangs her gear on the floor, and will talk of victory or maybe defeat . . . whilst, a singularly gracious hostess will tell of the first snowdrops seen in the garden, and of occasional lopping of trees.[9]

The objection to the improved public house is its inorganic imposition of a misplaced and idyllic stereotype. It was true that a large proportion of the population felt that the public house had acquired a disreputable character within the space of forty or fifty years or so. Unfortunately, the transformation from diagnosis to proscription was achieved by the use of a *non sequitur* which arose from the acute class divisions present in English society at the time.

'The English Inn was fallen from the high place it had once occupied in the social life of the community. . . . The only lasting and beneficial reform will come when the sociologists and legislators recapture the catholic spirit that made the inns an integral part of the life of Merry England.'[10] It barely warrants pointing out that an attempt to recapture the 'catholic spirit' of a bygone age is bound to fail, if that bygone age had never existed other than as the wishful thinking of a particular coterie of a particular class.

Before and after pictures of improved houses will, to the modern eye, look better before than after, but we cannot judge history according to our taste. There was no reactionary backlash against improvement, no campaign to defend public houses from being improved – unlike today, when refurbishment of public houses continues apace, much to the detriment of the pubs concerned, in the opinion of the pub preservation lobby. There clearly was a consensus. Popular morality was in sympathy with market realities in the interwar period. Improvement made commercial sense.

In the 1920s and early 1930s, when much attention was still directed at the Carlisle Scheme and there were frequent calls for further nationalisation of the trade, and when brewers were frequently mistrusted as monopolists, the defence of the tie was the main priority. Much effort was made to convince the government that the tie was in the industry's interests.

It is remarkable how many persons are ignorantly attracted by the lure of the word 'free'. The tied house system is in reality only a method of rationalization by which capital can be most economically and effectively applied. Without this system there would hardly be any improvement . . . as . . . there is nothing in principle to prevent retailers in free houses from spending money as liberally as the brewers but the truth is that they have not got the money.[11]

In the second place, improvement was a defence against the increase in competition provided by clubs. From 1905 to 1935 the number of clubs rose from 6,554 to 15,657, with a combined membership in excess of 5 million. Clubs also frequently depended upon loan ties, and so provided guaranteed outlets for brewers' beer. This was useful from the point of helping the brewer to run his plant to nearer capacity, but it was not necessarily a great help to his profits. Many clubs entered the field of 'cooperative' brewing and many were non-profit-making bodies. There was, therefore, stiff price competition to get into this market, which was regarded as a serious threat to the public house. Profits were very low on club sales, and brewers and licensed victuallers both preferred to see people drink in pubs and not clubs.

There had always been a reluctance in the brewing industry to engage in price competition, even in periods like the interwar years, when the overall market for beer, as for most other products, was declining. Improvement was a further method of safeguarding market share, but that only affected the distribution side of the brewers' business. Falling output also had effects on the supply side.

In 1900 there were 6,390 breweries. In 1910 there were 4,482, by 1914 there were 3,650; 2,889 in 1920; 1,418 in 1930, and by 1939 a mere 885. Mergers and takeovers had reduced the numbers of breweries to one-seventh the 1900 level in under forty years. Prior to 1900 acquisitions and mergers had been entered into to finance expansion. In the period after 1900 the process slowed down as brewery debenture holders often blocked plans for mergers. In the contracting postwar market, gains could be made by cutting costs and rationalising production. Mergers and takeovers were again the solution.

As early as 1911 the *Brewers Gazette* of 3 July was pointing out that

It is clear that brewing costs can be reduced by this method and the closing down of breweries within the metropolitan area and the concentration of brewing operations for a number of companies in a few of the largest and best equipped plants would be calculated to assist in the financial regeneration of companies. For with amalgamating they will, in a majority of cases, be associated with the extinction of capital unrepresented by assets.

As time went by and demand continued to decline, the pace of mergers accelerated again between the late 1920s and mid-1930s. Those firms most avariciously acquiring others were emphatically those not associated with the expanding part of the trade – the clubs. Ind Coope, Allsop, Simonds, Brickwood, Matthew Brown and Watney, Combe, Reid were all active acquirers at this time, while Bass, Worthington, Guinness and William Younger were all closely associated with the club trade. What the club suppliers had that others had not was bottling capacity. Bottled beer was an increasing proportion of a declining market, but bottling was a capital-intensive operation. These companies had a lead, and the familiarity of the club drinkers with their products meant they were being asked for in the pubs of other brewers. Thus, large firms were able to establish themselves without the need for acquisition.

In 1934 Ind Coope and Allsop combined to become the country's largest brewer and one of only two with capital valuation in excess of £10 million. This merger had been desired for a long time and was necessary to maintain the firms' productive capacity. Mergers undoubtedly assisted the increase in efficiency of firms. So too did improved roads, the introduction of cheaper commercial vehicles and other such innovations that reduced the cost of transport – always a high proportion of the variable cost of the production of beer as a result of the very bulk associated with the product – and allowed the viable acquisition of houses further afield. Small breweries on the edge of a larger brewer's domain could then be acquired along with their houses, and, in such fashion, the capacity of the larger brewery maintained. Familiar names such as Greene King, Brickwood, Vaux and Fremlins defended themselves in this fashion.

The emergence of the preference for bottled beer and the reluctance to compete on price grounds had a further effect on the public house – the disappearance of inn signs. Ever since the general increase in literacy in the late nineteenth century, breweries had started to advertise their brands of entire or pale ale on the outside of their houses. The world's first registered trademark was the famous red triangle of Bass's Beer and in the days before widespread literacy Bass faced tremendous problems with the piracy of their mark due to its very effective level of market recognition. By the 1930s the habit of writing the names of beers on the exteriors of pubs had become quasi-traditional, so that the most dominantly displayed item outside the pub was the brewing company's trademark, frequently in the form of a lantern over the door, examples of which survive today.

The Times ran a debate throughout the 1930s on the vanishing pub sign, a phenomenon that must be counted as a result of the growth in advertising and marketing techniques rather than as a result of improvement, and which, if anything, was noticeable as a trend running counter to the improvement ethos of the time. This may well explain the tone of rebuke adopted by *The Times*.

The owner who is proud of his inns and ambitious for their character and popularity will not let slip the chance of using his inn sign to show that he regards his guests as persons of polite habits and good taste. But an inn sign which is nothing but an advertisement for beer is open to the interpretation that the inn is only a beer house.[12]

Such a comment was designed to sting the 'improving' brewers into feeling shame. Even the licensed victuallers were aware of the disappearance of the sign, and the cause of it. In 1932 the *Monthly Bulletin* was explaining that 'the old inn signs were vanishing because the brewers were too intent upon displaying their trade marks to remember the former amenities.'

However, not all the blame could be laid at the door of the brewers. Other factors had contributed to the decline of the rural inn sign.

When the roads fell into disuse and the inns into neglect the signboards fell with them. Anyone born before the era of the motorcar, may remember signboards that were boards with no signs, because dirt and the weather had hidden or destroyed the painting. The inn had become a local beerhouse, and the local drinker could find it without a sign.

A renewed interest in inn signs, therefore, was partly a result of a renewed use of roads, whereby the neglect of many decades was finally noticed. The works of H.V. Morton and the comments of Stanley Baldwin directed the focus of the nation towards the countryside. People were reminded of the importance of the sign in the history of the public house. Quotations, like this from Goldsmith, were dusted off and pressed into service.

An alehouse keeper near Islington, who had lived under the sign of the French King, upon the commencement of the last war pulled down his own sign and put up that of the Queen of Hungary. Under the influence of her red nose and golden sceptre, he continued to sell ale, till she was no longer the favourite of his customers; he changed her, therefore, some time ago for the King of Prussia (Frederick the Great), who may probably be changed in turn for the next great man that should be set up for vulgar admiration.[13]

Vulgar admiration also meant vulgar education. People were reminded that inn signs were the story boards of English history, and a vocal campaign to defend the inn sign was got up. In 1936 *The Times* sponsored an exhibition of signs at the Building Centre, Bond Street, and for a while many a public-house sign post supported no sign, as hundreds of the nation's best remaining signs went on loan to London. The exhibition was a great success, and although the brewers still preferred a trademark to an inn sign on their cheaper properties, they did take note of the strength of public feeling, holding their own competition for signs at their 1938 exhibition, judged by Sir Edward Lutyens, so that today the inn sign is still a major feature of English heritage.

All this is not to say that the inter-war years were an entirely bad period. Some pubs were actually improved by improvement and many were doubtless preserved as a result. Improvement was as much a defensive measure resulting from depression and declining sales as it was a sop to the chief constables and magistrates who enthused over it. The increase in beer consumption between 1919 and 1920, when restrictions were lifted, was in excess of 11.8 million barrels. The output in 1920 of 35,047,974 bulk barrels had by 1933 fallen to 17,950,303 barrels. In other words, the depths of the Great Depression produced a fall in demand to a level even lower than could be achieved by legislation during the First World War (lowest output was 19,085,043 in 1918). In 1933 the average OG, at 1039°, was equal to the 1920 average. The massive fall in consumption, 50 per cent in thirteen years, illustrates the scale of surplus brewing capacity that there was and helps place the policy of acquisition and merger as a means of maintaining capacity output at the core of the business in its proper perspective.

These figures also illustrate the extent of the difficulty the brewers and landlords found themselves in. During the Depression the brewers were very anxious to guard their sales. They frequently employed men to watch the arrivals and deliveries from their rivals' yards to try to gauge how much business they were doing. In 1937 the Bolton Brewery visited by Mass Observation was openly running at less than full capacity, a fact which caused concern to the brewery manager. By 1937, however, appeasement was giving way to rearmament, and just as rearmament provided a financial stimulus to pull the nation out of recession, so it also proved to be thirsty work, for that year saw consumption rising once more.

Chapter 23

THE SECOND WORLD WAR: MODERN TIMES

Not drunk is he who from the floor
Can rise again and still drink more,
But drunk is he who prostrate lies
Without the power to drink or rise.

On 26 February 1991 the Prospect Inn, Minster, Kent went under the auctioneer's gavel. It was the last of ten public houses to be sold off by Whitbread that day, and like half of them it failed to reach its reserve price. The Prospect, like the other nine pubs, had suffered a decline in barrelage over a number of years, and implicit in the sale was the understanding that the property need not remain a public house in the future. When it was built by the architect Oliver Hill, it was the favourite darling of the public house movement. Styled on the bridge of the Queen Mary, its plans were reproduced in building journals, brewery trade publications and architectural magazines. Today it is an architectural oddity, a historical anachronism, very much like its floating inspiration.

Although the Prospect was a 1930s creation, in many ways it belongs to a wider era. It was built with the future in mind. It was very much regarded as the way things were to go. It was the first modern theme pub, a pub built for architects and marketing men rather than the drinking public.

The postwar era was more a story of changing brewers than changing public houses. Consensus was largely unchanged, and per capita consumption continued to drop. The number of public houses continued to decline and was only offset by the rapid growth in the free trade in restaurants, clubs, off-licences and supermarkets.

The tendency to reduce licences also persisted after the war despite evidence that the 'better and fewer' policy was seriously flawed. It would be difficult to criticise the policy of 'better and fewer' for failing to curb drunkenness, but it would seem that drunkenness fell from 1915 onwards with the restriction of opening hours. It must be pointed out, however, that drunkenness was falling in areas where little or no improvement had taken place, notably in parts of the north of England.

What is interesting to note is that the period of improvement was also a period of declining beer sales and that improvement, as demonstrated previously, was a defensive measure forced on brewers by a combination of magisterial preference *and* poor sales. As such, improvement was a result of more moderate drinking rather than moderate drinking being a direct result of public house improvement, as the improvers would have people believe. Falling beer sales were also a function of the increase in alternative forms of recreation that started to proliferate through the 1920s and 1930s: radio, cinema, sporting clubs and societies, rambling and cycling clubs (who did, admittedly, boost rural pub sales), municipal swimming baths, greyhound racing and horse racing, public libraries and dance halls. If people were spending less time in public houses because they were spending more time at other places, then all improvement could be claimed to do would be to induce people to patronise the pub when they might otherwise have chosen an alternative. This, of course, was the complete opposite of what the improvers sought to achieve.

On the question of fewer houses the simple facts are that the argument that fewer public houses resulted in less drunkenness was simply erroneous. The logic which argued for fewer public houses was simple and understandable since drunkenness was greatest where public houses were most prevalent, but it was based on a misconception.

Poorer people drank more and got drunk; there were more pubs in poor areas because richer ones kept publicans out and opportunities were greater in poorer areas because poor people drank more. If we cast our minds back to the opposition to the early gin palaces, a common complaint was that they were perpetually teeming with people entering and leaving. Yet these complaints are descriptions of people patronising a scarce resource. In fact there is an inverse correlation between numbers of public houses per head of population and the incidence of drunkenness. In short: the more pubs there are, the less drunkenness there is. The figures for 1936 are quite conclusive, and are taken over all the licensing areas in the country.

Pubs per 10,000 pop.	Average no. of convictions per 10,000 pop.
0–10	11.02
10–	9.97
15–	8.01
20–	5.96
25–	5.51
30–	5.32
40+	4.11

Source: *The Pub and the People*, Mass Observation

Drunkenness was also more likely to be a factor of the extent of industrialisation of an area. In an industrial area the density of pubs would appear to be greater because of the density of population, giving the impression of a causative link between pubs and drunkenness, whereas the causative link was instead between the extent of industrial activity in a town and its drunkenness. Naturally, there is a close correlation between unemployment and drunkenness, with a very close correlation between increases in unemployment and increases in drunkenness. This correlation will be stronger in an industrial area where there is a reduced diversity of labour opportunities and unemployment is more of a shared communal experience.

It is possible to produce statistical evidence showing a closer correlation between the incidence of drunkenness and a variety of other criteria than between drunkenness and the number of premises. The level of marriages, changes in the bank rates, employment and even brewery shares have all fitted the bill at one period or another, not to mention fine weather (the finer the weather the greater the consumption, with the exception of December).

The realisation that the entire policy of 'fewer and better' was based on a misconception came as a bolt from the blue to the Mass Observation team, who had never doubted the social desirability of the policy before they examined the data. They were awakened to the reality of the situation, which has been the subject of criticism throughout this book, that licensing justices had a responsibility to determine the public interest, but isolated themselves from either the brewery trade as they were obliged to under the 1910 act, and the public house, which they did from inclination.

> They [the JPs] can, and do, use their discretion from the angle of their own opinions, unfettered by public intervention or appeal. The public of this democracy have no nominee, no representative, no effective voice in this as in so many other matters which concern them. The result is a continual inhibition, a conservatism from necessarily aged persons who are also automatically too high up the social scale to know much, if anything, about ordinary pubs. Not only pubs but hotels and restaurants all over the country are affected even to the detriment of tourist traffic.[1]

The vagaries of the bench had become increasingly ludicrous. In the early part of the century they rejected an application for one landlord's licence because the tenant's quarters contained a combined WC and bathroom instead of separate ones. Yet the Royal Commission on Licensing (1929–1931) clearly laid down the duty of justices: 'The sole issue which the licensing justices have to consider in such circumstances is whether, having regard to all circumstances, it is in the public interest that the licence should be granted.'[2] The magistrates felt free to let their prejudices override their obligation. Sadly, the Second World War did little to alter their opinions.

During the Second World War, like the First, there was a dramatic and necessary rise in beer duties. Unlike the First World War, beer consumption rose between 1939 and 1945. In April 1933 the duty on a barrel of beer of $1027°$ was 24s, rising by 2s per extra degree of strength. By September 1939 duty was 48s; by April 1940, 65s and rising by 2s 6d per degree. July 1940 saw duty rise to 81s and 3s increments. By April 1942 duty was 148s 1½d with increments of 4s 4½d, and in April 1943 duty stood at the 138s 4½d with increments of 5s 1½d.

In the war period the average strength fell from a peak of $1041°$ in 1939, to 1034.34 in 1943, with duty on an average barrel rising from 52s to 174s 3d. In 1943 beer production was fixed at the 1938 level of output, but due to the reduction in strength the output in 1943 was actually 5 million standard barrels greater than that for 1938.

The biggest jump in consumption during the Second World War came in 1942. American troops started to arrive in significant numbers only at the end of the year, and so they are unlikely to account for the entire increase in consumption for that year. Other factors were also at work. A nation fighting for its life was a thirsty nation. People in abnormal circumstances are less likely to make provision for their needs during impromptu arrangements, and what institution is better suited to the satisfaction of impromptu needs than the pub. Soldiers were billeted in pubs, something that would have been unthinkable in 1914. Barley and hops were not such scarce commodities as they were during the First World War, though the labour to turn the barley into malt and pack the hops into pockets was scarce. In rural areas, at least, should beer shortages occur, cider was often available as a stop gap.

Part of the reason for the increase in drinking was the character of the war. In 1940 London was in the front line. People died in the nightly raids, so that, on one level, shunning hard liquor for the sake of our long term health meant little if each night could be your last; on another, the blitz kindled a camaraderie which gave the pub a social pre-eminence it had not enjoyed since the early nineteenth century. The appeal of Vera Lynn was truly classless. In wartime people sought out human contact, and what better place to do so than the pub. With food, clothing and petrol items all rationed, beer was virtually the only item that many people could find on which to spend their incomes.

In many ways the pub stood as a symbol of the blitz, for its traditional corner location meant it suffered disproportionately from blast damage compared with other buildings. The licensing laws also did not make allowance for war and the law was strict on a licensee's obligation to open. To see partially demolished premises open for business if they could find two crates of beer and a trestle was not an unusual sight in London's East End, though the bombing of public houses was met with almost undisguised pleasure by some improvement elements.

The *Monthly Bulletin* in 1942 saw bombing as an opportunity for pub improvement. 'Licensed houses new and old will then have to be fitted into the planning schemes of postwar reconstruction. There will be an appreciable redistribution of licences. We could ask for nothing better.' One wonders how a publican felt on reading these words after his pub had been bombed. He must have wondered which side the improvers were on.

With the end of the war, redistribution and improvement were again the watchwords of the day. Indeed, under a socialist government committed to planning, a return to improvement was completely natural. In 1942 a committee was established, under Herbert Morrison, to consider the planning of postwar licensing requirements. In welcoming planning the improvers managed, once more, to commit some logical *non sequiturs*.

> No sane person wants to rebuild the destroyed houses exactly as they were. Although there is a well inspired movement now against oversized houses, it is more or less certain that new houses which are to satisfy modern ideas must mostly be larger than old ones. Rather fewer houses, therefore, will be required. Again there is the possibility of some desirable accommodations among brewery firms – desirable because some licences are unnecessarily kept alive by rather expensive competition. Skillfully handled, this possibility might develop into an economic carve up.[3]

To assume that no 'sane' person would desire a return to the pre-blitz status quo is presumptuous in the extreme. It is a statement without any supporting evidence, or any attempt to consider that many of the residents of British cities bombed during the blitz might well wish for their old pubs to be restored, more or less, to what they had been, although it must be allowed that building materials were in short supply and that housing, not pubs, was the priority. The improvers recognised that there was a backlash against the brewers' Tudor and neo-Georgian styles, but dismissed it as merely 'well inspired' without caring to accommodate the thought that improved public houses could be anything other than in tune with public demand. They go on to state that in spite of increased demand for a change of policy, no such change will occur and implicitly suggest that now the policy of fewer and better is to be replaced by fewer and cheaper. Accommodation that will reduce competition will be encouraged and it is desirable because expensive houses are sustained by competition that would otherwise not be required, and the desirable end of reducing competition will, possibly, produce an economic boom.

It is hardly surprising that, in the light of such confused and tortuous wishful thinking, the rather sad history of the public house in the twentieth century allowed for no renaissance.

Chapter 24

LAGER, KEG AND CORPORATISM

I'm the man, the very fat man,
That waters the workers' beer,
What do I care if it makes them ill,
If it makes them horribly queer –
I've a car, a yacht, and an aeroplane,
And I water the workers' beer.

Paddy Ryan

In 1936 the East Sheen Tennis Club complained to Watney's that since they only sold beer at weekends they were suffering a lot of wastage from beer going out of condition during the week. Watney provided them with a barrel of their new trial pasteurised beer that Watney were experimenting with which was meant to supply troops in India, not the home market. Bass had undertaken a similar, non-pasteurised experiment in the nineteenth century. The popularisation of that brew at home, which became known as India Pale Ale, could in no way be a portent of what was to happen as a result of the popularisation of another beer by the genteel members of that well known vanguard of the British drinking public — the East Sheen Tennis Club. It became known as Watney's Red Barrel, a name now synonymous with all that was abysmal.

With the exception of a small supply to clubs, little was heard of Red Barrel until the late 1950s when other changes in the brewing industry made it a useful weapon in the armoury of the brewery in the attainment of their long-term strategy. In the 1960s the large breweries again went in for further periods of concentration, with the intention of reproducing themselves as national brewers rather than as London or Burton-based regional brewers. Although it was

288   AN INEBRIATED HISTORY OF BRITAIN

Flowers Breweries, rather than Watney, who were the first to heavily promote keg bitter, once one started the others were quick to follow, with the result that Watney, Ind Coope and Whitbread led the pack that dashed into the promotion of keg in the 1960s.

In 1959 the pasteurised sterile beer, wherein all secondary fermentation within the cask has been stopped, now known disparagingly as 'keg' was identified by its fizzy nature and method of being raised from the cellar by gas pressure, so dispensing with the need for the traditional long handled beer engine. It accounted for 1 per cent of beer sales. From this modest base it enjoyed a phenomenal rise. In this it was assisted by the increase in national market penetration by those brewers who produced keg, who were also the largest and most predatory; the prosperity of the 1960s which resulted in increasing beer consumption – keg reversed the decline in beer consumption; the desire to turn a collective back on the relative austerity of the 1950s, and especially the poor beer quality that had obtained since the war; improved domestic insulation, heating and refrigeration technology; the advent of the foreign package holiday; and aggressive promotion by the brewery companies. From a 1 per cent start it grew to 7 per cent in 1965, 8 per cent in 1966, 18 per cent in 1971 and 40 per cent by 1976, by which time lager also accounted for over 20 per cent of UK beer sales. This meant that once a further 23 per cent of bottled and canned beer was subtracted, draught beer, be it bitter, mild or stout, now accounted for only 14 per cent of all beer sales.

The success of keg was all the more impressive considering that it was, on average, two pence a pint more expensive in 1972 than pints of 'real ale', as traditional beer came to be known. Real ales, hand pulled cask conditioned beers, tended to have a stronger original gravity than their more expensive keg counterparts. The motives behind the heavy promotion of keg are not hard to see. It kept longer than real ale, was easier to handle and did not object to being bulk transported.

The acceptance of keg enabled the brewers to set about weakening the strengths of their established brands. Watney's Special fell from 1043.1° OG in 1960 to 1037.9° OG in 1971. This provided the brewery with an absolute cost saving of £2.64 per barrel over 1960. A further fall to 1036° OG in 1972 increased the saving to £3.08 at 1971 prices. Over the same period Ansells' Bitter also fell from 1045.3° OG to 1038.9° OG in 1971.

In 1959 lager accounted for 2 per cent of all beer sales; by
1990 it accounted for 50 per cent. Contrary to popular belief,
lager was not entirely a postwar entrant to the domestic scene. In
1900 there were already over a hundred small domestic lager
producers in England, but their numbers declined in the first
decades of the century, a typical example being the British Lager
Brewery Company Ltd of Devon Street, Liverpool, whose short
life lasted from March 1899 to 25 November 1902. The
Wrexham Lager Brewery was established in the 1880s and the
Glasgow Lager Brewery in the 1890s, so the drink was not the
stranger to these shores prior to the Second World War that
people often imagine. The popularisation of lager in the 1950s
was largely the result of the efforts of one man, the Canadian
brewery magnate E.P. Taylor.

Applying the principles of Adam Smith, Taylor saw in England
an opportunity to extend his brewing operations by the introduction
of Carling, complementing this innovation by the introduction of
bitter into his native Canada. In 1953 the Hope and Anchor
Brewery Company of Wadsley Bridge, Sheffield, was brewing and
bottling Carling for Taylor, but the brewery's estate of 150 houses
was clearly too small for Taylor's ambitious plans. In 1959
Northern Breweries came into being via the merger of the Hope
and Anchor Breweries, Hammonds United Breweries of
Manchester Road, Bradford, and John Jeffrey and Co. of the Heriot
Brewery, Edinburgh. The Hope and Anchor Breweries, had existed
since 1899 and had traded under the name since 1942 when it
had merged with Henry Tomlinson Ltd, whose Anchor Brewery,
Sheffield, was destroyed by bombing in 1940. Hammonds United
Breweries were a slightly older firm, having been incorporated
in 1889, while the brewery of John Jeffrey and Co. had been in
production since 1837. In their day Hammonds, whose brewery
has now been demolished, were an aggressive brewery firm, having
taken over the Ilkley Brewery and the Aerated Water Co. in 1923
with thirty-seven licensed premises, the Springwell Brewery Co.,
Heckmondwike, with its eighty-eight houses in 1929, Bently and
Shaw, Huddersfield, with their 192 houses in 1944, and Seth
Senior and Sons of the Highfield Brewery, Huddersfield, in 1947
along with their ninety-nine premises.

The Northern Breweries was to be a short-lived phase in the
history of the operation, which acquired a further sixteen brewery

companies between 1960 and 1962 when it was renamed United Breweries. By 1962 it had an estate of some 2,800 premises, which were added to that year when the brewery merged with the large east London firm of Charringtons (1738), which then combined with the Burton on Trent firm of Bass (1777). Bass, Ratcliff and Gretton had already combined with Worthington's in order to become the dominant Burton brewers in 1927, and in 1961 they merged with the Birmingham firm of Mitchell and Butler (1888). The 1967 merger of Bass and Charrington also saw the disappearance of Liverpool's Bents Brewery Co. (1889) who brought 514 premises with them, and whose brewery ceased production in 1975. The large merger produced Bass Charrington, which remained the country's largest brewery firm until Scottish and Newcastle took over Courage, a blow from which Bass's morale never recovered. Ind Coope (1708) became Allied Breweries in 1961 after merging with Tetley Walker, formerly Joshua Tetley and Son (1822) of Leeds and the Warrington firm of Walker Cain (1846) until their merger in 1960, Ansell (1857) and Friary Meux (1960) – from Friary (1895) and Meux (1888) – were added in 1963.

By 1970 Bass Charrington was able to get Carling Black Label into 9,736 on-licensed premises, and it owned a further 1,640 off-licences outright. Notwithstanding the large numbers of clubs and other free trade on- and off-licences which took its canned and bottled output, Bass Charrington was in a strong position to popularise Carling Black Label nationally. Other brewers were not slow to come up with their own branded alternatives.

Lager also benefited from the 1961 Licensing Act, which encouraged the proliferation of off-licences and bottle departments in grocers and supermarkets. The increasing penetration of television into British homes in the 1960s, combined with the relative ease with which lager could be canned with little detrimental effect on flavour compared with bitter, also greatly assisted the growth in the popularity of lager.

The Licensing Act of 1961, which removed restrictions on off-licences, prompted a popularisation of wines and spirits which had previously enjoyed very low levels of consumption. Interestingly, heavy fortified wines initially caught on faster, outselling table wine until 1970, when both types of wine sold approximately 24 million proof gallons, after which table wine began outstripping fortified wine consumption. This indicates that the 1960s and 1970s were very much an era of changing palates; eating out was becoming more popular and more accessible, a wider variety of exotic foods were on offer, and, by comparison, traditional English fare looked stodgy and heavy. In the 1980s this change in tastes towards lighter foods and lighter beverages was enhanced by the growth in demand for 'healthy' foods, which in the late 1980s and 1990s has also led to the demand – possibly brewery-led demand – for low alcoholic and non-alcoholic 'so-called' beers and lagers. (Strictly speaking, the 1948 Finance Act forbids anything with less than 2 per cent alcohol by volume from being called a beer, unless it is specifically ginger ale or ginger beer.)

For Bessie Beed, at the White Lion, Bradninch, the end of the war meant neither a return to improvement or very much by the way of immediate change. Her evacuees returned to what was left of Leytonstone, London, and she lost her US service clientele. Cigarettes and sweets were not back to normal until the 1950s, but such rationing as continued did not affect the life of a village pub too much. There were regular events which kept her occupied: the annual carnival, the blind school outing (paid for by the locals), the selling of *War Cry* in the pub by the Salvation Army, the village treasure hunt, the occasional travelling fair and the annual round of wedding receptions and Legion dinners, not to mention the annual harvest festival service which was held in the pub, and, of course, the Wednesday games night. These recreations, however, could not go on indefinitely and soon enough her brewery – Starkey, Knight and Ford Ltd (1887) with breweries at Bridgewater, Somerset and Tiverton, Devon – fell to the mercies of Whitbread in December 1962 along with its 400 house estate.

In the latter half of the twentieth century refurbishment was to mean a very different thing from what had gone on before. Work on the exterior was unlikely to be as extensive as previously. The sign might be updated or replaced by pre-moulded plastic lettering or an extension might be added, but no longer were attempts made to convert a building of a given period into one of another. Thanks to the war, there were plenty of destroyed pubs to be rebuilt completely in a variety of equally mediocre and unassuming styles. Most of the emphasis was on the interior of the pub, and here the tendency was for the increasing exclusion of the tenant from the design process, as the tenant came to be seen as a liability rather than an asset, and certainly as a smaller cog in the mechanism of the brewery machine than the designer or architect.

He may, in an extreme case, nearly break the hearts of architect, designer or brewer by introducing inappropriate, not to say deplorable furniture.

The introduction of deplorable furniture was to be entirely the preserve of management.

Convinced believers in management say that it is too chancy to commit the care of an improved public house to a tenant who may be indifferent to the architectural harmony and the various emblems of a cultivated taste which have been entrusted to him to cherish and preserve.[1]

This view was incorrect as it turned out. The preservation of a house was more likely to occur under a tenant than a manager. A tenant is usually one half of a couple who view the premises as their likely long-term home (average incumbency lengths having grown in the twentieth century). The tenants had a vested interest in the community and could afford to take a long-term view. They would often be fairly hard up for large amounts of capital to spend upon refurbishment, for even though the practice of paying goodwill to the outgoing landlord died out before the Second World War, moving into a pub entails much expense and frequently debt. For the postwar landlord extending credit was still a requirement when settling in, though credit giving, once the bane of the licensee, had now been squeezed out by modern financial discipline.

Managers, on the other hand, are employees of the brewery; they may or may not have a partner with them, but their loyalty is to the brewery rather than the community. They may be looking towards their career progress in the firm, or for a better posting if the house is not exactly to their taste. Therefore, their commitment to the premises will be more short term. The manager rather than the tenant will be the one who refurbishes the house in an undesirable fashion. The manager can often have greater call on brewery resources and is better placed to sell his proposals to his superiors, especially if he has a proven track record. He will not care if the regular customers are driven away and the public bar is converted into a disco area, or whether elderly customers are alienated by piped music or the ubiquitous juke box. The manager has already decided that pensioners do not spend enough money over the bar. He is trying to attract customers with a larger disposable income, which means young people. Frequently the nature of the refurbishment of pubs is, therefore, determined by the intent, not just to 'refurbish' the interior, but to change the character of the premises with a view to attracting a different type of clientele.

Managers of this kind made names for themselves in the 1960s, precisely when the brewery companies were subordinating the individuality of houses to the primacy of the corporate image.

> Illuminated perspex signs provided an effective and compar-
> atively cheap method of implementing the company and brand
> identity exercises that newly found awareness brought to the
> brewery giants. But the materials themselves were seldom
> compatible with the traditional materials of pub architecture. So
> the developing influence of marketing in the brewing world,
> compounded, in part, by the then current states of the art of
> corporate design and of sign technology obsessed with plastics,
> created a blandness and uniformity in pub design.[2]

Various issues of Watney's house magazine for the 1960s and 1970s – the appropriately named *Red Barrel* – described refurbishments. Its issue for August 1970 sings the praises of some completely ghastly houses.

> The bar names – The Cloisters, Jolly Friar and Merry Monks –
> reflect the general theme of the house, which is derived from
> nearby Barking Abbey.

> A false ceiling, new bar and back counter, carpeting and new
> furnishings have been installed, the general décor and pictures
> conjuring up Derby Day of years gone by.

This example does not sound too hideous, except that the Derby Day theme is in the Derby Arms, East Sheen, and the association is with the town of Derby or the Earl of Derby and not with the

Epsom races. The company were being lazy and this results in historical confusion. Inn signs are easy to decipher clues to local history. Refurbishment in the postwar era has too often replaced long-standing pub names with more snappy marketing department chosen names, so that local history is forgotten, or obscured by sloppy décor.

East Sheen got off lightly compared with what the brewers' designers unleashed on other towns. The Sutton Arms, Southend, suffered an appalling fate. 'Designed on a "cave" scheme, with imitation stalactites and stalagmites, and a bar called the "Cave Dwellers",' one can only assume that Watney's marketing department had identified a significant community of troglodytes in Southend, not previously identified as a fruitful market sector. However, in 1970 the Cave Dwellers was by no means the last word on the subject. 'Previously known as "The George IV", this rebuilt house is now decorated on the theme of the honeycomb, even the cash register being hidden inside an imitation wooden hive. The Honeycomb, Hounslow.'

By the 1980s the thinking behind such pub refurbishment was firmly established in the core of Grand Metropolitan corporate strategy. Many pubs were branded under the Chef and Brewer and the Open House groups, having approximately 750 houses each in 1985 (as of November 1993 part of Scottish and Newcastle). The former concentrated on traditional-type pubs, with an emphasis on food, especially the lunchtime trade. The latter operation embraced ten 'concepts', more closely identified with weekend drinking by the young, and it also tried to target young women as prospective customers, but the philosophy of Open House was intentionally flexible.

The approach has been to refurbish pubs following distinct design concepts which are contained in a master manual. A large proportion fall into the Open House style with an ambience far removed from the traditional brewery pub. One style called Barnaby's encompasses family restaurants (66 pubs). Other styles include 'Sports' (20) which offer facilities for the games enthusiast. Pub 80 (150) which aim to give a wine bar environment; Fashion Bars, Blitz (2) is an example of a Fashion Bar – it has a large food operation to attract lunchtime shoppers, and also has a 2 a.m. supper licence.[3]

Obviously, Grand Metropolitan are not alone in following this path. Their Berni Inns have their rivals in the Harvesters and Beefeaters owned by rival nationals. One cannot blame the brewers for indulging in market sector analysis, or market sector specific refurbishment of houses. One can, however, wish that the results of these refurbishments were not so awful, formulaic or confusing variety with gimmickry. It cannot always have been easy, given the mentality of many of those responsible. In the 1970s Roy Wilson-Smith, Watney's in-house designer, told the *Evening Standard*, 'I want to give people who use my houses a rare and primitive relationship with the raw forces of nature. People like to be awed when they enter a pub by a superior natural force – a strange sort of higher masochism.'

Chapter 25

THE MODERN ERA: THE NATIONAL BRANDS

Come Landlord fill the flowing bowl,
Until it doth flow over,
For tonight we'll merry, merry be
For tonight we'll merry, merry be
For tonight we'll merry, merry be
And tomorrow we'll be sober.

Since the end of the war the number of public houses has been in gentle decline, though the number of full on-licences has risen. The total number of licensed premises has also risen by around 70 per cent in this period, so that public houses, wine bars and hotels only account for some 40 per cent of alcohol sales, and among the public houses the number directly under brewery control is also declining. This has started another cycle of mergers and takeovers that led to the creation of the modern market with its national domination by a handful of monolithic brewing leisure combines, coexisting with some forty or so regional brewers.

As has been mentioned, the immediate postwar period was a time of declining per capita beer consumption, with relatively modest increases in consumption occurring in the early 1960s and more substantial increases later in the decade. Simultaneously, there was a change in drinking patterns, increased competition from other leisure amenities and a change in the profile of the drinking public away from older working-class males and towards younger professional people of both sexes.

While the last of these trends may have been actively encouraged by the brewers' companies, it was still, like the others, one to which they had to react. The policy from the late 1950s down to the early

1980s was to concentrate on holding on to estates. The arrival of keg enabled this to be achieved on a national scale. Marketing strategies were produced in order to come up with national brands, with the intention of increasing penetration of the free trade, while gradually the policy of having 'foreign' beers in tied houses – a hangover from the zoning regulations imposed in 1941 to reduce transport costs, whereby beer had to come from the nearest brewery, that created a culture of beer 'lending' – was gradually phased out. This policy had a brief revitalisation in the 1990s with the 'guest beer' policy which resulted from the 1989 Monopolies and Mergers Commission (MMC) report on the supply of beer.

From 1955 onwards mergers and acquisitions were the order of the day, formally ending in 1972 when Grand Metropolitan Hotels added Watney Mann (formed in 1958 from the amalgamation of Watney, Combe, Reid with Mann, Crossman and Paulin) to Truman, Hanbury and Buxton which it had acquired the previous year, and Imperial Tobacco acquired Courage, Barclay and Simonds. This had been formed by the 1955 merger of John Courage (1787) with Barclay, Perkins and Co (1781) – originally one of the big twelve London porter brewers – plus the 1960 acquisition of the Reading brewers H. & G. Simonds (1774), the 1961 acquisition of the Bristol Brewery (1788) and the 1970 acquisition of John Smith (1757) of Tadcaster, Yorkshire's answer to Burton upon Trent.

The entry into the trade of Grand Metropolitan Hotels and Imperial Tobacco was significant because it marked the end of breweries being solely concerned with a sale of beer to public houses. Now pubs and beer sales were merely diversified assets on much larger balance sheets of firms involved in the 'leisure industry'. These assets had to perform as well as any others in the group's holding and no allowance could be made for history, tradition, or sentiment, unless these could be converted into financial returns, even if they had, in the past, been characteristics which had given pubs the role they had occupied as social centres and places of continuity, and, indeed, had contributed to the survival of the houses during the precarious course of the twentieth century.

Gone were the days when a firm like Whitbread would act to prevent the asset stripping of a company like Cheltenham and Hereford Breweries, whose properties were valued in excess of the book value of company.

In 1955 Colonel W.H. Whitbread said:

A well managed company like the Cheltenham and Hereford
Breweries has a local tradition and is a human entity with staff
and employees who have worked with the company for many
years and their fathers and grandfathers in some cases before
them; they may also hope that their sons will be employed in
the organisation. It seems to me that a company such as this,
with all its staff and employees, is of great human importance
and it would not be in the best interests of the brewing
industry, or indeed the country, for such an entity to be
liquidated for the benefit of a quick profit for purely financial
interests. . . . I am convinced that the continuance of old
established concerns run on progressive lines, is in the public
interest and consequently sound business.[1]

In the 1960s and 1970s Colonel Whitbread turned out to be
correct. Under his management Whitbread adopted a more
federal structure, taking shares in companies rather than
acquiring them outright. Colonel Whitbread's intention was to
provide a protective umbrella for those companies in which he
invested. Initially it worked well and was welcomed by many
companies, but with his departure and the arrival of the
'accountants' the mechanism he established became a convenient
vehicle for takeovers. Whitbread closed a brewery every year
throughout the 1980s and indeed Whitbread had the worst
reputation among the national combines for acquiring remaining
independent producers with the intention of closing or
transferring their brewery capacity. However, to comply with the
Beer Orders, Whitbread has divested itself of the Whitbread
Investment Company and family involvement in the firm has
ceased. Whitbread and other brewers have been criticised for
claiming that beers brewed at new brewers and by different staff
are somehow the same as the beer produced in the closed plant.

In 1968 the seven largest companies had 73 per cent of the UK
beer sales. By 1976 that had risen, through further brewery
takeovers and aggressive marketing of brand names in the free
trade, to 91 per cent. In 1951 340 firms owned the 540 breweries
operating in the UK, compared to the 6,290 extant in 1903. The
companies which were to become the large nationals had 25 per

cent of output, regional brewers 35 per cent, small local brewers 38 per cent and club brewers and the state 2 per cent.

Company	No. of Breweries			% of Sales	
	1958	1970	1976	1976	1984
Charrington Bass	38	21	12	20	21
Allied Breweries	16	9	7	17	15
Whitbread	33	18	19	13	12
Grand Met	13	11	8	12	12
Courage Imperial	14	6	8	9	9
Guinness	1	1	1	9	6
Others	237	121	89	9	15
Total	360	190	147	100	100

Source: Peter Haydon

The fifty-eight breweries of the seven largest firms were, therefore, able to produce nine times the output of the eighty-nine breweries remaining in the hands of the independent trade and regional companies in 1976, i.e. on average, the large brewery firms' plant was 13.8 times as productive as the remainder of the industry. This gap has gradually increased, and with the decline in consumption seen in the recessionary years of the early 1980s, with a fall of 3.7 million bulk barrels being consumed from 1977 to 1984, predatory measures were embarked upon to measure excess capacity. Over the same period the total number of licensed premises increased from 170,039 to 185,700 in 1983, with full on-licences rising from 75,741 to 79,153. Of that 79,153 approximately 68,700 were public houses (compared with 70,000 in 1981), and of the 68,700 72 per cent were tied, with 28 per cent managed houses (13,850) and the remainder either tenanted (35,600) or free houses.

Clearly, the policy of the brewers was to become sufficiently large to achieve a national market, produce national brands, and acquire an estate to sell them in, while expanding sales through the free trade by aggressive branding. This policy did not preclude a fall in the number of public houses. Indeed, in the postwar era the main source of pub closures was no longer the magistrates but the brewers, the fall in the number of tied houses being propor-tionately greater than the fall in the number of free houses. Brewers have never been slow to close pubs in unprofitable areas. In the 1960s and 1970s redevelopment saw the destruction of many pubs, and in some areas brewers did not take up their full allocation of licences in new developments. Between 1963 and 1975, for example, the number of public houses in Salford fell from 250 to 185. The pubs built in place of those demolished were of a standard design and very much out of the brewery catalogue. Not one newly constructed pub was equipped to serve real ale. In rural areas the situation was also bad. Fewer houses meant brewery mergers tended to create regional monopolies. Between 1966 and 1977 in the Downham Marketing Division Watney's closed 27 pubs in 16 villages, leaving 31 remaining, of which 22 were Watney's houses.

A favourite 1970s trick in rural areas, where brewers were sensitive to the accusation that pub closures were severely detrimental to the amenities and social life of the village, was to persistently refuse to allow improvements to the premises on the grounds of low barrelage, until the state of affairs attracted the attention of the magistrates. Improvements demanded by the bench could then be portrayed as uneconomic and unreasonable, and the house successfully closed while the bench carried the bulk of the blame. The rate of pub closures as of 1985 stood at 0.8 per cent per annum. This figure includes those which reopened again as wine bars and restaurants, often under the same ownership.

These factors adversely affected the older public houses. In a 1974 survey the Victorian Society's Birmingham Group found only twenty-one pubs in that city with original surviving Victorian interiors. Many architecturally interesting pubs had been lost in the 1950s and 1960s to the policies of urban redevelopment and road building. Those that survived suffered varying degrees of vandalism by the brewers. Of the twenty-one remaining, twelve were under threat by roads or redevelopment. This is a staggering degree of loss, not just because of the paucity of Victorian pubs left in Birmingham, but because Birmingham Victorian pubs are not Manchester Victorian pubs or London Victorian pubs. The predominance of Mitchells & Butlers, Ansells and Holts during the building boom of the 1890s, the relatively small number of architects used and the fact that the building bubble did not burst, as in London, but receded, combined to give Birmingham's Victorian pubs a style of their own, characterised by much use of terracotta and faience. Their loss impoverishes not just Birmingham but Britain.

The huge productivity advantages of the national combines, plus the advantages that accrue from nationally recognisable brands and large advertising budgets, gave the nationals enormous influence over the industry. Since the dominant firms had always operated, more or less, as a cartel and eschewed price competition, they were free to manipulate the market to a degree not usually found in other industries. The Lloyds Bank Review of April 1974 summed up the strategy of the large firms as follows:

> More tied outlets and larger distribution areas intensified the problems of transporting and keeping the beer; these were tackled mainly by infusing draught beer with carbon dioxide at the brewery and serving the beer under pressure. These keg beers keep longer and can be widely distributed. The extra outlets and larger areas also required the customer to be persuaded to accept national products, recognizably different from traditional ales, and this factor increased the role of marketing and advertising. If demand could be increased for a single brew, yielding economies of scale in production, it simultaneously diminished the demand for local brews, whose producers could not afford comparable advertising expenditure. The financial power of the major companies, especially in marketing, is a crucial factor in recent years.[2]

The brewers were able to push lager and keg aggressively without too much difficulty for a number of reasons. First, ever since the First World War people had been less concerned about the quality of their beer than its price. For most of the population outside large cities, choice was always restricted, both as regards origin of supply and variety of drinks available – in London and large cities a huge variety had always been available. In the late 1930s Mass Observation reported that, 'For the great majority of drinkers, taste and quality of beer are not the major factors; were they so most of the big popular pubs in the town would have to go out of business. . . . Most pub goers simply drink the cheapest available beer, while a minority exists for whom quality is most important.'[3]

Although this is partly true today it is a reversal of the traditional position where quality was an important consideration and a matter of regional pride. War and depression had been partly responsible for producing this reverse, but it also reflected the decline of beer as a central part of people's lives and diet. With the emergence of the national brands and the decline in the number of beers available, there was an increase in the variety of types of drinks. Lagers, ciders, wines, vermouths, aperitifs and spirits were more widely available. This process, of course, continues today, most notably in the bottled lager market where 'lifestyle' lagers were heavily marketed in the 1980s, where drinking from the bottle so others could see what brand you were drinking was supposed to indicate that you were making a 'statement about yourself'.

In the 1970s the emergence of national brands of lager and keg bitter coincided with an increase in prosperity, a change in tastes away from 'heavier' foodstuffs and increased affluence among the young, who could be weaned onto lager without ever having really tried ale at all. Thus, for a whole swathe of drinkers quality was an issue that was completely side-stepped, since quality was seen in reference to other national brands and not against any traditional yardstick. Keg had been accepted by the public because the quality of traditional ale was variable or poor. The blandness of keg was preferred to the decidedly changing quality of 'real ale'; besides it more closely resembled the bottled beer that had been becoming increasingly popular.

It was the threatened elimination of real cask condition beer from the national scene and the emergence of consumer campaigners, notably the Society for the Preservation of Beer from the Wood and the Campaign for Real Ale, that raised public awareness of the potentially superior quality of cask conditioned ales and the policies of the large brewers. In the more sophisticated 1980s and 1990s, with an ever increasing number of brand names, quality was again a useful weapon in the armoury of the small brewers and regionals in defending themselves against predatory interests.

Prior to the implementation of the MMC Report's recommendations (*The Supply of Beer Orders*) brewers still avoided price competition since they all traditionally accept that other forms of competition are better able to serve their interests. Beer prices rose by twice the level of inflation during the 1980s and, in the depths of the recession of the early 1990s, they rose by 9.6 per cent in a little over a year. Further evidence is found in the disparities in price to be found throughout Britain, where prices can vary by around 50 per cent between regions. Prices were maximised to the limit of what the market will bear rather than set at levels that would maximise demand, despite surplus capacity in some sectors of the industry.

Competition was carried on by securing outlets, and when the national brewers became so large that the continued acquisition of premises brought them into conflict with each other, competition took place through the improvement of amenities rather than price cutting. The 1960s and after saw a mix of policy aims in the continued improvement of public houses. On the one hand,

> Until comparatively recently the pub was regarded as the social centre for those working-class men whose main relaxation was drinking beer in congenial company. With the coming of a more affluent society the traditional pub has had to face competition from the new entertainment industry. . . . This external competition requires of the brewers that they do more than maintain existing houses to a traditional standard. . . . Increasingly they are providing amenities to suit the locality, and the appropriate 'mix' of beers, wines, spirits, soft drinks, food, music, games and so on to meet consumer preferences. In practical terms this involves capital expenditure, both by brewer and licensee, not only on the maintenance of existing amenities but also on the provision of new amenities.[4]

Between 1974 and 1977 five of the national companies spent £277 million on improvement, almost three times their expenditure between 1966 and 1969. Competition between breweries was part of the story, but it was never aggressive enough to degenerate into price competition, since it was primarily competition against other leisure activities. History was repeating itself, as in the 1930s 'improvement'.

The *Morning Advertiser* of 1 January 1970, quoting the Brewers' Society, outlined the policy within the industry. 'If pubs are to combine to attract more customers, they must retain their competitive position in the leisure industry, and this means more money continuously being spent on their improvement.'[5] Interestingly, the description could as easily fit the 1890s as the

1970s and the first decade of the twenty-first century. The word 'improvement' is still active in the argot of the brewing trade.

What we are seeing is a return to the process of competition that occurred in the pubs of the 1880s and 1890s, when the impetus for improvement was market led. The result is the provision of amenities desired by those sections of society with a certain level of disposable income, rather than the imposition of amenities by people who did not patronise the pub at all. As a result, the amount of money invested in refurbishments rose greatly during the 1980s and 1990s, and the frequency with which certain pubs are refurbished has increased.

Indeed the history of the 1960s onward has vindicated the view that architectural improvement was a chimerical blind alley for the temperance movement. The improved houses have not stood the test of time as well as the Victorian and Georgian public houses they sought to replace. The architectural style of the country is a different matter altogether, and antiquity is praised for its own sake in a way that it is not in the towns.

Of course it is natural to value the achievements of the last generation but one, while despising the efforts of the previous one. This is what traditionalists have done to the improved houses, just as the improvers belittle the Victorian gin palaces in the admiration of the 'merrie England' of the coaching inn. None of this has made it any harder to modernise public houses of whatever age, though it must be said that we live in an age where our popular conception of a town pub is dominated by the pub style of the 1890s.

On the other hand, pursuing this policy of external competition had wider advantages than just bringing more people through the doors.

They [the brewers] spent heavily on the pubs, making them attractive to women and therefore doubling the potential numbers of customers. Young people deserted the coffee bars for the pubs too, once the pub had shrugged off the old image, that branded it a place that only the middle-aged and older people would find amenable. The survival of the pub as a 'leisure centre' in the face of the onslaught of the television age . . . bears witness to the marketing skills the brewers employed during the hectic years of change.[6]

It also bears witness to the enduring place the public house enjoys at the heart of British popular culture. There is little doubt that the range of amenities did expand rapidly over the 1970s and 1980s. One need only compare the range and quality of food on offer in the vast majority of public houses today with the menus of the early 1970s.

Improvement has paid off from a twofold aspect. First, it has restored the pub to the centre of the social environment where it had always rightly belonged, but from whence it had been driven by the stigmatising of Victorian bourgeois morality. Secondly, it achieved the aim stated in the *Morning Advertiser* of 1 January 1970. Between 1969 and 1975 per capita beer consumption rose by 4.1 gallons per annum, most of which was lager. Improvement proved to be capable of counter-cyclical resilience, since demand was not a mere function of money invested in public houses or of the size of advertising budgets, as much as the current economic climate. Therefore, although in the recessionary and health conscious early 1980s the bulk barrelage consumed was declining and money values of beers consumed was tailing off in real terms, the turnover of public houses was rising in real terms too.

There are several reasons for this. Although there has been a constant and long term decline in the number of visits to pubs by regular drinkers and of the number of drinks they consume, there has been a corresponding increase in the number of visits by occasional drinkers, a trend that continues to this day. This has the effect that the second group of people will likely spend more per visit. This has been especially true with the increased availability of food, the popularisation of wine and the resulting improvement in quality and choice of pub offerings. Women's drinks are usually more expensive than men's – especially since the explosion of the Premium Packaged Spirit (such as Bacardi Breezers) in the 1990s.

Apart from the popularisation of higher margin drinks and improvements in food, turnover has also increased because of the success of brewery and pub operating companies in keeping price increases ahead of inflation.

Chapter 26

THE END OF THE ROAD: A PERSONAL SUMMARY

When you have lost your inns
then drown your sorry selves,
For you will have lost the last of England.

Hilaire Belloc (1870–1953)

Ever since the fifteenth century the number of people directly involved in brewing has been in relative decline. From the 6,000-odd breweries which were emitting steamy aromas into the hearts of British cities, towns and villagers in 1900, only 115 of a size large enough to be run by firms controlling some form of estate were still operating in 1989. These were owned by a mere 72 companies, ranging from Bass Plc, at one end, with 13 breweries, more than 100 identifiable brands, over 20 per cent of all national beer sales and 7,190 public houses, to the Butcombe Brewery in Avon, with 1 brand and 1 public house. In 1985 the nationals and the major brewers without tied estates – Guinness and the Northern Clubs Federation Brewery Ltd – accounted for 83.3 per cent of all beer domestically brewed, excluding micro brewery production and domestic home brewing. This amounted to some 30,475,000 bulk barrels out of the 36,611,000 total produced. (There are many micro breweries also without estates, and indeed one of the positive aspects of recent years is the increase in small breweries, many of which were founded as a reaction to the policies of the nationals.) The UK imports approximately 10 per cent of its total domestic consumption.

Given such concentration in the industry, the point must eventually be reached when it can no longer proceed in such a fashion.

The industry thought that point was reached in 1989 with the attempted take-over of Scottish and Newcastle by the Australian brewery combine Elders IXL, who already owned Courage, as an outlet for their globally branded Fosters lager, and who weigh in as the smallest of the Big Six, in sales terms.

If the prospect of the Big Six becoming the Big Five was not so alarming to those who regard the operation of the laws of monopoly capital as a threat to their traditional enjoyments, it would have been quite amusing. The sight of Scottish and Newcastle, themselves highly avaricious predators, fending off unwelcome advances from a firm whose production was a mere 80 per cent of their own, pleading quality, tradition and the worth of the workforce as reasons why the takeover should not be allowed to proceed, was most edifying. It was Scottish and Newcastle who declared that the continuance of brewing at Matthew Brown and Co. was 'sacrosanct' at the time of their takeover of the Blackburn firm in 1987, only to cease production at Matthew Brown's in 1990.

The Monopolies and Mergers Commission found that the merger of the two combines would result in 'a reduction of consumer choice and competition between brands leading to a large increase in the scope of the control of a single brewer. A reduction in the competition for the supply of the free trade, a restriction of competition in the market to supply beer to off licences and the creation of a second major beer, which together with Bass, would control over 40% of the supply of beer.'[1]

In summary the commission concluded that: 'We have found no significant advantages to the public interest arising from the merger to offset these detriments.' Had the hundred-year-old history of merger and acquisitions in the brewery industry finally run into the buffers?

The relief felt by Scottish and Newcastle was short lived, for in the same month as the commission saved their bacon it also produced the weighty 500-page report *The Supply of Beer*, which concluded that Scottish and Newcastle, as well as Bass, Courage, Allied, Grand Metropolitan and Whitbread, were guilty of conspiring to perpetuate a 'complex monopoly situation' which resulted in 'serious public interest detriments' requiring essential 'structural changes'.

The brewers were flabbergasted. The last person to admonish them so publicly was Elizabeth I. To compound matters the then Secretary of State for Trade and Industry, Lord Young, announced that he was 'minded' to implement the recommendations of the commission in full. This was more than the brewers could bear. Were they not the largest corporate benefactors to the Conservative Party? The entire lobbying and publicity machinery of the brewers was mobilised to ensure that the commission's recommendations were torpedoed in the water. No one will ever know the extent of the back room arm twisting that went on. However, against a background cacophony of corporate chequebooks snapping shut, Lord Young quickly changed his mind about being 'minded' and disliked being reminded about being 'minded'.

The public machinations of the brewers were of a very high profile indeed. A massive forty-eight sheet poster threatened dire consequences if the commission got its way. Billboards depicted felled Royal Oaks and axe men's blocks threatened King's Heads. One magazine advertisement showed a traditional nineteenth-century London pub dwarfed by encroaching office blocks above a blurb promising that pubs such as this would cease to exist should implementation of the misguided commission's pernicious recommendations be allowed to proceed. Closer inspection revealed the pub in question to be the Prince Albert, in Victoria Street, Westminster. A former winner of the prestigious *Evening Standard* 'Pub of the Year' award, its wide staircase is lined with portraits of British Prime Ministers and the red uniforms of Chelsea Pensioners are frequently spotted among its busy throng. In short, the Prince Albert is among the most profitable pubs in the country. If the recommendations of the MMC would have resulted in the closure of the Prince Albert there would not have been a single pub left open in Britain.

The commission concluded that although the existence of tied houses and loan ties contributed to a monopoly that 'restricted competition at all levels' and 'served to keep the bigger brewers big and the smaller brewers small', they also recognised that the tie, having been in place for over one hundred years, was essential to the survival of the smaller brewers, given the huge inequalities that pertained since 'wholesale prices are higher than they would be in the absence of the tie' and that subsequently 'free houses cannot offer effective competition to the brewer's own managed and tenanted houses.'

Instead of advocating the abolition of the tie, an option they clearly considered, the commission decided that no estate should be in excess of 2,000 houses, and that the Big Six should have three years in which to divest themselves of the 22,000 odd houses they owned, over and above the 12,000 they were to be permitted. They also recommended the abolition of the loan tie and the introduction of a 'guest ale' (which landlords would be free to purchase from whomsoever they chose) and that wholesale price lists should be published.

The commission concluded that 'these measures will increase competition in brewing, wholesaling and retailing, encourage new entry, reduce prices and widen consumer choice, but that if no changes are made we believe it is inevitable that a very small number of brewers will increasingly dominate the supply of beer in the United Kingdom.'

That paragraph turned out to be prescient, for as it has been pointed out repeatedly in this book, history conspires to favour the brewer. The guest beer policy has been the most visible result of the Supply of Beer (Tied Estate) Order 1989 – the Statutory Instrument which implemented the recommendations of the report. This has not been successful. Only 25 per cent of eligible pubs adopted a 'guest beer', and initially much resistance from brewers was experienced. Tenants were intimidated by overzealous area managers who placed prohibitions on serving guest beers through brewery-owned equipment, or mounting the taps on a brewery-owned bar counter, or who hinted that stocking guest beers would result in an unfavourable rent review.

The universally reviled report did serve one useful purpose. It enabled the drinker to confirm what he or she had long suspected.

The price of beer in a public house had risen too fast in the last few years; the high price of lager is not justified by the cost of producing; the variation in wholesale prices between regions of the country is excessive; consumer choice is restricted because one brewer does not usually allow another brewer's beer to be sold in the outlets which he owns; this restriction often happens in loan-tied outlets as well; consumer choice is further restricted because of brewers' efforts to ensure that their own brands of cider and soft drinks are sold in their outlets; tenants are unable to play a full part in meeting consumer preferences, both because of the tie and because the tenant's bargaining position is so much weaker than his landlord's; and independent manufacturers and wholesalers of beer and other drinks are allowed only limited access to the on-licensed market.[2]

Ten or more years on, one is tempted to say *plus ca change*. Between 1979 and 1989 the price of a pint of bitter increased by 15 per cent over inflation, and between 1985 and 1986 this increase over inflation was a staggering 4.8 per cent. This process continues and has got worse, *vide* the drop in strength after the change in duty collection of June 1993, for having defeated the intention of the Beer Orders, the brewers believe they can act with impunity and do so. Not only is beer overpriced but lager is doubly so. In 1987 the average pint of lager was, and remains, ten pence dearer than bitter, yet, 'There is only a marginal difference in the cost of producing bitter and lager . . . some ales indeed cost more to produce than lagers of broadly similar strengths, produced by the same company.' For the brewers, however, a lot is to be gained by promoting lager instead of bitter. 'Lager is a higher margin product than ale. The average contribution per draught barrel of lager for the national brewers appears to be between 20 to 50% higher than that for draught ale, depending upon which trade channel is being considered.'

If these two seemingly contradicting positions are confusing, then so is the indifference of the brewers to their own products.

We [the Commission] believe that it is important to distinguish between a wide range of brands. The Brewers' Society disputed this, saying that 'from the point of view of the satisfaction of the consumer's needs in on-licensed outlets the choice of manufacturers is irrelevant and what matters is the product range available.' We do not believe, however, that, for example, a 1040 gravity bitter produced by one brewer tastes exactly the same as that produced by another. It follows that the products of all manufacturers combined is wider than that of any single manufacturer.[3]

This clearly demonstrates that, for the brewers, the 'carve up' is of greater consideration then either their products or their customers. Quality, by this standard, is not a goal to be aimed at but merely a level that must be maintained as long as the other players in the field agree to meet that level. It is no wonder that the Germans laugh at our so-called Pilsners.

In the intervening decade or so it is obvious that the much mangled Beer Orders had the opposite effect from that intended. Of the Big Six Grand Met did a pubs for breweries swap with Courage before being mismanaged out of the industry altogether. Later Courage disappeared into the maw of Scottish and Newcastle, leapfrogging the new entity over Bass into the number one slot. A shock from which Bass never recovered, especially after the DTI blocked its bid for Carlsberg-Tetley in 1997. Allied floundered for several years, living a lingering death for a while as Allied Domecq, until the spirits side became exasperated. It lives on, uncertainly, as Carlsberg-Tetley as a brewery with no pubs.

Bass and Whitbread survived the remainder of the 1990s, but the falling commitment to brewing of both was there for all to see. In 2000 the Belgian family firm Interbrew, and the first truly international firm to enter the UK market, bought both, but, in a move regarded as odd by just about everyone the MMC's replacement – the Competition Commission – recommended that the Bass deal be blocked.

As this is being written Interbrew is mounting a judicial review of the decision, and while its prospects of success are remote, it has the goodwill of the rest of the industry on its side. Whatever the outcome, Bass as a force in British brewing is finished: a fine end to one of Britain's once mightiest firms, but possibly no better than their performance in recent years merits. Whitbread has now renamed itself Enjoy!Whitbread; has moved out of its famous Chiswell Street HQ and even auctioned off much of its founder's furniture and paintings. It will emerge from its chrysalis as plain Enjoy!, a health club and hotel chain – disregarding the well-known fate of firms that choose to use punctuation in their titles.

It beggars the mind to consider the speed of the decline of these once mighty firms. As one Whitbread employee put it, 'It takes real talent to take firms of this size and turn them into nothing.' Where did it all go wrong? In the first instance the firms have no one to blame but themselves. From the instant the beer orders were passed they tried to climb out from under them. In doing so they unwittingly laid the grounds for their destruction, for they increasingly fell in thrall to the single biggest obstacle to economic growth, wealth creation and entrepreneurial flair in the UK outside the Treasury – the City of London.

Since the post-First World War brewing industry ceased to compete in terms of quality it had to compete in terms of quantity and price. Therefore, measures like the Guest Beer Provision were anathema. To escape it, and to comply with the requirement to reduce their tied estate, they started to sell pubs. In the early nineties a whole flotilla of pub companies were set up. The directors were often former managers of the brewery, and, invariably, they signed supply contracts with the same brewery. However, at the same time beer sales started to fall, largely due to the boom in alternative leisure, the growth of newly un-snobbed wine, and the nineties health fixation. Since the industry worked on a 'quantity is all' basis, this was a serious problem.

As increasing numbers of pubs were no longer brewery tied, and as supply contracts were of limited length, the pub owners realised that they could do well by shopping around. The 'discount system' was born. Second only to adulteration, this has been the most destructive practice in brewing for 1,000 years. Unlike adulteration, the brewers have actively gone along with it. As discounts were volume related, it was not rocket science, even for some of the people running pub chains, to work out that bigger was better. The mid-1990s was a period of massive pub company consolidation – just as the breweries consolidated after the famous Guinness floatation.

Since pubs were no longer the means to sell the brewers' beers, and since food was becoming an ever more important part of a pubs response to alternative recreation, along with the growth of female purchasing power that was such a feature of the 1990s; pubs were increasingly seen by their owners as units of working capital rather than outlets. In part this is understandable. Postwar brewers had been complacent. Many pubs even in the early 1980s still had a blokey image, and in reacting to this, by increasing investments and theming, which led to an ever shortening period before a pub could expect to be 'done over', it was natural that a pub should cease to be regarded in a traditional role, but as a unit.

Which, almost, brings us to the second villain of the piece – the City. Before we look at the City, however, it is worth examining what was happening in other areas of the market in the 1990s.

The Guest Beer Provision of the Guest Beer Orders opened up the beer market, or specifically, the cask ale market, by allowing all tenanted pubs of brewers owning more than 2,000 tenancies the right to take a guest ale of their choice. In the late 1970s a few pioneers, led by the likes of David Bruce of the Firkin Brewpub chains and Peter Austin of Ringwood Brewery, started opening microbreweries, so reversing the trend of falling brewery numbers that had been the norm since the 1880s. When the beer orders were passed the number of microbreweries in the UK stood at 140. The Beer Orders encouraged the creation of scores more breweries. Over 700 in all, of whom some 390 were in business at the start of 2001.

The 140 breweries present in 1990 produced some 2 per cent of all the beer produced in the UK. However, the 390 breweries trading in 2001 produced between 1.5 and 1.8 per cent of a reduced UK output. How could this be so?

The simple fact of the matter was that as soon as this new niche market was called into existence then the breweries and the new pub companies actively set about trying to shut it down. Breweries divested themselves of thousands of pubs to companies who were not obliged to take guest beers. Few continued with the policy, preferring to consolidate volume in the increasingly small number of heavily marketed national brands, in order to maximise discount.

In another part of the market regional brewers actively set out to capture market share by buying up free houses and tying them, so excluding the new wave of micros in the process. The net result was that while there was an increasing number of entrepreneurs and small businessmen prepared to try their hand in the microbrewery market – many of whom were inspired to set up by the belief that they could brew better beer than the big brewers (which wasn't hard) – they were all trying to enter a shrinking market.

The obvious analogy is with trying to see how many rugby players will fit in a phone box. The answer is not many. Once the box is full the only way to increase the number is to reduce the size of the bodies in the box. This is precisely what happened. In the late 1980s and early 1990s the market entrants were businessmen seeking to build successful businesses based on growth, and today's largest micros all date from that period. The microbrewers founded in the late 1990s and the ones being set up today, however, are both smaller in terms of initial size and in ambition, and are much more likely to be brewpubs with little aspiration to supply anything other than the pub out front and the occasional beer festival.

Nearly all the microbreweries were set up to supply a local market. Growth was postulated in local terms, and few of them ever believed there was virtue in shipping beer long distances. However, as they lost, and continue to lose, local accounts due to the activities described above, they were forced to travel further and further to sell the same volumes of beer and to rely on wholesalers to find markets for them – albeit at reduced margins. This meant that any local market saw an increase in small brewers trying to sell beer. Effectively there are two beer markets in the UK. Beer supplied to pub companies, managed and tenanted houses by regional and national brewers, where competition is limited by the fact of pub ownership and the length of supply deals, and the free trade market into which all brewers compete, but in which the smaller brewers increasingly compete against each other, without the benefit of tied and managed house sales at higher margins to subsidise discounts into the free trade. It takes guts to be a microbrewer, but it also takes guts to be a tenant.

The big difference between the pub companies and the brewers was that, whatever the changing face of the pub, they still had an interest in selling beer. Take beer out of the equation and what is a pub? A piece of property. In truth the pub companies – with the single exception of Wetherspoons, which operates managed rather than tenanted houses – are nothing more than property companies deriving revenue from rent. However, unlike other landlords they also have the right to tie their tenants and charge a premium – the discount – to a supplier who wants to sell products to their tenants. The record of the pub companies in passing on a portion of this discount to their tenants is abysmal, and the mechanism for doing so is normally via retrospective volume bonuses.

No one has yet asked why the pub companies should have this right, now that the traditional reasons for the tie (forcing brewers to run responsible houses and preventing adulteration) have broken down. Indeed, at the start of the new century, like the two before it, adulteration is again on the increase (frequently the modern adulterant is air).

The Duke of Westminster is a big landlord. He charges his tenants rent. He does not, however, tell them where they must shop, if they are individuals, or where they must buy their supplies, if they are companies. Neither does he charge those shops and suppliers a premium for the privilege. Why then should these new property companies have extra privileges merely because the properties they own are pubs?

An increasing number of tenants are starting to ask this question, and the blame for the increase in that number can be laid squarely at the door of the City. The City likes homogenous units, they are quantifiable. The more uniform they become the better they are, as each becomes easier to measure against the other. Having warned against pubs in the mid-1990s the City rediscovered them in the late 1990s. The tool that enabled it to do so was the bond securitisation market.

Securitisation was a financial tool developed in the US in the early 1980s. Put simply it is a method of raising finance by pooling a large number of income streams (such as mortgage payments and credit card repayments) where the risk is quantifiable, and increasing the credit rating of the whole income stream by a process called 'cross-collateralisation', whereby all the other income streams underwrite any that default. The nineteenth century system whereby publicans paid a levy to subsidise their own suppression is not dissimilar. Pubs are ideal securitisation vehicles. Their performance is easily analysed, and they are regulated so, therefore, have a scarcity value. As brewery pub disposals increased as a result of the Beer Orders, and as the big brewers favoured large scale disposals, it made sense for some of the brighter players in the pub market to finance the purchase of the pubs out of their future revenue with securitised funds. No small wonder therefore that the UK's largest pub owner is the Japanese bank Nomura.

The problem with this approach is that the pub company then has to generate a revenue stream back to the securitisation bond holders. There are two ways of doing that. First, continue to increase the size of the estate to maximise the discounts available and rents received. Second, appropriate as much of the value of the business as possible.

All the pub companies – except Wetherspooons and Wellington, which is under the umbrella of the second largest owner, Punch Taverns – rely on tenants. A tenant, or in his increasingly common reincarnation: the lessee, is a businessman or woman in his or her own right. Or that is the theory. Increasingly they are being manoeuvred into the position of self-employed managers. Forced to install meters on their beer lines, linked electronically to pub companies' central offices, tied into agreements whose terms are ever more slanted towards the landlord, with full repairing obligations, upwards only rent reviews, proportions of takings of fruit machines and pool tables also being appropriated to service the cash requirement of the bond securities market.

This is the market in the present day. Truly we have come a long way in the last thousand years. From the days when beer and the alehouse was the core of everything that defined us as a nation, increasingly the publican and the pub goer is impotent in the face of the demands of global capital.

Let us conclude this book on a personal note. When I first decided to write the book that I had always wanted to read in 1989, I knew no one in the brewing industry. All I knew was that I loved pubs, and I still do. Thanks to the first edition of this book, I was gradually drawn into the industry and ended up with the best job in the world, General Secretary of the Society of Independent Brewers, charged with representing Britain's slowly growing army of microbrewers, like-minded people who all want good beer in good pubs. From the point of objectivity in this book, therefore, nothing much has changed other than the final chapter. It has been re-edited, tightened up and corrected where necessary. The views expressed are still the ones I had ten years ago. Having said that, this chapter has been the hardest of all to write, not because I might cause offence: in some quarters I hope it does. Rather because some things will have changed between the time of proofing and printing. The modern industry is moving as fast as that.

I shall finish, therefore, with a few predictions for the future, made just after the 2001 budget. The forced Interbrew sale of Bass Brewers will become a rather messy affair and everyone will realise that letting Interbrew have it was the best thing all along, though the need to save political faces may mean this does not happen. Small brewers will see a Progressive Beer Duty regime introduced in the 2002 budget (a system operated in many European countries, whereby smaller brewers pay less beer duty than larger ones), which will have profound effects on the well-being of the smaller end of the sector and rescue the idea of competition and choice in the market, though it will not be a panacea and may not be enough to save some of the established regionals above a certain size who will continue to fall victim to the City's short-termism.

The consolidation of the brewing sector in the 1990s will be mirrored by a consolidation of the retail sector in the following decade (no brave prophesy this, it is already underway). However, two factors will affect this trend. Firstly, the large pub companies will face a recruitment crisis as prospective tenants are less willing to sign up to ever harsher terms dictated by the need to finance City repayment terms rather than their own incomes (again no great prescience needed here). The pub company owners will seek to cash in their assets via stock market floatation, and where one leads the rest will follow. (Why is it that anyone starting a business today is already expected to have planned their 'exit strategy'?)

The purchasers of the new stock in these companies will come in for a nasty surprise, as the share prices they pay will have been based on the expectation of extracting equal or greater returns from the assets – or pubs as we used to call them – they have purchased. Sadly, they will discover that these assets have been milked dry in order to build a floatation prospectus and pay the securitised bond liabilities.

With a bit of luck, this will end the City's love affair with the pub sector and the only people interested in buying pubs will be those people who should only ever have been interested in buying pubs; namely publicans and people who have a genuine love for them, and actually have an empathy for the pub, the people in it, the beer it serves and the place it has in our society and culture. Freed of the dead hand of managerial control many will be free to run pubs on traditional lines, by which I mean in a way that feels natural to British people, others will reinvent the pub in a new idiom, breaking free of some of the constraints that the pub has laboured under throughout the twentieth century. We may turn our noses up at them for a while, and then, in all probability, sniff, comment – without the eloquence of our forebears – enter and soon forget what the fuss was about.

Currently we are living in wild times, but if pubs can survive plague, taxation, civil war, Puritan and temperance fanatics and class condescension they can survive the City of London. After all, in the City, which came first, the pubs or the banks? You only need to look at all the old ground floor banking halls between Bishopsgate and Threadneedle Street that are now converted into bars and pubs to know which is the more resilient.

Today there are enough people who still care about each other, our culture and, therefore, our pubs to ensure that there will be great pubs that will continue to survive. The only real threat to the pub will be if we ever cease to care about ourselves.

Peter Haydon
London, October 2001

THE WOES OF THE PUB COMPANY TENANT

Do you have a lease with a Pub Company, or are you thinking that way? Beware.

Can you make a reasonable living? At the time you sign the lease is it made crystal clear what you are taking on?

At the time did you realise that it would be impossible to compete with managed houses, free houses and the large supermarket-type pubs?

The price you pay for your tied beer is full RETAIL i.e. up to £50 more expensive per 22 gallons.

The goverenment made the breweries sell off a large percentage of their tied houses to break their monopoly. Does the government now know that we now have a cartel dictating the price? Who sets that price? The brewery. Can you smell a rat?

The pub companies have a buying power so large it makes Wetherspoons look like a corner shop. The discounts that the pub company get are HUGE. Do they pass them on? No. They let you struggle and pocket the cash.

Pub company tenants are to them chaff and fodder.

If the tenant tries hard, increases the trade, spends money, improves their pub and turnover, come rent review up goes the rent. How many bankruptcies are they responsible for?

Now is the time to unite and fight back for our rights to run our own businesses on a level footing.

An e-mail circulated around the pub trade in 2000 by a disenchanted pub company tenant.

NOTES

CHAPTER 1

1. Gayre, G.R., *Wassail! In Mazers of Mead* (Phillimore & Co. Ltd, 1948).
2. Monckton, H.A., *A History of English Ale and Beer* (Bodley Head, 1966).
3. French, R.V., *Nineteen Centuries of Drink in England* (Longman, 1884).
4. Ibid.
5. Monckton, H.A., *English Ale and Beer*.
6. Fisher, T. and Hackwood, F.W., *Inns, Ales and Drinking Customs of Old England* (Unwin, 1909).
7. French, R.V., *Drink in England*.
8. Ibid.
9. Ibid.
10. Monckton, H.A., *English Ale and Beer*.
11. Ibid.
12. Ibid.

CHAPTER 2

1. Monckton, H.A., *A History of the English Public House* (Bodley Head, 1969).
2. Plaistead, A.H., *Ale Feasts and Country Taverns* (Medenham, 1962).
3. French, R.V., *Drink in England*.
4. Ibid.
5. Ibid.
6. Monckton, H.A., *English Public House*.
7. Plaistead, A.H., *Ale Feasts*.
8. Ward, E., *London Spy* (1704).
9. Simon, A., *A History of the Wine Trade in England* (Wyman and Sons, 1906).
10. Ibid.
11. Monckton, H.A., *English Public House*.

CHAPTER 3

1. Monckton, H.A., *English Ale and Beer*.
2. Ibid.
3. Monckton, H.A., *English Public House*.
4. Fisher, T. and Hackwood, F.W., *Inns, Ales and Drinking*.

CHAPTER 4

1. Monckton, H.A., *English Ale and Beer*.

CHAPTER 5

1. Morwyng, P., *Treasure of Evonymous* (1565).
2. Brander, M., *The Life and Sport of the Inn* (Gentry Books, 1973).
3. Morwyng, P., *Treasure of Evonymous*.

CHAPTER 6

1. Fisher, T. and Hackwood, F.W., *Inns, Ales and Drinking*.

2. French, R.V., *Drink in England.*
3. Ibid.
4. Samuelson, J., *The History of Drink* (Trücker & Son, 1878).
5. Prynne, W., *Healthes' Sicknesse* (1628).
6. French, R.V., *Drink in England.*
7. Monckton, H.A., *English Public House.*
8. French, R.V., *The History of Toasting or Drinking of Healthes.*
9. Ibid.
10. Clarke, P., *The English Alehouse* (Longman, 1983).
11. King, F.A., *Beer Has a History* (Hutchinson, 1947).
12. Monckton, H.A., *English Ale and Beer.*

CHAPTER 7

1. Richardson, A.E., *The Old Inns of England* (Batsford, 1934).
2. French, R.V., *Toasting.*
3. Lennard, R. (ed.) *Englishman at Rest and Play: 1558–1714* (OUP, 1931).
4. King, F.A., *Beer Has a History.*
5. Ibid.
6. French, R.V., *Toasting.*
7. Monckton, H.A., *English Public House.*
8. Timbs, J., *Club Life of London* (1886).
9. Mendelsohn, D.A., *Drinking With Pepys* (Macmillan, 1963).
10. Madder: a red dye from the root of the plant *Rubia tinctorum.*
11. Red Sander: a red dye from sandalwood – *Santalum album.*
12. Elecampane: the bitter, aromatic root from the sunflower-like plant *Inula helenium.*
13. *Licensed Victualler's Monthly Guide No. 1* (February 1834).
14. Dekker, T., *Belman of London* (1608).
15. Jope, E.W., *Studies in Building History* (Oldham, 1961).
16. Simon, A., *Wine Trade.*
17. Collon, C., *Compleat Gamester* (1674).
18. Guildhall Library, Norman Collection.
19. Timbs, J., *Club Life in London.*
20. Ward, E., *London Spy.*
21. King, F.A., *Beer Has a History.*
22. Longmate, N., *The Waterdrinkers* (Hamish Hamilton, 1968).

CHAPTER 8

1. Boston, R., *Beer and Skittles* (Collins, 1976).
2. Herbert, Sir A.P., *Mr Gray's London* (Ernest Benn, 1948).
3. Boston, R., *Beer and Skittles.*
4. French, R.V., *Toasting.*
5. Werthman, M. and Cantor, N.F., *The History of Popular Culture* (Collier-Macmillan, 1968).
6. Ibid.
7. Malcolm, J.P., *Manners & Customs of London* (London, 1808).
8. Monckton, H.A., *English Public House.*

9. Simon, A., *Bottlescrew Days: Wine Drinking in England in the Eighteenth Century* (Duckworth, 1926).
10. Webb, S. and B., *History of Liquor Licensing in Britain* (Longmans, 1903).
11. Simon, A., *Bottlescrew Days*.
12. French, R.V., *Drink in England*.
13. Williams, G.P. and Brake, G.T., *The English Public House in Transition* (Edsell, 1982).
14. Webb, S. and B., *Liquor Licensing in Britain*.
15. Ibid.

CHAPTER 9

1. Nouse, T., *Campania Felix* (1706).
2. Ward, E., *London Spy*.
3. Ibid.
4. King, F.A., *Beer Has a History*.
5. Samuleson, J., *Trade Unions and Public Houses* (Longman, 1871).
6. Bickerdyke, J., *The Curiosities of Ale and Beer* (Field & Tuer, 1886).
7. Collon, C., *Compleat Gamester*.
8. Harper, C.G., *Half Hours with the Highwaymen* (Chapman & Hall, 1908).
9. *The Times* (19 January 1785).

CHAPTER 10

1. Boston, R., *Beer and Skittles*.
2. *The Story of Whitbread* (Whitbread & Co., 1964).
3. Mathias, P., *The Brewing Industry in England: 1700–1830* (Gregg Revivals, 1993).
4. King, F.A., *Beer Has a History*.
5. Ibid.

CHAPTER 11

1. Eliot, G., *Felix Holt* (Penguin, 1995).
2. Dickens, C., *Pickwick Papers* (Penguin, 1996).
3. Bruning, T. and Paulin, K., *Historic English Inns* (David & Charles, 1982).
4. Harper, C.G., *Old Inns of Old England* (1906).
5. Brander, M., *The Life and Sport of the Inn* (Gentry Books, 1973).
6. Dickens, C., *Sketches By Boz* (OUP, 1987).
7. Bruning, T. and Paulin, K., *Historic English Inns*.
8. Moritz, P., *Travels Through England* (1782).
9. Guildhall Library, Norman Collection.
10. Moritz, P., *Travels Through England*.
11. Bruning, T. and Paulin, K., *Historic English Inns*.
12. Everitt. A., *Perspectives in English Urban History* (Macmillan, 1973).
13. Clark, P., *The English Alehouse*.

CHAPTER 12

1. Boswell, J., *Life of Johnson* (Oxford, 1953).

2. Simon, A, *Bottlescrew Days.*
3. Werthman, M. and Cantor, N.F., *The History of Popular Culture.*
4. Boniface, O., *Ebritatis Encomium* (London, 1723).
5. King, F.A., *Beer Has a History.*
6. Ibid.
7. Richardson, A.E. and Eberlein, H.D., *The English Inn, Past and Present* (Batsford, 1925).
8. Ward, E., *Quack Vintners* (1712).

CHAPTER 13

1. Cruickshank, G., *My Sketchbook*, vol. 1 (Chorly Tilt, 1834).
2. Boston, R., *Beer and Skittles* (Collins, 1876).
3. Spiller, B., *Victorian Public Houses* (David & Charles, 1972).
4. Guildhall Library, Norman Collection.
5. Elwall, P., *Bricks and Beer: English Pub Architecture 1830–1939* (British Architectural Library, 1983).
6. French, R.V., *Drink in England.*
7. Harrison, B., 'Pubs' in H.J. Dyos (ed.), *Victorian City* (Routledge, Kegan, Paul, 1973).
8. Spiller, B., *Victorian Public Houses.*
9. Harrison, B., 'Pubs'.
10. Girouard, M., *Victorian Pubs* (Studio Vista, 1975).
11. Ibid.

CHAPTER 14

1. *Licensed Vituallers' Monthly Guide No. 1* (February 1834).
2. Girouard, M., *Victorian Pubs.*
3. Elwall, P., *Bricks and Beer.*
4. Loudon, J.C., *Encyclopedia of Farm, Cottage and Villa* (Longman, Rees, Orme, Brown, Green & Longman, 1836).
5. Harrison, B., 'Pubs'.
6. *Licensed Victuallers' Monthly Guide*, No. 1 (February, 1834).
7. Ibid.
8. Cruickshank, G., *Sunday in London* (Effingham Wilson, 1833).
9. Ibid.

CHAPTER 15

1. Cruickshank, G., *Sunday In London.*
2. Spiller, B., *Victorian Public Houses.*
3. Harrison, B., 'Pubs'.
4. Spiller, B., *Victorian Public Houses.*
5. Ibid.
6. Harrison, B., 'Pubs'.

CHAPTER 16

1. Longmate, N.R., *The Waterdrinkers.*
2. Smith, J.M., *Nuts to Crack For Moderate Drinkers* (1890).
3. Ibid.
4. Samuelson, J., *History of Drink.*
5. *Licensed Victuallers' Monthly Journal* (1869).
6. Spiller, B., *Public Houses.*
7. French, R.V., *Drink in England.*

CHAPTER 17

1. Asquith, G.R., *British Taverns* (1928).
2. King, F.A., *Beer Has a History*.
3. Asquith, G.R., *British Taverns*.
4. *Licensed Victuallers' Official Annual* (1984).
5. Girouard, M., *Victorian Pubs*.

CHAPTER 19

1. Wilson, B., *Alcohol and the Nation* (1940).

CHAPTER 20

1. Asquith, G.R., *British Taverns*.
2. Oliver, *Renaissance of the English Public House* (Faber & Faber, 1947).
3. Ibid.
4. Ibid.
5. Williams, E., *The New Public House* (Chapman & Hall, 1924).
6. Elwall, P., *Bricks and Beer*.
7. Yorke, F.B.W., *Public Houses: Their Planning and Equipment* (Architectural Press, 1949).
8. Williams, E., *The New Public House*.
9. Oliver, *Renaissance of the English Public House*.

CHAPTER 21

1. Monckton, H.A., *English Ale and Beer*.
2. Brander, M., *The Life and Sport of the Inn*.
3. Selley, E., *The English Public House As It Is* (Longman, 1927).

4. Shadwell, A., *Drink in 1914–1922: A Lesson in Control* (Longman, 1923).
5. Selley, E., *The English Public House As It Is*.

CHAPTER 22

1. Beed, E., *Seventy Years Behind Bars* (1984).
2. Elwall, P., *Bricks and Beer*.
3. Guildhall Library, Norman Collection.
4. Elwall, P., *Bricks and Beer*.
5. A Monthly Bulletin, vol. 3, 1931.
6. Ibid.
7. Mass Observation, *The Pub and the People* (Cresset Library, 1987).
8. Ibid.
9. Ibid.
10. Ibid.
11. Ibid.
12. *The Times* (9 May 1936).
13. *Inn-Signia* (Whitbread & Co, 1948).

CHAPTER 23

1. Mass Observation, *The Pub and the People*.
2. Ibid.
3. A Monthly Bulletin vol. 12, 1942.

CHAPTER 24

1. A Monthly Bulletin, 1931.
2. Boulting, N., 'Company Identity to Corporate Image', in Binney, M.

NOTES

324

and Milne, E. (eds)
Time Gentlemen Please
(SAVE Britain's Heritage
and CAMRA Ltd,
1983).
3. Mansukhani, R., *The
Pub Report: British Pubs in
the 1980s* (Euromonitor
Publications Ltd,
1985).

CHAPTER 25

1. Hawkings, K.H. and Pass,
C.L., *The Brewing Industry*
(Heinemann, 1979).
2. Boston, R., *Beer and Skittles.*

3. Mass Observation, *The Pub and
the People.*
4. Hawkings, K.H. and Pass,
C.L., *The Brewing Industry.*
5. Williams, G.P., and Brake,
G.T., *The English Public House
in Transition.*
6. Hawkings, K.H. and Pass,
C.L., *The Brewing Industry.*

CHAPTER 26

1. Monopolies and Mergers
Commission, *The Supply of
Beer* (HMSO, 1989, CM651).
2. Ibid.
3. Ibid.

INDEX